THE
OBAMA
HATERS

THE
OBAMA
HATERS

Behind the Right-Wing Campaign of Lies, Innuendo & Racism

JOHN WRIGHT

Potomac Books, Inc.
Washington, D.C.

Library of Congress Cataloging-in-Publication Data
Wright, John.
  The Obama haters : behind the right-wing campaign of lies, innuendo, and racism / John Wright. — 1st ed.
      p. cm.
  Includes bibliographical references and index.
  ISBN 978-1-59797-512-4 (hardcover : alk. paper)
  1. Obama, Barack. 2. Right-wing extremists—United States. 3. Racism—United States. 4. United States—Politics and government—2009- I. Title.

  E908.W75 2011
  973.932—dc22

                                                        2010049225

Printed in the United States of America on acid-free paper that meets the American National Standards Institute Z39-48 Standard.

Potomac Books, Inc.
22841 Quicksilver Drive
Dulles, Virginia 20166

First Edition

10 9 8 7 6 5 4 3 2 1

A man is supremely blessed when he has the grand and loving counsel, companionship, and wisdom of his parents to temper his impetuousness and simultaneously nurture his ambitions. I have been thus endowed by the uncompromising and limitless devotion from my father and mother, Richard and Helen, who will always serve as shining examples of the way to treat and serve others with an open heart, fairness, and dignity.

Thou shalt not bear false witness against thy neighbor

—Exodus 20:16. The ninth of the Ten Commandments.

CONTENTS

PREFACE

The 2008 presidential election was the longest and most expensive in U.S. history. It was also among the nastiest. Barack Obama, not even midway through his freshman term in the U.S. Senate, announced his candidacy on February 10, 2007, nearly two years before Inauguration Day. He wasn't even the first. Obama joined other candidates from both major political parties already scurrying around Iowa and New Hampshire to persuade voters with the first opportunity to size them up. Pollsters and fund-raisers were already pestering voters and donors.

Voters hungered for change from George W. Bush, unpopular wars in Iraq and Afghanistan, an imploding economy, mistrust after utter incompetence in the handling of Hurricane Katrina, and worldwide scorn against the United States. Conditions were ripe for change as Americans searched their souls about whether they were ready to elect someone of African descent as their leader.

Beneath the radar of most Americans and news organizations lurked a sinister stealth campaign to destroy the reputation and candidacy of Obama, who was still largely unknown. During his 2004 race for the U.S. Senate, scant attention was paid to a slur portraying him as a Muslim. Another early smear via chain e-mail purported that Obama was born outside the United States, which, if true, could disqualify him from becoming president.

The Obama campaign worked to prevent either lie from influencing voters. By the time he won the Democratic nomination, these two unbelievable aspersions had morphed into a hydra-headed monster, with dozens of smears getting attention from websites, e-mails, talk radio, TV, and the flapping tongues of political opponents.

Obama overcame the outrageous slander. Americans wanted their new president to resolve the nation's pressing problems; many, in fact, even hoped he could share power with Bush immediately after the election.

Following the election, I was driving to a Thanksgiving celebration through rural back roads, where the only radio station available played Rush Limbaugh. Instead of telling listeners to wait and see what Obama does before passing judgment, he ranted, "We know that everything we have said about Obama is true." I was dumbfounded by his brazen inaccuracy; each and every mean-spirited accusation spit out during the campaign had been proven wrong.

After Thanksgiving dinner, my family had a heated debate, split between Obama supporters and haters. I heard things like: "I don't trust him. . . . He's un-American. . . . He associates with people who hate America. . . . I'm afraid he will do to America what Hitler did." The arguments against Obama were all falsehoods spread by chain e-mails, talk radio, and Fox News. I was determined to explore how things got this way and who was behind it.

I spent Obama's first twenty months in office researching this book, astounded by the willful distortions and the blatant effort to undermine the new president. Many people asked my why I was writing this book. After all, everything is already out there on the Internet, isn't it? I came to realize that the Internet is just a bunch of jumbled facts and falsities, a massive phone directory listing things at random with no semblance of order. Furthermore, most of what's out there is dead wrong. So this book is a faithful endeavor to serve as a historic record.

My goal in writing this book is not to make everyone love Obama. I realize that people with differing views will not like him, and that is healthy. We live in a participatory democracy, not autocracy with forced allegiance. But opinions, whatever their nature, should be based on facts, not lies. Thus, my book is dedicated to that basic purpose and simple premise. You can disagree with everything Obama has done as president and still condemn the Obama haters.

People inquired about what I was writing. One person asked whether it was fact or fiction. My quick answer: "It's a nonfiction book about a lot of fiction."

There's a lot more to it than that. My attempt to set the record straight required shining bright headlights on misinformation and liars as well as compiling a record of the most insidious attacks against Obama.

I do confess, moreover, to having a grander scheme in mind. Seeing that elections can turn on smears, as did the 1988 and 2004 presidential contests, and knowing that Obama's detractors have vast financial resources available to try to dispose of him, my goal is to prevent their lies from dominating the 2012 elections. That sometimes feels like a Sisyphean task considering the headway they have already achieved.

"What will you do if you find the criticism of Obama to be true?" bellowed my father, whose political views have moved steadily distant from mine over the years.

"Then that's what I'll write. That's what the publisher expects," I responded. I told my agent that I had only one demand of my publisher: that this book be the simple, unvarnished truth. All the conclusions I have reached are mine alone. The publisher has not told me what to write or what not to write.

My editor made it clear that this book must be objective, not clogged with political screeching. She insisted on "some acknowledgment that not all criticisms of Obama are rooted in racism or even in right-wing politics."

I am not shy about criticizing Obama where I find it appropriate.

Now for a few thoughts about the title: some people asked why I named it *The Obama Haters* and thought the title was too strident. I briefly considered anodyne titles such as *Obama Phobia* but stuck with my original title to describe the tangible, visceral hatred of our president.

Merriam-Webster's Collegiate Dictionary defines hatred as "prejudiced hostility or animosity." That sums it up accurately and succinctly. The hatred is obvious. Yet equally evident is that much of the hatred is misplaced due to fatuous reasoning.

A personal note: since I graduated from college in 1974, I have worked as a journalist for community newspapers, then as a foreign correspondent for major news services. Everywhere I worked, a simple, deeply held allegiance to the facts and unwavering fidelity to the truth guided me. I was a reporter in the field and an editor directing reporters in far-flung places. Whenever we got something wrong, we always corrected our mistakes right away.

Forcing myself to spend day after day, week after week, month after month, listening to Rush Limbaugh, watching Fox News, and reading scurrilous information on websites and in deceitful books was exhausting and emotionally draining. I felt as if I were locked in an insane asylum, the only rational person in search of the exit door. Conducting the research for this book was like diving into a sewer.

I have little patience for extreme ideologues after spending years in Latin America, where left-wing and right-wing death squads murdered anyone they suspected of getting in their way, and where military rulers ignored basic human rights.

Could it happen here? It already has, to a lesser degree. We've always had political violence surrounding race, religion, labor, abortion, and wars. A very real and tangible fear is that it could spin out of control. The Obama haters keep upping the ante. In their playbook, it's acceptable to call the president a communist, a fascist, a terrorist, or a traitor with total disregard for the facts. Incredibly, some even think it's okay to tote guns to a political rally.

But we can find common ground, as we have done in the past. When conservatives inspire us with a grand vision, I applaud. I didn't vote for President Reagan, but I cheered when he told the Soviet goons to "tear down this wall" in Berlin. But the other side is less fair-minded. When Obama, like Reagan before him, demands human rights in countries where such calls are ignored, the right wing bashes him. Today's Republican leadership, tragically, toadies up to the fringe elements and opposes everything Obama does automatically.

I pray that Obama can prevail in inspiring what Lincoln called our "better angels," thwarting his political enemies in their attempts to stoke hatred and fear. If Obama is successful, we all win and my yet-to-be-born grandchildren will inhabit a better world. If the Obama haters succeed through their bullying tactics of lies and intimidation, we all lose and I will shudder for the future of our great nation.

ACKNOWLEDGMENTS

This book would not exist without the wise counsel of my multi-talented agent, Alison Picard, who helped me shape and market my idea and guided me through the process of transforming a great but sketchy idea into reality. Nor would it exist without my editor, Hilary Claggett, who saw potential in my proposal and my ability to complete the task.

My uncle, Bernard James, is the most talented writer I know; his wisdom resides in every well-crafted word and phrase in this book, and his encouragement has been monumental. Maria is the great love of my life, who bestowed upon me the gift of Juliana and Joseph, who have infused purpose into my life. Juliana is a young woman of poise and dignity of whom I am keenly proud. Joseph is a hard-working college student, the best son a father could want. Both my children have given me clever ideas for promoting this effort. Lia, Marcella, and Bruna regularly make me recognize the value of my family connections. My brothers, Rick and Stephan; my sisters, Roxane and Cathy; and their spouses, Rhonda, Sharmon, Casey, and Craig are all precious to me and all contributed to the end result. My mother-in-law, Juliana, is a stellar example of how to live as I seek to emulate my late father-in-law, José, even knowing I will always fall short of his example. Dave Carpenter helped me sharpen and fine-tune important details. Jenni Clark made irreplaceable contributions; she believed in this undertaking even when my own faith was flagging and prospects were waning. Carolyn and Matthew Clark were highly supportive. Tony Mercandetti and Keith Sawyer pulled me into their lifeboat and offered me shelter from the swirling storm when I needed it most. The late Herschel M. "Pete" Wilson and Howard Seemann imparted real-world wisdom and prepared me for my chosen profession. John Ross, Jean van de Walle, and Sue Ishikawa offered valuable advice at a difficult turning point in my life. Annie Skipper arranged a place to get away from the frantic pace of life when I needed it most, and Maharishi showed me how to find peace and stability within.

This book is stronger for insights, suggestions, and generosity from many people, including Abe Amoros, Dave Cole, Adela Yarbro Collins, Noam Chomsky, Mike DeCesare, Wiley Drake, Michael Dukakis, Karmen Frisvold, Jonathan Haidt, Molly Hanchey, Alexander Lamis, Jim McDermott, Bernard McGinn, Michael Medved, Gerald C. Meyers, Gary Miller, Kristen Monroe, Sing Oldham, David and Rhoda Orme-Johnson, Russell Pang, Gene Policin-ski, Ed Rendell, Laura Rico, Larry Sabato, Rene Schoof, Hari Sevugan, Emily Schwartz Greco, Brian Sieben, Ben Smith, Margaret Talev, Kip Tew, Jim Tran-quada, Mike Weisman, Tom Wilkinson, and Isaac Wood. To all those who helped and I failed to acknowledge, I offer my sincere gratitude.

John Wright, Seattle
September 2010

INTRODUCTION

How a Positive Campaign Faced the Onslaught of
Smears and Still Remained Positive

I hear that every cycle, you know, that people are fed up with
negative advertising. But the fact is that while they say that, it
motivates them, it persuades them, it compels them.

—Mark McKinnon

He is described as the Antichrist, a Muslim, a traitor, a socialist, a fascist, a communist, an America hater, a racist, a baby killer, a "pal of terrorists," a sexual libertine, the devil, mentally unstable, and even a foreigner with a forged birth certificate. His wife is said to be "angry" and is accused of using racial slurs and having a "hit list" of people to destroy. Some believe she hates America. One of their young daughters is depicted as "ghetto trash." His father is called a revolutionary; his mother is seen as an atheist. Her mother is believed to be a voodoo priestess. This family endures the most ferocious racist taunts a century and a half after the Emancipation Proclamation.

Who are these people? Suspicious characters skulking in the shadows? Wily radicals on the lam from the law? No, these are descriptions of Barack Hussein Obama, forty-fourth president of the United States; his wife, Michelle; and their preteen daughters.

Strangely and sadly, millions of people believe these smears, which have no basis in fact. These are the monstrous caricatures contrived by anonymous websites, acid-tongue commentators, political enemies, and propagandistic anti-Obama media.

The man who won scholarships to Columbia and Harvard also was described as "a poor ignoramus" by one critic and setting in motion "a nuclear war plan" by another. A third hissed, "Obama and his administration have sown new seeds to increase hatred and revenge on America."

Who uttered those words? Shady bloggers? Republican leaders? Conservative columnists? No, those remarks were spoken by Venezuela's Hugo Chávez, North Korea's Kim Jong-Il, and Osama bin Laden, respectively. Anyone who can distinguish between the rhetoric of Obama's domestic foes and statements by these infamous world-class thugs should win a prize.

An alarming segment of America's Religious Right even calls for Obama's death in public prayers, quoting biblical verses with insufficient condemnation from their brethren. Not even psychopathic foreign dictators go that far.

Obama's candidacy and election unleashed a tide of unbridled hatred from America's underbelly. Researching this hysteria made me feel like a proctologist examining the body politic.

Rip Van Winkle, upon awakening and hearing such exaggerated rhetoric, might envision a scowling, pathological, Nixonian menace rather than this brilliant, charismatic, natural leader with a knock-'em-dead smile and infectious optimism.

Anyone can take potshots at Obama for any reason without foundation. Right-wing media echo and amplify the smear with no questions asked, no checking of facts, and no attempt to learn the truth. The sky's the limit, and anybody can join the blood sport. Nobody has proof that Obama has done anything wrong, but the Obama haters, like a clever ambulance chaser in a courtroom, throw out invective and innuendo to muddy the waters and instill doubt. They have proudly raised ignorance to an artform.

The most extreme, egregious propaganda gets "mainstreamed" through the "baton march of the bogus," as described by Craig Crawford of *Congressional Quarterly*. "A crazy rumor or story would start in a blog or a gossip rag somewhere on the Internet, then it would move to English newspapers, then it would move to a tabloid here, and pretty soon it's on the network news," he said on October 20, 2009, on MSNBC's *Countdown with Keith Olbermann*.

Mainstream news organizations "get hammered for covering up the story," which in most cases is not really news, forcing them to act, even if only to explain why they are not covering it. "Pretty soon the story's in the mainstream media and becomes real," Crawford explained.

Some news organizations, such as the *New York Post,* are active partisans. In her lawsuit against the newspaper, former editor Sandra Guzman stated that she was told by Washington bureau chief Charles Hurt that the paper's "goal is to destroy Barack Obama. We don't want him to succeed." The tabloid is part of the media empire belonging to Rupert Murdoch, who also owns, you guessed it, Fox News.

When challenged, conservatives insist they are only engaging in tit for tat after liberals ridiculed George W. Bush. That's nonsense. Vice President Joe Biden's gaffes elicit plenty of laughs. Even Obama committed foolish blunders, such as making light of the Special Olympics and Nancy Reagan's penchant for astrologers. Verbal pratfalls are fair game when a politician not only inserts foot in mouth but also leaves room for an entire shoe store. The dumbest statements get attention, irrespective of the babbling bungler's ideology.

Here is the key distinction: when fringe elements concocted nonsensical blather about Bush, they were quickly denounced by Democrats. Republican leaders, however, don't bother to herd their own sheep and rarely rein in their most extreme elements.

Bush the Lesser had smooth sailing early on. During the 2000 election, most Democrats found him inoffensive. He got much better press (what liberal media?) than Democratic opponent Al Gore. He did not stoke the wrath of the Left until Republican legal trickery intervened in Florida, which millions of Americans still believe was legitimately won by Gore but stolen when the U.S. Supreme Court disgracefully aped banana republics by outlawing the democratic tradition of vote-counting. Bush took office amid the biggest protests (including this author) since the Vietnam War era. Once he invaded Iraq on phony, trumped-up assertions and called everyone who disagreed with him unpatriotic, there was no reconciling with the enraged and growing opposition. No one can equate criticism of Bush with Obama, who won decisively in a clean election and suffered outrageous taunts long beforehand.

Some view the right-wing stunts as buffoonish entertainment, but it can't be dismissed as harmless. After Bill O'Reilly on Fox News showed pictures of abortion-provider George Tiller and called him "Tiller the baby killer" numerous times, the doctor was gunned down on May 31, 2009, in his church by Scott Roeder, who was later convicted of first-degree murder after defending his actions with his religious beliefs.

James von Brunn allegedly killed a security guard at the Holocaust Memorial Museum in Washington, D.C., on June 10 after frequenting racist anti-Obama websites and being convinced that the president's birth certificate was a forgery.

After Glenn Beck ranted that Obama conspired to imprison political opponents in concentration camps, people took it seriously. "If you have any kind of fear that we might be heading towards a totalitarian state: look out. Buckle up. There's something going on in our country that ain't good," Beck said on March 3, 2009, on *Fox & Friends*. Nancy Genovese was arrested on July 30 of that year while scouting out Francis S. Gabreski Airport at an Air National Guard base on Long Island. She carried an XM-15 assault rifle, a shotgun, 500 rounds of ammunition, and had posted a clip of Glenn Beck on her Myspace page; she was ordered to undergo a psychiatric evaluation. Beck later debunked the concentration camp story after feeding the frenzy for weeks.

Obama haters used increasingly violent and incendiary imagery, encouraging threats against Obama and his allies. Blacks in Congress were called "nigger," spat upon, and threatened with lynching. Beck warned that Obama planned to "stir up" violence and "cause trouble."

Minnesota Congresswoman Michele Bachmann told her zombie-like followers to be "armed and dangerous." Sarah Palin's Facebook page showed symbols for snipers' crosshairs on the districts of targeted Democrats.

Federal agents arrested nine members of the self-described "Hutaree Christian Warriors" in late March 2009 in Michigan, Ohio and Indiana and charged them with seditious conspiracy, intending to "levy war against the United States." The group said it was preparing to battle against the Antichrist. Calling Obama the Antichrist is one of the most insidious accusations by the Obama haters (see chapter 5). Federal officials said activity by militia groups surged to unprecedented levels once Obama became a presidential candidate.

Nobody made these deranged people commit (or plan) violence, but challenging the legitimacy of the president, labeling a physician a murderer, and telling uninformed people that their country has been stolen away from them inspires unbalanced people to fancy themselves as patriotic heroes.

It's much easier to grasp complicated politics when we reduce it to a simplistic morality play: our side blessed with high-minded, noble, self-sacrificing heroes, while the opponents are malicious, cunning charlatans. Everybody does that.

When examining people who hate Obama, we must first look inside ourselves. In his first inaugural address, Abraham Lincoln asked Americans to appeal to "the better angels of our nature." Many Obama haters are no better or worse than the rest of us. What distinguishes them is that most are woefully uninformed about who Obama is, what he stands for, and what his presidency means to them, allowing themselves to be manipulated by demagogues.

Instead of summoning our better angels, right-wing smearmeisters tap a vein in the dark side of our nature to exploit our own worst instincts. Their cult-like followers believe they are defending some essential element of their lives and nationhood by lashing out at Obama. When asked, Obama haters can't define what makes him a communist or what he has in common with Hitler. They haphazardly jumble facts to defend a position based on emotion. Pick apart their argument, and it boils down to an empty slogan from Fox News, talk radio, or an attack e-mail.

Even though I supported Obama, I long respected John McCain and believed that he had the experience, judgment, and character to be president. But I part company with Senator McCain and his vicious, deceitful, slanderous campaign against Obama. After all the baseless accusations, the singular moment that defined the 2008 contest came when McCain had to decide in a split second whether to be held hostage to the furious distortions unleashed by his campaign or show his spine and stand up for the truth.

"I can't trust Obama. I have read about him. . . . He's an Arab," an ill-informed woman spit out at an October 10 rally in Lakeville, Minnesota, swayed by the onslaught of lies by the McCain campaign and its minions. McCain artfully grabbed the microphone and interrupted, nodding his head while saying, "No ma'am. He's a decent family man and citizen that I just happen to have disagreements with on fundamental issues, and that's what this campaign is all about."

Bravo! McCain distilled his distinguished career in a single breath. It's sad, however, that the entire bipolar campaign was not waged in this unpretentious, candid fashion.

Although his campaign was inexcusably foul, McCain, to his credit, refused to exploit racial friction surrounding African American preacher Reverend

Jeremiah Wright (see chapter 5). Fox News and others incessantly tied Obama to Wright's polemical rhetoric with no proof that the candidate agreed with a single word.

Newsweek's Evan Thomas wrote in his account of the campaign, *A Long Time Coming:*

> McCain was sincere. He did not want to win by playing on racial anxiety. He had too vivid a memory of being smeared in South Carolina in 2000. His wife had an even more searing recollection. She personally blamed Karl Rove, Bush's political guru, for unleashing the old Lee Atwater attack machine, using anonymous smear artists to spread around leaflets suggesting that her adopted daughter, Bridget, was the love child of a black prostitute. At a private gathering in Aspen, Colorado in the summer of 2007, a friend asked Cindy whether she would stab Rove in the back if he walked by. "No," she answered. "I'd stab him in the front."[1]

By October 10 emotions gushed uncontrollably from the broken-sewer rhetoric. At rallies for McCain and his vice-presidential running mate, Alaska governor Sarah Palin, people yelled "Kill him" and "Terrorist" at the mention of Obama's name. Palin's daily mantra at her public appearances—as if a robot on steroids—chanted that Obama "pals around with terrorists" and challenged his patriotism to these mini-mobs and the fawning media. The Republicans tried to make a major issue of William Ayers, a former 1960s radical who had served on boards of charitable organizations (which met a few times a year) along with Obama.

Despite McCain's words of tolerance, a robo-call during the campaign said, "Hello. I'm calling for John McCain and the RNC because you need to know that Barack Obama has worked closely with domestic terrorist Bill Ayers, whose organization bombed the U.S. Capitol, the Pentagon, a judge's home, and killed Americans. And Democrats will enact an extreme leftist agenda if they take control of Washington. Barack Obama and his Democratic allies lack the judgment to lead our country. This call was paid for by McCain-Palin 2008 and the Republican National Committee."

The McCain team decided to go all out with the Ayers smear in late September. Palin seized the hatchet, and she slashed with orgasmic gusto. *The*

Battle for America 2008: The Story of an Extraordinary Election, by Dan Balz and Haynes Johnson, depicted Palin's enthusiasm for a memo from campaign strategist Nicolle Wallace, a veteran of the Bush White House.

"The attack on Ayers unleashed the nastiest seven days of the campaign. McCain launched attacks on Obama's honesty and seemed to question his character. 'Who is the real Barack Obama?' he asked," Balz and Johnson wrote.[2]

"Finally after a week of William Ayers and talk of treason and terrorists and lack of patriotism, everyone stood down. The campaign dialogue returned to a more peaceful ground and to arguments more central to the country's real problems," the authors added.[3]

Filching a line from *The Untouchables,* Obama said that "if they bring a knife to the fight, we bring a gun," but employed heavy artillery only for defensive combat. Campaign manager David Plouffe told in his 2009 memoir *The Audacity to Win: The Inside Story and Lessons of Barack Obama's Historic Victory,* that Obama was angered over release of a negative video about McCain because he wanted to maintain a positive tone. Obama's campaign never impugned McCain's patriotism or dignity. When a slippery-tongued liberal blogger made an unsubstantiated comment— for instance, publication of a rumor that Sarah Palin's baby was borne by her daughter Bristol—Obama promptly and sharply rebuked the smear.

"I have said before and I will repeat again, I think people's families are off-limits. And people's children are especially off-limits. This shouldn't be part of our politics. It has no relevance to Governor Palin's performance as a governor or her potential performance as a vice president," Obama said at a September 1, 2008, press conference.

"Even in the final days of the election the candidate pointedly refused to hack back," wrote Richard Wolffe in his book about the campaign, *Renegade: The Making of a President:*

Fresh with cash, Obama's campaign expanded the battlefield as Election Day approached. They took out TV ads in Georgia and North Dakota—where they had previously pulled out—and in McCain's home state of Arizona, where the polls now suggested the race had narrowed between one and four points. On his regular late-night conference call, the candidate was skeptical. "Is this for real? Do we really stand a chance in Arizona?" he asked. When we heard about the polls he relented but set down a clear marker. "Well, put up a positive ad, then. Nothing negative. We're not going to keep a boot on his throat," he said. His aides pushed back, wanting to go in for the kill. "No," he insisted. "I feel strongly about this. We're not going to do that in Arizona." Obama ended up losing Arizona by almost nine points."[4]

Obama generally responded to attacks via surrogates. Instead of striking back in kind, his campaign launched its Fight the Smears website to counter the monumental disinformation (see chapter 10).

Smear tactics are nothing new in politics. In the 1800 election, pamphlets published by Federalists said, "If Thomas Jefferson is elected president, murder, robbery, rape, adultery, and incest will be openly taught and practiced." Remember the Hamilton-Burr duel? There was a time when you fought fire with real gunfire. Father Charles Coughlin red-baited Franklin D. Roosevelt at the height of the Great Depression.

Democratic Massachusetts Governor Michael Dukakis traversed the same high road as Obama, but it was his death knell. In 1988 he fell from a seventeen-point lead in the polls when his opponent, Republican Vice President George H. W. Bush, launched one of the most effective napalm bombings in political history on the advice of campaign manager Harvey LeRoy "Lee" Atwater.

Atwater honed his fangs in the employ of segregationist South Carolina Senator Strom Thurmond, where he learned anti-Semitic and racist attacks, according to the 2008 documentary *Boogie Man: The Lee Atwater Story*.

Dukakis was vanquished by his opponent's exploitation of racial fears. A previous governor, Republican Francis Sargent, had begun a furlough program in 1972 for prisoners, allowing them to leave on temporary passes before eventual release. A black convict, Willie Horton, was granted a weekend furlough in June 1986 but did not return. In April 1987 he raped a woman in Maryland and bludgeoned her boyfriend. Although Dukakis had no direct connection to Horton, the Bush campaign turned it into a major issue after testing on focus groups. Bush himself mentioned Horton first on June 9 by saying Dukakis had allowed Horton to "terrorize innocent people."

Atwater famously said he would "make Willie Horton his running mate" and "strip the bark off the little bastard."[5] Numerous states, including California during Ronald Reagan's years as governor, also had programs in which furloughed prisoners had committed violent crimes. Furthermore, the federal government had a similar furlough program during the Reagan-Bush years.

Dealing other trick cards up his sleeve, Atwater spread false rumors that Dukakis had been treated for mental illness and that his wife, Kitty, had burned the flag during a protest against the Vietnam War. The Bush crew also blasted Dukakis for vetoing legislation that required all students to recite the Pledge of Allegiance. Dukakis cited a 1943 case (*West Virginia State Board of Education v. Barnette*) in which the Supreme Court had ruled that compulsory recitation of the Pledge was unconstitutional.

David Bossie (see chapter 8) masterminded the Willie Horton ads. "I was hired by a political action committee called 'Americans for Bush,' and they asked me to craft some ads for them," Bossie said on a CNN special *Campaign Killers: Why Do Negative Ads Work?*, aired on November 28, 2007. He said the ad caused poll numbers to change "though the nightly tracking poll."

Dukakis blames himself for being blindsided. "I made a basic decision that I wasn't going to respond to the attack campaign and was mistaken. You've got to be ready for it. You've got to deal with it. As Obama was, by the way, to his credit," he told me.

At the time, he believed the high road "preferably turns the attack campaign into a character issue with the guy that's doing it." Later, he recognized that confronting smears is crucial. "So you've got to be aware of this, you've got to be alert to it. And as I discovered, to my great dismay, if you leave these attacks unanswered, then don't be surprised if at least some people begin believing them," Dukakis recalled.

Four years later Bill Clinton's campaign was ready. It learned from Dukakis's mistakes; Clinton had overcome mendacious opponents in Arkansas. Clinton was lucky he did not have to face Atwater, who had died in 1991. Some Republican strategists believe Clinton could never have won had Atwater still been alive.

The 1993 documentary *The War Room* showed how Clinton's chief strategists—James Carville, George Stephanopoulos, and Paul Begala—blunted the negative campaigning. The rapid-fire response strategy, crafted around the insatiable twenty-four-hour cable TV news cycle, was to not leave any charge unanswered. The Clintonistas handled tough issues, such as the Pentagon leaking Clinton's letter to the draft board during the Vietnam War, accusations that Clinton led anti-U.S. demonstrations in Moscow, and numerous "bimbo eruptions."

Later, another Bush employed even dirtier campaign tricks. After his father left the White House, W. ran for governor of Texas against incumbent Democrat Ann Richards. She had delivered the keynote address at the 1988 Democratic National Convention that nominated Dukakis. Her most memorable line mocked the then–vice president's patrician roots and inability to measure up to Reagan's oratorical genius. "Poor George. He can't help it— he was born with a silver foot in his mouth."

The son wanted to avenge daddy's humiliation, and the silver-coiffed Richards paid dearly for her silver-tongued wit. With Atwater acolyte Karl Rove managing the 1994 Bush gubernatorial effort, Richards was portrayed as a lesbian.

In the 2000 election, Bush fell short in the New Hampshire primary to his more experienced rival, McCain, so the South Carolina primary became a showdown. A whisper campaign alleged that McCain's adopted daughter was the offspring of a liaison between the senator and a black prostitute, and that McCain got favorable treatment at the expense of fellow war prisoners in North Vietnam.

In 2004 Massachusetts Senator John Kerry's campaign against Bush was torpedoed by the Swift Boat campaign that distorted his heroism in Vietnam. The beneficiaries of these misrepresentations were President Bush and Vice President Dick Cheney, both deserving Olympic gold medals for the speed at which they sprinted away from service in Vietnam.

It took the Kerry campaign two weeks to respond. By then, the damage had been done.

"When I first saw the ads, I thought, this is crazy. There's no way that these accusations are going to hold up," Stephanie Cutter, communications director for the Kerry campaign, said in *Campaign Killers*. "The old rule of crisis communications is that you don't respond to an attack, otherwise you elevate it."

Official records from the U.S. Navy and eyewitness accounts by other sailors who served alongside Kerry proved the smears to be lies. But news media played clips from the snazzy attack ads over and over again (yet another example of liberal bias?), which heightened the attention and impact.

"Who would have thought that they would have attacked a genuine war hero on behalf of a guy that was reading magazines in Alabama during the war, with a running mate who was one of the most notorious draft dodgers in American history?" Dukakis recounted. "And John today will tell you. He just wasn't ready for it, didn't think people would take it seriously. Well, you can't make that assumption."

Obama would not repeat the same mistakes. Dukakis said Obama "learned from my experience and John's experience. They never left an attack unanswered. Never. And you've got to do it with a fairly coherent strategy."

The late comedian George Carlin had a profanity-laced routine called "Seven Words You Can Never Say on Television." Many parents who would refuse to expose their young children to such obscenities—which they probably hear on the playground—permit their children to hear filthy lies about Obama.

Do they not know that lies harm us all? Lies. Falsehoods. Fibs. Prevarication. Misrepresentations. Fallacies. Canards. Mendacity. Sophistry. Speciousness. Untruths. Liars, when indulged, are parasites that drain the blood from democracy, thieves which steal our faith and pump hate into the heart of democracy.

"You've got to live with it. There's nothing to live with but mendacity, is there?" Big Daddy growls in one of the most riveting scenes ever performed on stage, in Tennessee Williams's *Cat on a Hot Tin Roof.* We have a choice to claw back against mendacity like Big Daddy, refusing to let the life drain out of his dying body, or let it overcome us.

The lies that anguished Big Daddy often slink below the surface. They are cleverly camouflaged as little morsels of truth buried deep within thick gobs of propaganda. "The truth, cleverly told, is the biggest lie of all," Thomas Hardy observed in *The Return of the Native* back in 1878. Nothing has changed since then.

The Obama Haters: Behind the Right-Wing Campaign of Lies, Innuendo & Racism is not another political attack by one side demeaning partisans on the other side. I praise Republicans when they stand up for the truth and criticize Obama and other Democrats when they make mistakes.

If Democrats ran a scorched-earth campaign calling John McCain or Bob Dole a traitor and a coward and demeaning their war heroism, I would pro-

test. Yet few Republicans publicly denounced the patently dishonest charac-
terizations of Dukakis, Kerry, Clinton, or Obama.

John McCain and fellow Republican Senator Chuck Hagel honorably
and vigorously defended Kerry in 2004 from the right-wing snipers. In 2000
then-senator Joe Biden and other Democrats defended McCain from the
Bush-Rove slander.

Did any Republicans come to Obama's rescue during the 2008 contest?
Before the election, one in ten voters believed Obama is a Muslim; in heavily Republican Texas, one-quarter of voters believed it. This, comically, despite loud complaints about controversial sermons by Reverend Wright. Then
again, 6 percent of the population believe the moon landing was faked and 7
percent think Elvis Presley is still alive.

If I watched Fox News or listened to Rush Limbaugh every day without
contrary information, I would probably think Obama was corrupt, stupid,
vain, and dangerous. Fox makes few attempts to correct its mistakes or distortions. The right-wing smear machine plays by its own murky rules. Listening
to them is like playing horseshoes blindfolded: lots of clanging, banging, and
clashing sounds that rattle the nerves, but almost never a ringer that slides on
target cleanly.

Obama, nevertheless, moves beyond the naysayers, even as they crouch
down into the mud for inspiration while he reaches for the stars and encourages others to do the same. Like all presidents and leaders, Obama falls short.
The most successful leaders suffer withering setbacks and even the least successful enjoy some successes.

Ideally, an American president should have the wisdom and foresight of
the Founding Fathers, Dwight Eisenhower's military might, Woodrow Wilson's academic depth, Lyndon Johnson's legislative accomplishments, Herbert Hoover's cabinet experience, Ronald Reagan's communication skills,
Bill Clinton's superior intellect, and Harry Truman's everyman common
sense. No matter how well prepared, they all fall short. George H. W. Bush
was arguably better suited for the presidency than any predecessor: he served
in Congress, was a war hero, was an ambassador to the United Nations and
China, was the head of his party, and was vice president. He was Mr. Résumé,
yet voters made him walk the plank following a single mediocre term, even
after public opinion polls earlier gave him nearly 90 percent approval thanks
to victory in the first Gulf War.

A memorable moment in our history occurred when Lincoln paraphrased the Bible ("A house divided against itself cannot stand") in his losing 1858 Senate race. We know that the nation became divided to the point of civil war just a few years later.

How divided are we now? A handful of cuckoos in Texas threaten secession, and the state's governor suffers the fools gladly. Huge numbers hate Obama palpably, but even more like him. The nation is split about how to proceed in Iraq and Afghanistan. Health care issues stoke the passions of millions. Abortion cleaves the country. Will Obama unite the country behind a common vision, or will unity crumble due to divisions and partisan bickering?

We all are willing to believe anything bad about a person we don't like. Now magnify that gossip with the Internet, with professionals manipulating facts to malign someone. That is what politicians face today at the hands of other politicians as well as professional gossips, malcontents, and organized campaigns which have no compunction about wounding a political leader, fairly or not.

Did the positive nature of Obama's winning strategy consign negative campaigning to the dustbin of history? Hardly.

Mark McKinnon, an aide to Bush and McCain, pointed to the effectiveness of attacks. "They work all the time. They've worked in the beginning. They've worked in the middle. And they've worked in the end. And they're going to continue to work," McKinnon said in *Campaign Killers*. "I hear that every cycle, you know, that people are fed up with negative advertising. But the fact is that while they say that, it motivates them, it persuades them, it compels them."

1

How an Unknown Inspired Hope in Millions and Became a Target for Hatemongers

The Internet and the kind of unfiltered, unedited junk that travels from coast to coast and around the world in the blink of an eye encourages some of this [violence]. It really feeds the crazies. Often people get this nutty stuff and they actually believe it. They think that the stuff being said is true, and, of course, it isn't.

—Larry Sabato

Most Americans felt good about the election of Barack Hussein Obama as the forty-fourth president of the United States on November 4, 2008. The nation had finally overcome its most hurtful, shameful, and enduring legacy—the enslavement of one group of people by another. Even after emancipation, there continued to be decades of denying equal rights, prejudice, overt and hidden racism, and lynching. The heirs of slaveholders, and everyone else, agreed to be governed by a man sharing racial heritage with former slaves. The vast majority of Americans were ready to do what Martin Luther King Jr. preached a half-century before: to judge a person by the content of his character and abilities without regard to race.

Americans, seeking a change from the past, entered a new era. Or so they thought. Yet the shape of things to come became obvious before the votes were counted on election night, when people started getting e-mails linked to an "Impeach Obama" website. Simultaneously, racist websites attracted record numbers of readers.

Obama was the least likely of candidates. Born in Hawaii as the son of a Kenyan immigrant and a young white woman from Kansas, he spent part of his youth in Indonesia. He studied on scholarships at Occidental College, Columbia University, then Harvard Law School, and was only forty-seven years old when elected president, before completing even one full term in the U.S. Senate. Previously, he served for eight years as an Illinois state legislator.

He faced an array of stunningly qualified top-tier candidates for the 2008 Democratic nomination. Hillary Clinton had completed seven years in the Senate and, as former first lady, was privy to valuable inside knowledge about the White House. Telegenic John Edwards had been the Democratic nominee for vice president four years before. New Mexico Governor Bill Richardson had a lengthy, highly impressive résumé as energy secretary, ambassador to the United Nations, congressman, and crisis troubleshooter around the world. Joe Biden had been a senator since Obama was in grade school, was an expert on just about everything, and knew most world leaders personally. Christopher Dodd was also a fixture in Congress for many years and was respected by people across the political bandwidth. At the start of the campaign, this youthful relative-unknown appeared to be a featherweight dwarfed by the Spanish Armada of political heavyweights.

Still, the most impressive résumés can be trumped by personal characteristics such as charisma and emotional factors. How else would someone with George W. Bush's mediocre résumé have topped the eminently better-qualified Ann Richards, John McCain, Al Gore, and John Kerry?

Voters, political know-it-alls, and professional bookmakers laying real money on the race presumed Clinton would easily win the Democratic nomination with an excellent chance to become the first female U.S. president.

Nonetheless, Obama captured a hard-fought nomination running on a platform of restoring hope and opportunity to a disillusioned populace. He nabbed 365 votes in the Electoral College and more than 69 million popular votes, or 52.9 percent, against 45.7 percent for McCain, his vastly experienced Republican opponent.

As primary season neared, Clinton's right-wing enemies sharpened their fangs, salivating at the chance to harass another chief executive for four or eight more years. After forcing the impeachment and humiliation of President Bill Clinton over a personal indiscretion, they couldn't wait to dig their claws into fresh carrion. Presumably, Obama's short résumé left little to exploit, except his lack of experience and race. While race-baiting was still popular among the dwindling ranks of never-give-an-inch racists, most Americans rejected such attacks. So there seemed little to target.

Obama attracted voters who were disgusted by the same old crowd running Washington. Many Democrats, worn out by the drama surrounding the Clintons, were weary of right-wing attacks against the couple, whether justified or not. For millions of Americans, it was time to move on and start anew.

Obama proved his muster by taking on frontrunner Clinton. As Obama overtook his rivals, the *scheisse-slingers* changed gears deftly and began to sully him. For two decades the right wing had relied on painting every Democratic presidential nominee as unpatriotic. In Obama's case, that was only one spike in a multi-pronged pitchfork of attack.

Public Policy Polling released a survey on October 21, 2009, which said 59 percent of Americans believed Obama loves America and 26 percent believed he does not. Among Republicans, only 27 percent believed he loves America, 48 percent said he does not, and 25 percent were unsure.

A Research 2000 poll of Republicans released on February 2, 2010, found 39 percent think Obama should be impeached. *Sacré bleu!* Did he start a war on false pretenses or disclose the identity of an undercover CIA agent? Other findings: 63 percent see Obama as a socialist, one-quarter are convinced Obama "wants the terrorists to win," 53 percent find the grotesquely and frighteningly unqualified Sarah Palin qualified to be president, one-quarter think their state should secede from the United States, and 77 percent believe the Bible should be taught in public schools. Only 42 percent admit that Obama was born in the United States; the rest are unsure or believe he is foreign born. Roughly one-third believe Obama "is a racist who hates white people," a third believe he is not, and the same proportion are unsure. Are these the opinions of people with a grip on reality and awareness of the cold, hard facts?

Fox's Bill O'Reilly—incapable of fathoming the shrill irony of his remarks—labeled the Research 2000 poll a plot to make Republicans look silly. Fox treats denying the legitimacy of Obama's birth certificate as worthy of debate. Fox's Glenn Beck called Obama a racist "who hates white people." Fox commentators and guests—including those on O'Reilly's own show—

regularly brand Obama as a socialist, communist, or fascist without rebuttal. Fox News, clearly, is a major factor in spreading smears against Obama with no basis in reality. Furthermore, the Research 2000 survey is consistent with numerous polls cited throughout this book regarding opinions about Obama held by Republicans with no factual underpinnings.

Who are these Obama haters detected in the polls? Some are unrepentant racists who refuse to accept a successful black person outside of sports or entertainment. But what about the rest? Why do they feel this way? Who puts such radical, bizarre, and untrue thoughts in people's heads? And why is this venom so powerful?

It would be easy to conclude, based on such polling data, that right wingers have declared war on the truth. Remember that the Bush administration looked askance at the "reality-based community" when Karl Rove bragged, "We create our own reality."

In this book, I investigate this phenomenon in unprecedented depth, connecting current events to rancorous right-wing smear tactics in the past. I will shine a harsh spotlight on the haters' and fearmongers' tactics and show how the Internet and right-wing media give a soapbox to every keyboard-pounding crackpot.

Profound words by a Nobel Prize–winning poet can be disseminated as far and wide and quickly as vulgar profanity by a racist, hatemonger, or pornographer. And many people just can't distinguish the difference.

The Obama haters often use words and descriptions that don't stand up to scrutiny, so I define words that are misused. I draw mostly from *Merriam-Webster's Collegiate Dictionary, Eleventh Edition*. Standard, neutral descriptions are necessary because extremists of all persuasions hijack language and debase the meaning of words.

I will use the judgmental terms "right-winger" and "far-right" to distinguish from authentic conservatives, who are devoted to preserving the Constitution. I don't use those terms when describing a generally held conservative view. I object strongly when news organizations such as Fox News freely bat about terms such as "far-left" and "left-wing," especially to describe viewpoints held by a majority or a significant plurality and to demean people whose opinions differ from their meme. "Far-left" and "left-wing" are accurate only when describing fringe views. The right-wing activities I investigate represent views held by a minuscule segment of the population but are espoused by people who practice mouthfeasance with outsize megaphones and inflated egos.

Political hacks manipulate weasel words to give an impression without saying so directly. Study the language by the Bush-Cheney cadre leading up to the invasion of Iraq. Slick wordsmiths devised phrases to give Americans the impression that Saddam Hussein was in cahoots with the September 11 plotters, but after all of their arguments were proven wrong, they backtracked and claimed they never made such statements. When you examine their old arguments, it's obvious that they conflated unrelated events. This is demagoguery. The dictionary defines a demagogue as "a leader who makes use of popular prejudices and false claims and promises in order to gain power." The biggest of the bigmouths on the Right—in particular, but not limited to, Rush Limbaugh, Sean Hannity, O'Reilly, and Beck—practice demagoguery regularly.

Right-wingers invent terms and test them with focus groups to see which get the most emotional impact as a way to further their goals. Here are some examples of right-wing neologisms that constitute etymological malpractice:

Death panels: When health reform legislation contained a Republican-sponsored provision to require health insurers to pay for counseling over end-of-life decisions such as a living will, Palin and other right-wingers chanted falsely that Obama was establishing "death panels" of government bureaucrats to decide who lives and dies.

Death tax: Use of this expression tricked millions of people into thinking their humble possessions would be seized upon their demise. Inheritance taxes are levied only on estates totaling more than $3.5 million for an individual or $7 million per couple. Since when are Internal Revenue Service spooks lurking about mortuaries?

Democrat Party: This is used instead of Democratic Party to denote disrespect. Refusing to call a person or institution by its own chosen name is the height of impertinence. It would be comparable to someone saying Big Fat Idiot Party to describe the Republicans by naming the party after its mascot, Rush Limbaugh.

Partial-birth abortion: Use of this term was coined to maximize emotional appeal. You can't be partially pregnant, partially born, or partially aborted. The correct term used by medical professionals is intact dilation and extraction. Irrespective of your opinion about abortion, doctors, not political consultants, should define medical procedures. What if a political hack called prostate removal a "libido inhibitor?" That would not make it correct.

Small business: Republicans demagogue that Obama's tax plans will hurt "small business," conjuring up images of mom-and-pop shops, when in fact Republican tax laws allow companies such as Bechtel Corporation, the nation's biggest engineering firm with $31 billion in annual revenues, to qualify for tax breaks as "small businesses," according to Pulitzer Prize–winning author David Cay Johnston.

Whether attempting to cast its own ideas in a positive light or vilify opponents, the right wing pays top dollar to propagandistic manipulators adept at exploiting language with maximum emotional impact. When Bush lusted to wage war in Iraq, his advisers coined phrases such as "axis of evil," "weapons of mass destruction," and "We cannot wait for the final proof—the smoking gun—that could come in the form of a mushroom cloud." After such phrases were vetted by focus groups, the Bush administration and its toadies spread its propaganda via interviews with compliant media. Anyone who analyzed the policies instead of being railroaded by slogans was dismissed with "You're either with us or you're with the terrorists." With one phrase, they tossed Saddam Hussein, Osama Bin Laden, skeptical allies such as France, and domestic critics into the same bucket without distinction.

The Obama administration, by contrast, never accused domestic antagonists of being in league with hostile regimes such as North Korea or Iran.

When out of power, the right wing maligns its adversaries with simplistic one-liners. Inflammatory accusations are a proud part of right-wing repertoire, according to Saul Anuzis, former chairman of the Michigan Republican Party.

"We've so overused the word 'socialism' that it no longer has the negative connotation it had twenty years ago, or even ten years ago," Anuzis, who lost a bid to became national party chairman, told the *New York Times*.[1] "Fascism—everybody still thinks that's a bad thing." How many people think the words coming out of Anuzis's mouth are a bad thing?

The right wing has degraded into a single strategy: blind attacks. This shrunken, tireless, fanatic core of Republican Party nabobs, Tea Party leaders, right-wing news organizations and commentators, anonymous bloggers, fanatic preachers, and cockeyed crackpots lobs scurrilous salvos with a single purpose: to see who might land a fatal blow to President Obama's administration. Did the Founding Fathers envision this when they established First Amendment guarantees?

Antics by the Obama haters are as off-key as Groucho Marx singing, "Whatever it is, I'm against it" in *Horse Feathers*.

This debate is debased further when media outlets give a platform to the perpetrators of these smears. They might let "the other side" debunk the rumor, but there isn't always another side to basic facts. When an astronaut is interviewed, nobody seeks comment from a nutcase who insists the moon landing was staged. When victims of Hitler's Final Solution tell their tragic stories, news organizations don't let Holocaust deniers tell "the other side."

Then, why do they give a platform to someone who says Obama has a fake birth certificate, or that he is a Muslim, or that he pals around with terrorists? These are all canards without a shred of evidence. Interviewing liars only spreads the lie further. When the kook appears alongside a truth teller, they are given equal weight, but the truth is not equal to a lie.

As fast as Obama scrambles to fix the unprecedented mess Bush left him, the right wing keeps greasing the path and sticking out their feet to trip him. Like that arcade game Whac-A-Mole—where players pound on moles with a mallet, only to find another popping up elsewhere—I will whack at numerous pesky moles in this book, but they just keep surfacing somewhere else.

After Obama haters cheered Chicago's loss of the 2016 Olympics, Paul Krugman wrote in the *New York Times*:

> The episode illustrated an essential truth about the state of American politics: at this point, the guiding principle of one of our nation's two great political parties is spite pure and simple. If Republicans think something might be good for the president, they're against it—whether

or not it's good for America. How did one of our great political parties become so ruthless, so willing to embrace scorched-earth tactics even if so doing undermines the ability of any future administration to govern? The result has been a cynical, ends-justify-the-means approach."[2]

As this irritating noise engulfs the airwaves, many Americans scratch their heads. "There's been a transformation of the conservative establishment," Sam Tanenhaus, author of *The Death of Conservatism,* told Bill Moyers on PBS on September 19, 2009. Tanenhaus said the intellectuals have left the conservative movement.

"So, it's been dominated instead by monotonic, theatrically impressive voices and faces," he added. "It means it's ideologically depleted. What we're seeing now and hearing are the noisemakers, in [William F.] Buckley's phrase."

Tanenhaus compared the Tea Party movement to the John Birch Society of the 1950s and 1960s because both are "extremist, revanchist groups which view politics in a very conspiratorial way." He recalled that the Birchers considered President Dwight Eisenhower a Communist. In 1965 Buckley, a conservative intellectual icon (admired by this author) who died in 2008, denounced the John Birch Society. Where is today's William F. Buckley?

2

Falsehoods About Obama Echo Endlessly, Even After Debunking

Make the lie big, make it simple, keep saying it, and eventually they will believe it.

—Joseph Goebbels

Nearly everyone in public life has been smeared. Celebrities and average people have been cast into the limelight—perhaps thrown to the wolves—for their fleeting fifteen minutes of fame. Just ask Samuel Joseph Wurzelbacher, better known as Joe the Plumber, who obsequiously thrust himself before the klieg lights when Obama was campaigning in Ohio. Within days the whole world knew that Joe was not really named Joe and that most of the things he said about himself were fables. Without the opportunistic media attention, nobody would have heard about this man, who nonetheless used his undeserved fame to get a book deal and recording contract.

Those who seek the spotlight are often singed or even destroyed by it. Ordinary people are turned into monsters. Lawsuits for defamation are rarely successful and draw even more attention to outlandish accusations.

Anyone who seeks to be rich and famous should remember the dark side of celebrity: the cottage industry to destroy luminaries for fun, for profit, or maybe just for envy and spite. Anyone can jump in at any point and take potshots. Fire away.

Nobody is exempt, not even Mother Teresa, who tirelessly devoted her energies to the sick and dying, the untouchables of India's fetid slums. She remained single-mindedly devoted to her life's mission until she died at age eighty-seven without ever resting on her abundant laurels. None of this stopped Christopher Hitchens from attacking her in *The Missionary Position: Mother Teresa in Theory and Practice,* published in 1995. If even Mother Teresa is not immune from calumny, who among us mere mortals—with presumably many more faults, foibles, and weaknesses than Mother Teresa—can escape the wrath of someone with a fat mouth and computer keyboard, let alone well-financed, mean-spirited people with an agenda to crucify anyone they choose? How would Jesus fare in today's tabloid-driven Internet world?

The best-organized hate machine in American political history aimed all its ammunition incessantly at Bill and Hillary Clinton. The slime started flying when he was governor of Arkansas and never stopped: he smuggled drugs, ordered the murder of a White House aide, committed rape, swindled people in the Whitewater land deal, and had extramarital sex with women. Hillary was alternatively described as a lesbian, frigid, having a screw loose, or drug-addled. Of course, we know now that only the womanizer accusation against Bill Clinton was true, but it was nearly enough to topple a president. By the time Clinton was impeached for libidinal lying, millions of people believed he was guilty of real crimes but had somehow hidden the evidence despite the unblinking, searing spotlight on every corner of his life.

One might hope that after Election Day, the hatred against Obama would cease. After all, the McCain campaign had rolled up the carpet, turned out the lights, and gone home, its staff scattering to the winds. But for some determined individuals and groups unwilling to accept Obama's election, the party was just beginning.

PLEDGE OF ALLEGIANCE

Obama haters e-mail a photograph snapped during a September 16, 2007, political forum in Indianola, Iowa, that shows Obama's hands limply at his waist while Bill Richardson, Hillary Clinton, and Ruth Harkin placed their hands over their hearts. The e-mails are accompanied by these remarks: "He refused to not only put his hand on his heart during the pledge of allegiance, but refused to say the pledge . . . how in the hell can a man like this expect to be our next commander in chief?"

It looks damning until you learn that this was the National Anthem being sung at that moment, not a recitation of the Pledge. A video of this event shows Obama singing the anthem while the others stood mutely with their hands over their hearts.

"My grandfather taught me how to say the Pledge of Allegiance when I was two. . . . During the Pledge of Allegiance you put your hand over your heart. During the national anthem you sing," Obama explained in a November 7, 2007, interview with the Associated Press.

Other pictures were taken before and after this same event that show Obama with hand on heart during the Pledge. Long after this smear was debunked, saboteurs continued to circulate it.

FOREIGN STUDENT HOAX

A false news item e-mailed anonymously on April Fool's Day in 2009 purported to be an Associated Press story announcing that Obama had enrolled as a foreign student named Barry Soetoro at Occidental College. Even though this e-mail of undetermined origin was a fabrication, it ricocheted around the Internet and managed to convince some people that he is not truly an American.

> April 1, 2009 - AP- WASHINGTON D.C. - In a move certain to fuel the debate over Obama's qualifications for the presidency, the group Americans for Freedom of Information has released copies of President Obama's college transcripts from Occidental College. Released today, the transcript indicates that Obama, under the name Barry Soetoro, received financial aid as a foreign student from Indonesia as an undergraduate at the school. The transcript was released by Occidental College in compliance with a court order in a suit brought by the group in the Superior Court of California. The transcript shows that Obama (Soetoro) applied for financial aid and was awarded a fellowship for foreign students from the Fulbright Foundation Scholarship program. To qualify for the scholarship, a student must claim foreign citizenship. This document would seem to provide the smoking gun that many of Obama's detractors have been seeking.
>
> The news has created a firestorm at the White House as the release casts increasing doubt about Obama's legitimacy and qualification to serve as president. When reached for comment in London, where he has

been in meetings with British Prime Minister Gordon Brown, Obama smiled but refused comment on the issue. Meanwhile, White House press secretary Robert Gibbs scoffed at the report stating that this was obviously another attempt by a right-wing conservative group to discredit the president and undermine the administration's efforts to move the country in a new direction.

Britain's *Daily Mail* has also carried the story in a front-page article titled, "Obama Eligibility Questioned," leading some to speculate that the story may overshadow economic issues on Obama's first official visit to the U.K.

This is stuffed full of falsehoods. The AP denied the story immediately. There is no such organization called "Americans for Freedom of Information." The *Daily Mail* never published this story. Obama did not use the surname of his stepfather, Lolo Soetoro, outside Indonesia.

Occidental College proudly boasts that the future president attended from the fall of 1979 through spring 1981 registered as—who would believe this alias?—Barack Obama.

"All of the alumni I have spoken to from that era who knew him, knew him as Barack Obama or Barry Obama," Jim Tranquada, the college spokesman, told me. "At the time he studied here, there was a campus literary magazine called *Feast*. Two of his poems appeared under the name Barack Obama," he said. "Fulbright scholarships are for graduate study. They are not given to undergraduates. Obama was an undergraduate at Occidental."

Sadly, the truth has no bearing on the Obama haters, who impulsively believe anything that makes Obama look bad.

Free Republic, a right-wing website said, "LORD, GOD, PLEASE MULTIPLY THE SPREAD OF THIS INFO INTO EVERY EVEN PARTIALLY PATRIOTIC AMERICAN'S CONSCIOUSNESS, IN Your Name, Lord." Here is a rare case in which I wholeheartedly endorse the Obama haters' rhetoric. If Free Republic writers define themselves as "partially patriotic Americans," why argue with them?

THE TALE OF THE MISSING "THESIS"

Right-wing bloggers worked themselves into a tizzy when they were unable to unearth Obama's senior paper from Columbia University. Obama and the university allegedly did not save copies. David Bossie took out classified ads in Columbia University's newspaper and the *Chicago Tribune* in March 2008 searching for the "missing thesis."

There was no thesis.

On July 24, 2008, NBC News quoted Obama's former professor Michael Baron as saying, "My recollection is that the paper was an analysis of the evolution of the arms reduction negotiations between the Soviet Union and the United States. For U.S. policy makers in both political parties, the aim was not disarmament, but achieving deep reductions in the Soviet nuclear arsenal and keeping a substantial and permanent American advantage. As I remember it, the paper was about those negotiations, their tactics and chances for success. Barack got an A."

Critics label the missing paper a "thesis," even though Columbia University said undergraduates in 1983 did not write a thesis.

Rush Limbaugh, a college dropout, finally uncovered the "missing thesis" and informed his listeners on October 23, 2009, quoting Obama as having written about "plutocratic thugs with one hand on the money and the other on the government." The only trouble is that it was a hoax. Even after Limbaugh learned he had been punked, he said: "I don't care if these quotes are made up. I know Obama thinks it." Limbaugh finally demonstrated definitively that accuracy and truth have no influence on his words.

ANTOIN "TONY" REZKO

Chicago real-estate developer Antoin "Tony" Rezko was convicted in June 2008 of corruption in his dealings with the state of Illinois.

Rezko met Obama in 1990 when the developer made an unsolicited job offer to the Harvard Law School student. Obama turned it down. In 1993 Obama went to work for the Davis, Miner, Barnhill & Galland law firm, which represents developers and non-profits. Rezko was a client of that firm.

When Obama launched his campaign for the Illinois Senate in 1995, Rezko was an early supporter. Upon election to the seat in 1996, Obama's district included eleven of Rezko's thirty low-income housing projects. Rezko held a fundraiser in June 2003 for Obama's 2004 campaign for the U.S. Senate.

In June 2005 Obama paid $1.65 million for a mansion in Chicago, $300,000 below asking price. Rezko's wife paid $625,000 for an adjacent vacant lot. Six months later, when Rezko was under federal investigation,

Obama paid Rezko's wife $104,500 for a strip of land along their boundary to enlarge his yard. Obama later called the purchase a "bone-headed" move because it allowed critics to suspect impropriety.

Rezko was indicted in October 2006 on charges he sought kickbacks from companies doing business with Illinois Governor Rod Blagojevich. Federal prosecutors said Rezko donated $10,000 worth of kickback money to Obama, who later gave that money to charity.

Investigators and prosecutors never found any Obama involvement in Rezko's illegal dealings; Rezko never implicated Obama.

ROD BLAGOJEVICH

The Democratic Illinois governor became a poster boy for corruption, stupidity, and foul language when tapes of his attempts to "sell" Obama's open Senate seat to the highest bidder became public shortly after the presidential election.

Obama kept his distance from Blagojevich because of the governor's shady reputation.

Blagojevich was arrested on December 9, 2008, before appointing Obama's successor. U.S. Attorney Patrick Fitzgerald said Obama and his team were not implicated in the skullduggery. In fact, the governor was taped saying the Obama staff offered "nothing but appreciation," which makes it quite clear that Obama and his aides refused to play along with the scheme.

But that did not stop Fox News and the rest of the anti-Obama symphony from loudly contriving imaginary links. Sean Hannity said on December 9 that Obama is "all over" the criminal complaint against Blagojevich: "The pres—the word 'president-elect' is mentioned forty-four times in the document. Pretty troubling." Hannity just moved on to the next smear and never explained what he found "troubling" in a report that convincingly cleared Obama.

GUNS

After Obama's election, legal gun sales surged due to fears that Obama would outlaw firearms purchases. The National Rifle Association ran an ad saying Obama planned to "ban use of firearms for home self-defense," eliminate the right to carry weapons, "ban the manufacture, sale, and possession of handguns," "close down 90 percent of gun shops in America," ban commonly used ammunition, and appoint judges who "share his views on the Second Amendment."

Obama did nothing to take away gun rights and never said he would seize weapons from law-abiding citizens. The gun lobby, however, prefers to inflame passions rather than speak the truth, even if it triggers murderous rampages by unbalanced followers.

Richard Poplawski, twenty-three, of Pittsburgh, believed the NRA lies. He was described as a paranoid white supremacist who allegedly killed two police officers and wounded three others on April 4, 2009, out of fear that Obama would seize his guns.

THE "BABY KILLER"

Anti-abortion advocates say Obama practices infanticide because he supports legalized abortion. The controversy stemmed from 2001 legislation in Illinois (SB-1082) that was intended to "protect" infants who were "born alive" during an abortion.

A law already on the books in Illinois (Illinois Compiled Statutes, 720 ILCS 510/6) stipulated:

> No abortion shall be performed or induced when the fetus is viable unless there is in attendance a physician other than the physician performing or inducing the abortion who shall take control of and provide immediate medical care for any child born alive as a result of the abortion. Subsequent to the abortion, if a child is born alive, the physician required to be in attendance shall exercise the same degree of professional skill, care and diligence to preserve the life and health of the child as would be required of a physician providing immediate medical care to a child born alive in the course of a pregnancy termination which was not an abortion.

Therefore, Obama was not backing infanticide by opposing a bill that duplicated a law already in effect. But that has not stopped his enemies from calling him a baby killer.

Opponents of legal abortion should recognize they are outnumbered five to one and that Obama's views coincide with the overwhelming majority of

Americans. These numbers have been consistent since annual polling on the issue began in 1975.

The annual Gallup poll, taken in 2010, showed 54 percent favor legal abortion with restrictions, 24 percent want no restrictions and 19 percent want all abortions banned.

Conservatives rail against "activist liberal judges," but five of the Supreme Court's members were appointed by Republican presidents and four by Democrats. Republicans appointed 60 percent of federal appeals judges, with a majority on every circuit. Despite this Republican advantage on the courts, they have not banned abortion.

MENTALLY UNSTABLE

Talk about instability is one of the more contemptible lies against Obama, since he has never lost his cool in public and is not known for behaving any differently in private.

On July 21, 2009, Limbaugh said, "Obama is showing signs of being unhinged and signs of instability." Take it from Limbaugh, an expert on instability. In 2003 he admitted an addiction to narcotics and buying opiates illegally. In another incident involving drugs, Limbaugh was detained by a customs officer for possessing Viagra with a prescription in someone else's name. Do stable people behave this way?

The same day, Ann Coulter dittoed Limbaugh on Hannity's TV show. "You can see he's becoming unhinged," she said.

On July 23 Bill Sammon, Fox's Washington bureau chief, said, "There is a whiff of panic" in the Obama White House. A few hours later, Obama gave a press conference that embodied a 1960s deodorant commercial: cool, calm, and collected.

It is the Obama haters, in fact, who have a scary habit of melting down on the air.

As a host on *Inside Edition* in the 1990s, a younger Bill O'Reilly, sporting a blow-dried pompadour that would win first place in a Gomer Pyle–look-alike contest, flipped out over an apparent technical glitch. In frustration, he exploded, "We'll do it live, fuck it. Do it live. I'll write it, and we'll do it live. Fucking thing sucks." After that, O'Reilly composed himself long enough to read the show's closing lines and then flailed his arms as he bolted out of his chair.

O'Reilly went berserk on May 18, 2009, on his radio show when a caller

challenged his remark, "I've been in combat." O'Reilly said that as a journalist, he was "in the middle of a couple of firefights in South and Central
America . . . people were shooting at me." When the caller said that O'Reilly
phrased his remarks in a way to make people think he was a military veteran,
O'Reilly blew up, saying, "Hey listen Roger, you know what? You can take your
little fair and balanced snit remark and shove it. Okay? You're not getting on
this air. And you, mister macho man, would have never come close to anything I've done down where I've been. Okay? So take a walk."

On July 22, 2009, O'Reilly said on his Fox News program, "I think my
head is going to explode." Did he mean to imply that it had not exploded
already?

While O'Reilly pretentiously nicknames his program "the no-spin zone,"
whenever he appears on TV, his head is always spinning faster than that of
Linda Blair's character in *The Exorcist*.

Coulter crash-landed on August 24, 2006, on Fox's *Hannity & Colmes*
when a guest host challenged her statement that Osama bin Laden was "irrelevant." Coulter began to talk loudly over the other guests, turning her head
wildly, saying, "Good night. It was nice being here. We're done," and stormed
off the set. Do families of 9/11 victims—who Coulter attacked by saying "I've
never seen people enjoying their husbands' deaths so much"—think bin
Laden is irrelevant?

Glenn Beck turned himself inside out July 15, 2009, when a caller challenged him about mocking people unable to get health care. "Cathy, get off
my phone. Get off my phone you little pinhead. I don't care. You people don't
care about the trillions. Get off the phone. I'm going to lose my mind today,"
he screamed. He was honest, just this once, about his own mental state.

Michael Savage has lost his head so often on the air that it's not clear
whose head he uses these days.

I'm not a psychiatrist, so I can't define their mental state, but one has
to wonder if these on-air personalities act this way because they are truly deranged, or if it is a put-on so their unbalanced fan base feels a kinship.

OBAMA'S "VICTIMS"

Gerald Walpin was fired as inspector general for AmeriCorps in June 2009 after investigating alleged misuse of federal grants by Sacramento mayor Kevin
Johnson, an Obama ally and former pro basketball star.

Beck and Laura Ingraham made it a cause célèbre, insisting that Obama ordered the hit on Walpin. Of course, they never mentioned that a Bush-appointed U.S. attorney said Walpin withheld exculpatory evidence, that the case against Johnson was settled before Obama took office, or that Ameri-Corps's board of directors, not Obama, ordered the dismissal.

Beck compared it to Soviet oppression. "Our government will destroy whoever they have to destroy to get their way. It's the latest example in a long line of people destroyed by this government," he drooled, with scary music playing in the background.

The screen then showed a video montage of Obama's other "victims." It started with the David Letterman/Sarah Palin flap over a distasteful joke (see chapter 8). Letterman is a government agent? Palin was destroyed? Was this before or after she grabbed millions for an autobiography she didn't write and lip-synched the words of others at speaking engagements?

Next Beck showed "Joe the Plumber," who told candidate Obama during the campaign that his tax program would ruin Joe's plans to buy a business. It turned out that Joe did not have a plumbing license and did not have the financial resources to buy a business as stated. It was not the government that uncovered Joe's misrepresentations, and Obama was not in charge at that time. Somehow, Joe got a book contract and a recording deal in Nashville. Joe was not destroyed. He enjoyed far more money and fame than his meager talents would have ever earned him without throwing himself in Obama's path.

Viewers then saw former General Motors CEO Rick Wagoner, who resigned as part of the bailout to fix the mendicant auto manufacturer. It was Wagoner, not Obama, who made disastrous decisions for eight years that brought the auto giant to the cusp of collapse. Who is the victim: Wagoner, who walked away from GM with a $20 million retirement package, or the thousands of people who lost jobs due to Wagoner's mismanagement? If Wagoner is a victim, let me be the first to offer myself to suffer his great misfortune.

Beck was inventing connections—following his nasty habit—between unrelated events, and painting people as victims who instead profited handsomely despite their utter failure, incompetence, and mediocrity.

YOU LIE!

Whenever attacks against Obama appear to reach a limit, someone zooms further into the Twilight Zone. When the president spoke before Congress about the need for health care reforms on September 9, 2009, Republican Congressman Addison Graves "Joe" Wilson of South Carolina drowned out the president by yelling "You lie!" when Obama said health reforms did not include illegal immigrants. Historians called this outburst unprecedented. Wilson apologized, and Obama graciously wanted to drop the matter, but the right-wing echo chamber egged on Wilson, saying Democrats had accused George W. Bush of lying. Bush did lie to Congress about the invasion of Iraq and his numerous violations of the Constitution. Yet not one Democrat ever yelled at Bush in Congress.

The sincerity of Wilson's apology must be called into question. Before his infamous words stopped echoing in the halls of Congress, he was already exploiting his impertinence to raise money for his reelection and for fellow Republicans.

Not all Republicans were knee-jerk supporters of boorish behavior toward the president.

"Make Joe Wilson pay. And by pay, I mean beat his sorry ass at the polls and send him to the private sector. That is the only way to change the political discourse in America today. Because as long as louts like Joe Wilson can spout off and call the president a liar and get rewarded with reelection, then louts will continue to spout off. And we will continue to claw our way to the very bottom of the political swamp," Mark McKinnon, a former adviser to Bush the Second and John McCain, wrote at The Daily Beast.[1]

TAKE BACK AMERICA

Right-wingers put their most intolerant extremists on display at the "How to Take Back America" conference in September 2009. Among the issues were "How to Counter the Homosexual Extremist Movement," "How to Stop Socialism in Health Care," and "How to Recognize Living Under Nazis and Communists."

Anyone who knows the first thing about dictatorships would tell this crowd to be thankful they live in the United States, where they can regurgitate such brainless pap, because a tyrant would have jailed them.

Speakers were a who's who list of congressional Republicans comprising the sludge of the IQ barrel: Tom McClintock, Tom Price, Steve King, and Michele Bachmann, along with Joe the faux Plumber. Even Mike Huckabee did a gigantic belly flop into the Obama-hating cesspool after previously tiptoeing around the edges.

Phyllis Schlafly, a one-time flunky for the far-right John Birch Society, said Americans don't want "our country to be run by czars," which she called "a Russian idea." She seemed unaware that George W. Bush appointed as many "czars" as did Obama and that the nickname for presidential advisers has no connection to Russia (see chapter 6).

Huckabee said of the United Nations, "It's time to get a jackhammer and to simply chip off that part of New York City and let it float into the East River, never to be seen again!" Huckabee did not mention whether he had discussed this plan with Osama bin Laden, who sought to carry out Huckabee's wish on 9/11.

Trent Franks, a Republican congressman from Arizona, declared that Obama "has no place in any station of government and we need to realize that he is an enemy of humanity."

Kitty Werthmann, Eagle Forum South Dakota president, told people to "buy more guns and buy ammunition, take back America."

Who better reflects the values of our nation, and who sounds scarier: Obama or this ship of fools?

NOBEL PRIZE

The Nobel Peace Prize is perhaps the most prestigious honor in the history of mankind. People the world over applaud the award and its recipients. When Obama was bestowed this great tribute on October 9, 2009, people questioned whether he deserved it, only nine months into his presidency. Many people wondered if his deeds measured up. That's a fair question, but this achievement became an excuse for racism and hatred.

"I did not realize the Nobel Peace Prize had an affirmative action quota," Erick Erickson scribbled at RedState.[2]

While other networks compiled reaction from around the world that day, Fox News spent nearly two hours covering, via helicopter, police chasing a truck in Texas. Will history books record that Obama won the Nobel Prize on this day or recount a routine police chase in Texas?

Limbaugh led the buffoonery by saying, "Our president is a worldwide joke," and agreed with the Taliban by condemning the award. Rush freely admitted that his interests and what's good for America are polar opposites.

Beck chimed in on Fox News that the award instead should go to the Tea Party movement that was duped into participating in corporate-funded protests against health care reforms.

O'Reilly said, "There are times when what's good for America should trump partisan politics. President Obama was honored today, and deserved or not, the world is hearing America and peace in the same sentence, and that's good." Fair enough, but five minutes later, he blurted out: "The Nobel Peace Prize committee has now said to the world, 'We are a joke, we don't know what we're doing, we're in business to promote liberal politics.'"

Chris Wallace, the usually serious host of Fox News Sunday, said of the Nobel Committee, elected by the Norwegian Parliament. The Norwegian Parliament is a very left-of-center, left-leaning organization, and the people who are on this are very left leaning."

Past recipients include Martin Luther King, the Dalai Lama, Mikhail Gorbachev, Aung San Suu Kyi, Nelson Mandela, Elie Wiesel, Lech Walesa, Mother Teresa, Anwar El-Sadat and Menachem Begin, Andrei Sakharov, Henry Kissinger, and Dag Hammarskjöld. Who is undeserving? Where is the pattern of left-leaning people?

John McCain was one of the few Republicans who simply praised the award without lacing his words with strychnine: "As Americans, we're proud when our president receives an award of that prestigious category."

I have personally met one Nobel recipient, Óscar Arias of Costa Rica, who brokered lasting peace accords in Central America in the 1980s. He is truly worthy of the award for working tirelessly to stop the bloodshed that afflicted millions of people. Most people around the world, outside the Obama haters, hope and pray that Obama will manage to do likewise.

It was not enough for people to criticize Barack Obama as a candidate or as a president. The Obama haters also thrust their swords into his wife, Michelle; his grandmother, Madelyn Dunham; a distant relative, Zeituni Onyango; and even the Obama children.

MICHELLE OBAMA

The most tasteless smear against the first lady was the accusation that she used the term "whitey" to describe Caucasians. "I now have it from four sources (three who are close to senior Republicans) that there is video dynamite—Michelle Obama railing against 'whitey' at Jeremiah Wright's church . . . I am told there is a clip that is being held for the fall to drop at the appropriate time," Larry Johnson wrote on his blog at the No Quarter website. This despicable smear ping-ponged around the right-wing echo chamber. If she spoke this way in a packed church, why did nobody corroborate it? After all, nobody hid Reverend Wright's controversial words. This fictitious video never materialized.

Instead of bursting out in anger, Michelle handled the incident with dignity, grace, and wit by referring to 1970s TV sitcom *The Jeffersons*: "I mean, 'whitey?' That's something that George Jefferson would say. Anyone who says that doesn't know me. They don't know the life I've lived. They don't know anything about me."

O'Reilly said on September 16, 2008, on his TV show, "I have a lot of people who call me on the radio and say she [Michelle Obama] looks angry. And I have to say there's some validity to that. She looks like an angry woman."

Such comments fit racial stereotypes without resorting to name calling, yet can't be refuted. Don't racists love to demonize an "angry black" as an object of fear? O'Reilly, like any coward, artfully deflects blame to his callers. O'Reilly and his Fox cohorts look and act a lot angrier than Michelle.

The *New York Post* reported on its "Page Six" gossip page on October 17 that Michelle had gorged on lobster and caviar at the Waldorf Astoria two days earlier. Rupert Murdoch's tabloid reproduced an alleged $447.39 bill for room service that listed lobster hors d'oeuvres, two whole lobsters, Iranian caviar, and Bollinger champagne at the midtown Manhattan hotel. The scandal sheet retracted the story a week later. Michelle was not even in New York at the time of the alleged incident, but rather on an airplane en route to a campaign event in Fort Wayne, Indiana.

A year later, right-wingers were still repeating this smear as if it were valid.

The cover of *Globe*, a *National Enquirer* wannabe, read "Michelle Obama's SECRET HIT LIST!" The July 6, 2009, issue carried the byline Randy Jernigan, but it looked like a plant by a dirty Republican trickster. This is not the typical story about two-headed goats, space aliens, or walking mummies. It was laced with well-researched political invective with a definite goal.

"Shockingly, the 45-year-old First Lady has devised a detailed plan that has Barack winning a second term FOLLOWED by Michelle becoming the first woman president, sources reveal. She is determined to keep the Obamas in the Oval Office until 2024, say insiders," the article stated.

The article also revived a vicious lie by ex-con Larry Sinclair, which got scant attention because it is so outlandish and uncorroborated. *Globe* said, "And she's desperately trying to cultivate a wholesome image for her husband, who has been accused of using cocaine and having a gay sex fling with the author of a controversial book."

Two out of three Americans held a favorable view of Michelle, even when the president himself fared below 50 percent in late 2010. That didn't stop Ingraham from attacking Michelle as a guest host on *The O'Reilly Factor* by saying "the co-presidency makes people uncomfortable," on October 30, 2009. She was mischaracterizing a *New York Times Magazine* profile in which the president said he discusses policy with his wife, a graduate of Harvard Law School. Yet Ingraham did not voice any complaints when it was revealed that oil field roustabout and "first dude" Todd Palin was allowed to make policy decisions when Sarah was governor of Alaska.

GRANDMA "TOOT"

Madelyn Dunham, who Obama affectionately called "Toot," tragically never lived to see her cherished grandson elected president. She died on November 2 at age eighty-six during the weekend before the election. But her advanced age and frail health didn't stop the attacks against her.

Larry Sinclair on Obambi.com alleged that Dunham had died two weeks earlier. He wrote, "It has been reported that Maya Ng (Obama's half-sister) and Hawaii officials knowingly and intentionally falsified death records of Madelyn L. Dunham who had actually died prior to Barack Obama arriving on Thursday, October 23, 2008 for his claimed visit." Knowing the end was near, Obama suspended his campaign temporarily to visit his grandmother one final time.

"According to sources employed in the coroner's office Madelyn Dunham died on October 21, 2008 and was cremated on Friday, October 24, 2008. It is further claimed that the death records of Madelyn L Dunham were falsified at the direct and specific request of Barack Obama and Maya Ng," Sinclair alleged.

What would be gained by falsifying the date of his grandmother's death? Why would doctors, coroners, and Hawaiian public officials engage in such an elaborate, unnecessary cover-up? Somebody would surely squeal if that were happening.

ILLEGAL ALIEN AUNT

The federal agency that enforces immigration laws leaked information to embarrass Obama. Three days before the election, news reports surfaced that one of Obama's aunts, Zeituni Onyango from Kenya, was living in Boston illegally. Shortly after the election, Julie Myers, head of Immigration and Customs Enforcement (ICE), resigned under fire for the revelations, although the leaker was never identified. Prior to this incident, Myers awarded "most original costume" to a white government employee who wore blackface to a Halloween party.

MALIA OBAMA

For once, I thought Fox News got it right, standing firm on principle instead of shallow rhetoric and sloganeering, when panelists on O'Reilly's show moaned about "unfair attacks on her children." They appeared to be talking about recent slurs from a right-wing website, which referred to eleven-year-old Malia Obama as "a typical street whore" and asked, "Wonder when she will get her first abortion?" I was already moaning along with the pundits, pleased that after watching Fox every day to monitor the Obama-bashing, I would get to praise them.

I was wrong.

They were not discussing the vilest attack ever made against any member of a politician's family. Instead, they were rehashing the David Letterman wisecrack about Bristol Palin that happened a month before, for which the late-night comic had groveled apologetically twice. The Foxies were having another pity party for Palin but did not utter a single word about the unspeakably cruel assault against Malia.

Was I surprised? Not at all. But I was truly disappointed. Because I am an eternal optimist, despite subjecting myself every day to these nattering nabobs of nonsense, I held out hope for an instant that they could distinguish between a bawdy joke and a truly vicious attack.

A commenter on the website Free Republic on July 9, 2009, wrote, "We're being represented by a family of ghetto trash . . . looks like a bunch of ghetto thugs . . . a stain on America. . . . What we are now sending the ghetto over to represent us. And if so who the hell is that flea bag who looks to be dragged from the trash dumpster. . . . You could go down any ghetto right now and see exactly the same. . . . They make me sick. . . . The whole family . . . mammy, pappy, the free loadin' mammy-in-law, the misguided chillin'. . . . This is not the America I want representin' my peeps."

The website also showed a picture of the first lady speaking to Malia with the racist caption, "To Entertain Her Daughter, Michelle Obama Likes to Make Monkey Sounds."

Free Republic later yanked the offensive material "pending review." The website, however, refused to apologize. Rather, it blamed the foul-mouthed degenerates given free rein on its site, saying, "Opinions expressed on Free Republic are those of the individual posters and do not necessarily reflect the opinions of Free Republic or its operators."

Kristinn Taylor, a spokesperson for Free Republic, offered no mea culpa. "I think you exaggerated the vileness of some of them. I'm not defending them, but you said they were the worst of the worst, and I would differ on that," Taylor said in a July 13 interview on MSNBC. He gave no examples of anything worse; would any decent person call complaints about those reprehensible slurs "exaggerated?"

3

Barack the Magic Negro: How Racism Oozes from Extremists into Mainstream Media

Darkness cannot drive out darkness; only light can do that. Hate cannot drive out hate; only love can do that.

—Dr. Martin Luther King Jr.

After electing the first president of African descent, most Americans wanted to see their country evolve into a post-racial society in which people are judged by the content of their character rather than the color of their skin, as Dr. Martin Luther King Jr. famously saw in a dream. The Obama haters, however, don't want to move on. They hurl filthy racial epithets and have the chutzpah to accuse the president himself of harboring racial animosity.

Obama had not even declared his candidacy for president when the first racist salvo screeched across the bow. "Barack Obama has picked up another endorsement: Halfrican American actress Halle Berry," Rush Limbaugh wise-cracked on the radio on January 24, 2007. "Halfrican" became one of Limbaugh's favorite lines, and he gorged himself regularly on racial taunts, so Obama knew what he was getting into before he announced his candidacy three weeks later.

After *Los Angeles Times* columnist David Ehrenstein wrote March 19, 2007, that Obama was reminiscent of a stereotypical benevolent "Magic Negro" who is "like a comic book super hero," Limbaugh showed off how he could get away with saying "Negro." Like an insolent schoolboy, he said "Magic

Negro" twenty-seven times that day. Soon after that, he began playing a parody, "Barack the Magic Negro," sung to the tune of the 1960s hit "Puff the Magic Dragon."

During the battle for the Democratic nomination, Limbaugh made double entendres degrading to blacks and women on January 15, 2008: "Obama is holding his own against both of them [Bill and Hillary Clinton], doing more than his share of the 'spadework,' maybe even gaining ground at the moment, using not only the spade, ladies and gentlemen. But when he finishes with the spade in the garden of corruption planted by the Clintons, he turns to the hoe. And so the spadework and his expertise, using a hoe. He's faring well."

"Spadework" is a common term for completing preliminary tasks, while "spade" has been a slur toward blacks for decades. "Hoe," or "ho," is slang for whore. If it was unintentional, why did he keep repeating spade and hoe for emphasis?

"It is clear that Senator Obama has disowned his white half," Limbaugh said on March 21. He called Obama "unqualified" on August 19 and said "I think it really goes back to the fact that nobody had the guts to stand up and say no to a black guy." He described Obama's nomination as "perfect affirmative action." If nobody "had the guts" to "say no" to a black presidential candidate, why did Shirley Chisholm, Jesse Jackson, and Al Sharpton not become president?

Limbaugh was the loudest voice in a synchronized chorus of racist remarks.

At the ironically titled Values Voter summit in Washington, D.C., in September 2009, the Family Research Council sold boxes of "Obama Waffles" showing a caricature of Obama wearing a Muslim headscarf with the inscriptions "Change you can taste" and "Point towards Mecca for tastier waffles." The drawing resembled Aunt Jemima racist stereotypes. What kinds of "values" condone brazen hatred?

A local Republican official in California distributed "Obama bucks," a parody of food stamps, showing Obama's face along with drawings of stereotypical fried chicken, watermelon, and ribs. The Republican Party in Sacramento posted a picture on its website in October with two captions: "The only difference between Obama and Osama is BS," showing pictures of bin Laden and Obama, and "Waterboard Barack Obama."

Election night saw scattered ugly incidents. The car belonging to a black family near Pittsburgh was torched as they watched Obama's victory speech on TV. Vandals spray-painted "Obama" across the trunk of the car and threw an Obama yard sign through the family's window. On Staten Island in New York City, seventeen-year-old Ali Kamara, a black Muslim, was beaten with baseball bats by white men yelling "Obama."

Other racist incidents ensued. A player on the University of Texas football team wrote, "All the hunters gather up, we have a Nigger in the White House" on his Facebook page, which earned his expulsion from the team. Two police officers in Durham, North Carolina, were investigated for posting racially charged remarks about Obama on their private Myspace pages. Not far away, at North Carolina State University in Raleigh, four students admitted spray-painting "Shoot Obama" and "Kill that Nigger" on a campus walkway.

Chip Saltsman, running for the chair of the Republican National Committee, sent out copies of "Barack the Magic Negro" to party elders. The number of elected Republicans who condemned Saltsman could be counted on one hand of a guy who's missing a couple of fingers.

The *New York Post* published a cartoon on February 18, 2009, that showed a gun-toting policeman standing over a dead, bleeding chimpanzee with the caption, "They'll have to find someone else to write the next stimulus bill." The image appeared to depict the president, using age-old imagery likening black people to apes. Some also saw the cartoon as encouraging Obama's assassination.

That same month, Dean Grose, mayor of Los Alamitos, California, sent an e-mail that showed a watermelon patch in front of the White House with the caption, "No Easter Egg hunt this year." Grose resigned after the incident.

In June Republican staff members of the Tennessee Legislature received an e-mail with a picture bearing the portraits of every president from Washington through Bush the Lesser. Obama was portrayed as a pair of bright white eyeballs peering through the darkness. Legislative staffer Sherri Goforth apologized, not for showing abysmal taste or judgment, but for sending it "to the wrong people." Goforth's job appeared to be safe with the aptly named Diane Black, a white Republican state legislator.

To make life easier for racists, maybe David Duke should start an e-mail service to specialize in sending these types of messages.

Obama gave a watershed speech on July 16 to the National Association for the Advancement of Colored People (NAACP), the oldest U.S. civil rights organization, urging African Americans to lift themselves and their communities up and not make excuses for failure. Right-wing commentator Laura Ingraham called Obama divisive. Unable to extract any divisive words or phrases, she instead ridiculed the president's superior rhetorical flourishes.

"Recently the president and his party have in different ways demonstrated that they're not above using race to advance their left-wing agenda. Last night, President Obama spoke to the NAACP and channeled his best Jeremiah Wright accent," Ingraham said the next night as guest host on Fox's *The O'Reilly Factor*. She played a clip of Obama praising people who struggled for civil rights through the years. There was no change in accent. Obama used the cadences of a masterful orator rather than the monotone a president seems to assume in the day-to-day affairs of the nation.

"It's a cheap attempt to pander to an audience that already supports him," Ingraham added.

What's cheap—and tragic—is the beating Obama endures from screwballs like Ingraham when he addresses vital issues and tries to motivate people to improve themselves to create a better America. It might be a given that Ingraham thinks "they all look alike," but why does she insist that all black people are stereotypical Stepin Fetchits who sound alike?

Right-wingers had multiple orgasms after Obama weighed in about Dr. Henry Louis Gates, a prominent black historian who was arrested by a white police officer at his home near Harvard University on July 16 for disorderly conduct. The racial overtones boiled for more than a week, and Obama said at a July 22 press conference that the police had "acted stupidly." Two days later, he apologized for rushing to judgment and spoke with the police officer he had maligned, Sgt. James Crowley.

Despite the apology—something George W. Bush never offered for tormenting the world with his eight years of failure and incompetence—right-wingers refused to forgive Obama's blunder or acknowledge his speedy regrets. This became an opening to attack Obama right after his daughter Malia was humiliated by venomous racist slurs.

On the same day as Obama's apology, Sean Hannity said on his TV show, "So he doesn't have to apologize to Jesus? I apologize every time I do something wrong." When will Hannity apologize for the multiple times he has violated the Ninth Commandment about bearing false witness against thy neighbor? Or does he get to wiggle out because he has no black neighbors, ergo Obama is not his neighbor?

"He's got a chip on his shoulder," Limbaugh told Fox News's Greta van Susteren on July 23.

"When Obama is faced with a political setback, even one of his own making, he plays the race card," Limbaugh said on his radio show the next day, "You know me. I think he is genuinely angry in his heart and has been his whole life."

The incident stoked the most bizarre rant about race involving Obama, by Glenn Beck on *Fox & Friends* on July 28: "This president I think has exposed himself as a guy over and over and over again who has a deep-seated hatred for white people or the white culture. I don't know what it is."

A host disagreed with Beck, saying that Obama has many white friends, associates, and supporters.

"I'm not saying that he doesn't like white people. I'm saying he has a problem. This guy is, I believe, a racist," Beck retorted.

Instead of scolding Beck, Dr. Keith Ablow, Fox's in-house psychiatrist (if he's doing his job, why does that network resemble a loony bin?), justified the unjustifiable by calling Obama "someone who harbors anger and resentment toward white people" without citing a whit of evidence. Physician, heal thyself.

Joe Scarborough, a Republican former member of Congress and current MSNBC host, tweeted that day (on Twitter), "ARE YOU SERIOUS??? Did Glenn Beck really say the president has a 'deep-seated hatred for white people or the white culture?' Outrageous."

Ron Christie, a former aide in the second Bush White House, told MSNBC the same day, "Calling the president of the United States a racist is not productive, and frankly, I think it's kind of stupid."

The next day, Hannity said, "This goes back, and I don't want to keep bringing up Reverend Wright, but I think it's relevant here inasmuch as he sat in that church for twenty years."

Beck was vindicated when his boss, Rupert Murdoch, said in a November 9, 2009, interview with Sky News Australia that Obama "did make a very racist comment."

Racists always seek validation; Limbaugh, Beck, and Hannity give them cover, so they feel it's safe to come out and play. Dr. David McKalip sent an e-mail to Tea Party friends that superimposed Obama's head on the body of what appeared to be an African witch doctor festooned in feathered head-dress regalia but otherwise wearing only a loincloth.

McKalip was a member of the American Medical Association's House of Delegates. The AMA and Florida Medical Association distanced their organizations from McKalip's clownishness, and he later apologized.

"Republicans are struggling right now to find the great white hope," Republican Congresswoman Lynn Jenkins said at the University of Kansas on August 19. The expression originated a hundred years earlier when whites sought a "great white hope" to dethrone Jack Johnson, a black man who was the boxing heavyweight champion. Jenkins later retracted her words.

Mark Williams, who touted himself as a Tea Party leader, was asked by CNN's Anderson Cooper on September 14 why the rhetoric at anti-Obama rallies was racist and threatened violence. Defending his previous statement calling Obama "an Indonesian Muslim turned welfare thug and racist-in-chief," Williams blurted out, "That's the way he's behaving."

When black students beat up white students on a school bus, Limbaugh said gleefully on September 15, "In Obama's America, the white kids now get beat up with the black kids cheering, 'Yeah right on, right on, right on!'" Limbaugh recommended segregated buses and said, "I wonder if Obama's going to come to the defense of the assailants the way he did his friend Skip Gates."

Obama himself rarely addresses racial issues in public. Former presidents Bill Clinton and Jimmy Carter, however, were not shy about broaching the topic. After the lunatic fringe came out in full force against Obama, Carter sparked a conflagration by identifying racial motivations.

"I think an overwhelming portion of the intensely demonstrated animosity toward President Barack Obama is based on the fact that he is a black man," Carter told NBC News on September 16.

The next day he spoke at Emory University in Atlanta.

"When a radical fringe element of demonstrators and others begin to attack the president of the United States as an animal or as a reincarnation of Adolf Hitler or when they wave signs in the air that said we should have buried Obama with Kennedy, those kinds of things are beyond the bounds," Carter told students.

"I think people who are guilty of that kind of personal attack against Obama have been influenced to a major degree by a belief that he should not be president because he happens to be African American," Carter emphasized. "It's a racist attitude, and my hope is and my expectation is that in the future both Democratic leaders and Republican leaders will take the initiative in condemning that kind of unprecedented attack on the president of the United States."

Carter's searing remarks should have fomented an honest debate about race relations. Instead, partisan bickering ensued. Conservatives accused liberals of saying that every criticism of Obama is racially motivated, and liberals accused conservatives of saying there is no racism in America.

Clinton told ABC's *Good Morning America* five days later that racism was a factor in anti-Obama invective, but that "if he were not an African American, all of the people who were against him on health care would still be against him. They were against me, too."

Obama tried to defuse the imbroglio on September 21 on CBS's *Late Show With David Letterman* and quipped, "It's important to realize that I was actually black before the election."

Drew Westen, a professor of psychology at Emory University, said on September 17 on MSNBC's *Hardball with Chris Matthews*, "When you get down to things like the birther movement, it's pretty hard to interpret that as anything other than fairly overt racism."

We must be careful to distinguish blatant racism from harsh criticism in which racism may only be peripheral. Many, like Westen, see racism motivating the "birthers" who question Obama's citizenship. Race might be one reason why Obama haters question his legitimacy, but, oddly, a leader of this movement is fellow African American Alan Keyes. Others saw racism in the disruptive "town hall" protests against Obama's health care plan, but Clinton recalled that he was trashed for his own health reform proposals. Obama supporters should not play the race card unless they are holding the trump card: blatant racism. The argument gets weakened when peripheral implication gets mixed in with brazen racism. Bush was frequently ridiculed as a simian, so is it always racist to parody Obama in the same way?

Occasionally I glance at my TV screen, with sound on mute, and see Obama. Tears well up at the notion that our nation elected a black man. I clearly remember debating race relations as a twelve-year-old with adult neighbors who admired the John Birch Society. I lived in the hills above Los Angeles and watched dozens of tiny fires flickering from the Watts riots in the distance, reminding me of bonfires on the beach. One saying from those times sticks with me: "Give 'em an inch, and they take a mile." When I see Obama as president, I choke up about how far we have come as a country. And when I see ignorant, racist Obama haters, I choke up at the number of Americans who remain trapped in the Jim Crow past inhabited by my contemptible neighbors years ago, and I feel sad that their inexcusable hatred was not engulfed in the Watts fires.

4

Loons and Losers Challenge Obama's
Birth Certificate and Legitimacy

Barack Hussein Obama was born in Hawaii and is a natural-born American citizen.

—Dr. Chiyome Fukino, director of the Hawaii
State Department of Health

arack Hussein Obama II entered this world on August 4, 1961, at the
Kapi'olani Medical Center for Women & Children in Honolulu, Hawaii,
to mother Stanley Ann Dunham (born in Fort Leavenworth, Kansas)
and father Barack Hussein Obama, a Kenyan. It's easy to confirm. That's what
his birth certificate says.

Starting in the presidential campaign's infancy in 2007, however, anonymous e-mails began to question the legitimacy of his birth certificate and, therefore, his eligibility to be president. When this rumor started to command attention, the Obama campaign released his birth certificate based on the filing with the official registrar four days after his birth, confirmed by Hawaii officials. That document, which was inspected and verified by experts, is just a computer click away for anybody who wants to see it.

Honolulu's two daily newspapers, the *Honolulu Advertiser* and the *Honolulu Star-Bulletin* ran typical birth announcements on August 13 and 14, 1961, respectively: "Mr. and Mrs. Barack H. Obama, 6085 Kalanianaole Hwy., son, Aug. 4."

All this corroboration has not quieted the cranks who insist the birth certificate is tainted. These crazed fanatics—who make the Three Stooges look like serious guys by comparison—filed frivolous lawsuits in an attempt to disqualify Obama.

Even after Obama was sworn in and the election results could not be reversed, these crackpots brought further legal action based on spurious claims. One after another, the courts dispatched these cases to the garbage can, where they belonged; the U.S. Supreme Court dismissed three preposterous lawsuits.

What began as an Internet smear grew into a movement embraced by at least a dozen members of Congress and a vocal flock of fringe elements and misfits. Few elected Republicans are willing to swat off these pesky flies and instead humor the nutcases, an important Republican constituency.

If this happened in some third world backwater, we would all howl with uncontrolled laughter at ignoramuses who believed their president was unqualified to hold office. What does it show about our country that so many people believe such bizarre nonsense? And how many foreigners are laughing at our stupidity?

While normal people scoff at such an absurd notion, a psychopath might take it seriously. One of many grievances by white supremacist James von Brunn when he shot up the Holocaust Memorial Museum on June 10, 2009, was his belief that Obama's birth certificate was a sham.

This movement even begat a neologism: birthers. The whimsical word first broke through in mainstream media in Ben Smith's excellent March 1, 2009, *Politico* article, which lay bare the conspiratorial movement. From there, "birthers" blossomed into a derisive expression used by regular people to describe those who mock the validity of Obama's birth certificate. By that time, right-wing website WorldNetDaily, which trumpeted the birther cause, argued that 300,000 people had signed an online petition "demanding more information on Obama's birth."

The birther creed is a compendium of hysteria, crackpottery, wingnuttery, tomfoolery, unfounded conspiracy theories, non sequiturs, and outright lunacy. If we ask how such an illogical premise could ever gain ground, we must defer to Honest Abe about fooling all of the people some of the time and some of the people all of the time.

The impartial FactCheck.org said its experts viewed the original document at Obama campaign headquarters in Chicago. They verified that it has a raised seal and is stamped (rather than signed) on the back by Hawaii state registrar Alvin T. Onaka. The website's analysis and close-up photographs of the birth certificate are available online.

Some people insist that Kapi'olani Medical Center must divulge more information about Obama's birth, but the hospital cites privacy laws that prohibit such a release.

A book the size of *War and Peace* could be filled with all the senseless theories about Obama's birth from grandstanding nutjobs. Some argue the birth certificate is an outright fabrication obtained with complicity of government officials. Others contend that Obama's parents filed for the certificate using falsified birth information. An offshoot group of renegades keeps finding odd characters, spots, or other unexplained "irregularities" on the document. They claim that it does not have a raised seal, it is not signed, there are no creases from folding, there is a strange "halo" around the letters, the certificate number is blacked out, or the date of certification is suspicious.

The most prevalent accusation is that Obama was born in Kenya, while at least one kook claims he was born in Canada. Some people allege that his biological father was Malcolm X or poet Frank Marshall Davis. None of these fanciful stories have ever been verified.

Why does this matter? The president is required to be a natural-born citizen, according to Article 2 of the Constitution. That means a president must have been born in the United States or, if born outside the United States, be born to an American citizen as a parent. Because Obama's mother was an American, she would have conferred her citizenship to her son no matter where she gave birth. It's so simple, but beyond the grasp of some simpletons.

Title 8, chapter 12, Subchapter III, Part I, §1401 of the U.S. Code (Nationals and citizens of the United States at birth) confers natural-born citizenship automatically: "(g) a person born outside the geographical limits of the United States and its outlying possessions of parents one of whom is an alien, and the other a citizen of the United States who, prior to the birth of such person, was physically present in the United States or its outlying possessions for a period or periods totaling not less than five years, at least two of which were after attaining the age of fourteen years."

The U.S. Passport Agency sets this citizenship requirement to obtain a passport: "Your full name, the full name of your parent(s), date and place of birth, sex, date the birth record was filed, and the seal or other certification of the official custodian of such records." Obama's birth certificate meets those legal criteria.

If Obama was an imposter, the Bush administration had every political motivation—as well as legal duty—to expose such deceit.

Ironically, it was Obama's general election opponent who was born outside the United States. John McCain's father was a military officer stationed in Panama, but he was conferred American, not Panamanian, citizenship because the Canal Zone was then a U.S. territory and he was born to U.S. citizen parents. In fact, right-wingers had researched McCain's birth, hoping to disqualify him, but came up with nothing.

McCain, who had the most to gain if the Obama birth certificate smear proved to be true, never raised the issue in public. His campaign lawyers, in fact, looked into the birth certificate rumors but found nothing amiss.

Trevor Potter, who served as general counsel to McCain's presidential campaigns in 2000 and 2008, told the Washington Independent website:

> There were no statements and no documents that suggested he was born somewhere else. On the other side, there was proof that he was born in Hawaii. There was a certificate issued by the state's Department of Health, and the responsible official in the state saying that he had personally seen the original certificate. There was a birth announcement in the *Honolulu Advertiser*, which would be very difficult to invent or plant forty-seven years in advance.[1]

If Obama were born in Africa, as maintained by birthers, he could not have entered the United States without a passport issued by British colonial authorities or a travel document from a U.S. consulate unless he was delivered by a Kenyan stork. The Americans and British are both meticulous record keepers, and that information would be stored somewhere if it existed.

Although right-wingers make opposition to "frivolous lawsuits" an article of faith, they are the first crybabies to employ legal eagles when they don't get their way. Some lawsuits contend that Obama was born outside the United States; others assert that somehow he was a dual national, because his father was a foreigner, and therefore ineligible to be president. Obama never applied for British or Kenyan citizenship, so there is no conflict.

The number of lawsuits—approaching two-dozen—challenging the legitimacy of Obama's birth certificate exceeds the IQ of most birthers. Courts dismissed these cases for lack of standing, which means that the plaintiff does not have a dog in the fight. Most of the people filing the suits are nobodies, but a handful of infamous Obama-hating clowns—Andy Martin, Alan Keyes, Rev. Wiley Drake, Philip Berg, and Orly Taitz—have turned courts into a legal circus. The judges are not amused.

Martin was the midwife for the Muslim smear in 2004 when Obama ran for the U.S. Senate from Illinois (see chapters 5, 8, and 9). Keyes was Obama's Republican opponent for the Senate and ran for president in 2008 representing the America's Independent Party. Drake was Keyes's running mate for vice president and issued imprecatory prayers asking God that Obama die (see chapter 5). California lawyer Taitz and Pennsylvania lawyer Berg milked the birther movement to attract publicity.

One lawsuit asserts falsely that Obama was adopted by his mother's second husband, Lolo Soetoro, and became an Indonesian. No documentation shows any such adoption. Even if he were adopted, U.S. law does not allow a child to lose citizenship based on adoption. Only an adult U.S. citizen can renounce citizenship.

Berg brought suit in U.S. District Court, alleging that Obama was born in Kenya. Without citing any reasons for such suspicions, Berg questioned whether Obama was a citizen of Canada, Kenya, or Indonesia. The case was tossed.

Drake filed a suit asking California's attorney general to not certify California's election results. Drake said he had an audiotape (since debunked) of Obama's Kenyan grandmother describing how she had witnessed Obama's birth in that African nation. Keyes was also listed on the Drake case.

Martin filed a lawsuit in a Hawaii state circuit court demanding to see Obama's birth certificate. The court ruled that he had no standing.

Taitz sought an injunction in Georgia district court on behalf of Maj. Stefan Frederick Cook, who contended that orders to deploy to Afghanistan were illegal because Obama had no authority as commander-in-chief because he was not a U.S. citizen. Cook, however, signed up to go to Afghanistan after Obama took office. The army later revoked his orders, and the case was dismissed.

Taitz filed suit for another soldier, Capt. Connie Rhodes, to prevent her deployment to Iraq. Federal judge Clay Land, nominated by George W. Bush, dismissed the suit, saying, "Unlike in *Alice in Wonderland*, simply saying something is so does not make it so. Plaintiff's challenge to her deployment order is frivolous. She has presented no credible evidence...Instead, she uses her (lawsuit) as a platform for spouting political rhetoric." The judge said Taitz "is hereby notified that the filing of any future actions in this court, which are similarly frivolous, shall subject (Taitz) to sanctions." Land said Taitz was trying to make Obama "prove his innocence," contrary to U.S. legal tradition. Judge Land fined Taitz $20,000 for "misconduct."

In an August 4, 2009, interview with MSNBC, Taitz blurted out—incorrectly—that 85 percent of Americans doubt Obama's birth certificate and that "Obama's brownshirts in the media" are cloaking his deceptions.

In a September 16 interview with TPM Muckraker at TalkingPoints Memo.com, Taitz said, "somebody should consider trying [Judge Land] for treason and aiding and abetting this massive fraud known as Barack Hussein Obama . . . Judge Land is a typical puppet of the regime—just like in the Soviet Union."

After this outburst, Subodh Chandra, a lawyer and delegate to the 2008 Democratic National Convention, filed a formal complaint with the California Bar Association over Taitz's remarks about Judge Land and history of filing frivolous lawsuits. Taitz could face sanctions or even disbarment.

Taitz said in a January 7, 2009, press release that Obama's birth certificate is a forgery. She filed another lawsuit on August 2 in which she submitted what she purported to be a Kenyan birth certificate as evidence, but it contained numerous flaws. The document was allegedly issued by the Republic of Kenya, which did not exist when Obama was born; Kenya was a dominion of the British crown until 1963. Mombasa was identified as Obama's place of birth, but in 1961, it was part of Zanzibar, not Kenya.

At the time of the 2008 election, Hawaii's governor was Linda Lingle, a Republican. If the birth certificate were a forgery, wouldn't a Republican governor want to undermine Obama?

Dr. Chiyome Fukino, the state official in Hawaii who is responsible for public records, vouched for its authenticity.

There have been numerous requests for Senator Barack Hussein Obama's official birth certificate. State law (Hawaii Revised Statues §338-18) prohibits the release of certified birth certificate to persons who do not have a tangible interest in the vital record.

Therefore, I, as Director of Health for the State of Hawaii, along with the Registrar of Vital Statistics who has statutory authority to oversee and maintain these types of vital records, have personally seen and verified that the Hawaii State Department of Health has Senator Obama's original birth certificate on record in accordance with state policies and procedures.

Also negating the conspiracies is the simple question of how and why young parents of modest means concocted such a grand conspiracy with officials at the hospital and health department, or where they got the money to jet set between Hawaii and Africa.

A Research 2000 poll commissioned in July 2009 found that 77 percent of Americans believe Obama was born in the United States, 11 percent believe he was not, and 12 percent were undecided; 93 percent of Democrats said yes and 4 percent said no. Among Republicans, 42 percent said yes, 28 percent said no, and 30 percent were undecided. A majority of Americans in the Northeast, Midwest, and West all believed Obama to be a natural-born American citizen, but only 47 percent of Southerners agreed.

An August 2009 survey by Public Policy Polling in North Carolina found that 54 percent believe Obama is a natural-born American, 26 percent believe he is not, and 20 percent are unsure. Among Republican Tar Heels, only 24 percent said yes, 47 percent said no, and 29 percent are unsure. It found that 88 percent of Republicans in North Carolina believe Hawaii is a state, 7 percent deny Hawaii's statehood, and 5 percent are unsure. Have North Carolina right-wingers prohibited their children from learning geography as well as sex education and science?

Middle Tennessee State University released a survey in October 2009 which found one-third of Tennesseans believe Obama was born in another country. Among Republicans, 47 percent say Obama was born outside the United States. The same survey found 30 percent of people in the Volunteer State believe Obama is a Muslim, but 48 percent of Republicans believed that.

Asked whether Obama is a socialist, 46 percent overall answered yes and 71 percent of Republicans agreed.

WorldNetDaily publisher Joseph Farah solicited donations to erect billboards reading "WHERE'S THE BIRTH CERTIFICATE?" After collecting money, he put up similar signs in Louisiana, California, and Pennsylvania.

Before the Obama haters pushed this lie onto right-wing TV and radio, it circulated on blogs, websites, and e-mail. Larry Sinclair, who alleged gay sex and drug encounters with Obama (see chapter 8), jumped early into the equally discredited birther lie.

"Barack Obama, a good son of Africa was born in Mombasa, Kenya where his late father and mother were on holiday," Sinclair wrote on his Obambi blog.

In an October 16, 2008, telephone interview with Bishop Ron McRae of the Anabaptist Churches of North America, Obama's father's stepmother said through an interpreter that Obama was born in Hawaii. Nevertheless, Berg uses a tape of that conversation to allege that Obama was born in Kenya.

Robert L. Schulz placed full-page ads in the *Chicago Tribune* in December 2008 arguing that Obama was born in Kenya or that he subsequently renounced his U.S. citizenship.

The now-defunct website AmericaMustKnow.com encouraged the Electoral College to vote against Obama's confirmation as president. This effort was supported by WorldNetDaily, which also sponsored a letter-writing campaign to the Supreme Court.

Radio hosts Brian Sussman, Lars Larson, Bob Grant, Jim Quinn, Rose Tennent, Barbara Simpson, and Mark Davis—guppies in right-wing talk radio waters—have all disputed Obama's birth certificate. So have the killer sharks in that pond.

Convicted Watergate felon G. Gordon Liddy said August 26, 2008, on his radio show, "If they had a real birth certificate from Hawaii, the campaign would put it out, not rely on a phony thing Photoshopped by Daily Kos, you know."

Michael Savage said on October 8, "He won't even produce a birth certificate . . . It does not exist, they can't find it in the Hawaii government. It's never been produced. The one that was produced is a forgery."

Rush Limbaugh raised the issue on October 23, saying Obama was visiting Hawaii not to visit his dying grandmother, but rather "this birth certificate business, I'm just wondering if something's up." Then on June 10, 2009, he asked what God has in common with Obama, answering himself with, "Neither has a birth certificate."

Fox News legitimized the smear when it interviewed Jerome Corsi on August 15, 2008, when he claimed Obama's campaign "has a false, fake birth certificate posted on their website." Instead of fulfilling his role as a journalist and sparring with Corsi over the facts or allowing another guest to debunk him, Fox host Steve Doocy instead offered tea and sympathy. Draft dodger Corsi had co-authored *Unfit for Command: Swift Boat Veterans Speak Out Against John Kerry*, which in 2004 mutilated John Kerry's Vietnam War record in tandem with attacks by the Swift Boat campaign. This smear tactic became known as swiftboating after the vessel that Purple Heart winner Kerry piloted in the war. Doocy asked Corsi obsequiously, "And do you feel almost as if you yourself are being swiftboated?"

Fox's Sean Hannity decided to throw in his lot with the likes of Corsi and Taitz rather than rational people when he asked a listener on his radio show July 23, 2009, "Have you ever seen the birth certificate?"

The supermarket tabloid *Globe* ran the headline "Obama birth certificate is a FAKE!" on the cover of its August 17, 2009 edition. It theorized that his mother, who had graduated from high school in the Seattle area, had flown back to Seattle from Hawaii and sneaked over the border to give birth in Vancouver so her son would be eligible for U.S. and Canadian citizenship. There was no evidence of this, and no Canadian hospital has ever produced records to that effect.

The tabloid cited Pamela Geller, who runs the Atlas Shrugs website, as claiming that his real birth certificate is a forgery. *Globe* called Atlas Shrugs "the acclaimed watchdog website." Acclaimed by whom? *Globe?*

Globe quoted Geller as citing an unidentified forgery expert, whom she called Techdude, who asserted that Obama's birth certificate is fake. Curiously, experts have gone on the record to verify the authenticity of the document; no reputable expert has publicly contradicted these findings.

In late September 2009, the so-called United States Justice Foundation ran twenty-eight-minute infomercials in Texas claiming that Obama was born in Kenya. They featured the aptly named attorney Gary Kreep and Rev. Bill Keller, who runs LivePrayer.com. The infomercial seeks thirty dollars for a bumper sticker saying, "Got a birth certificate?" Money from the donation allegedly will pay for a phalanx of faxes to Attorney General Eric Holder and state attorneys general.

Joining the birther brigade was crooner Pat Boone in a June 29, 2009, article at Newsmax.com, where he asserted that "Obama's mother, about to have her child in Kenya, had booked a flight to Hawaii but was prohibited from flying because delivery was so imminent." That was nearly a half-century before Sarah Palin flew from Texas back to Alaska hours before son Trig's birth so he could be a "native-born Alaskan." Boone and his stragglers have no records to corroborate such insanity. Lest we forget, one of Boone's number one hits was "I Almost Lost My Mind."

Almost?

Republican members of Congress would rather pander to lunatics than speak the truth, but not a single elected Democrat joined this birther movement.

On May 15, 2009, Congressman Bill Posey introduced H.R. 1503, "a bill to amend the Federal Election Campaign Act to require beginning in 2012, the principal campaign committee of a candidate for election to the Office of President to include with the committee's statement of organization documentation (including a birth certificate) as may be necessary to establish that the candidate meets the qualifications for eligibility to the Office of President under the Constitution."

"The only people I know who are afraid to take drug tests are people who use drugs," Posey explained to Andrea Shea King of WorldNetDaily on her Internet radio show on June 18, 2009.

First the frivolous lawsuits; next, frivolous legislation to solve a problem that is not a problem, unless you are a birther.

Republican state legislators in Oklahoma, Tennessee, and Missouri proposed legislation that questioned Obama's birth certificate.

Tom DeLay, who was forced out as majority leader in the House amid ethics violations, outed himself as a birther on August 19, 2009, when he told Chris Matthews on MSNBC's *Hardball*, "I would like to see him provide his birth certificate."

Birthers disrupted a June 30, 2009, town hall meeting with then Delaware Republican Congressman Mike Castle. One woman insisted that Obama is a "citizen of Kenya," met by boisterous hoots and hollers of support from the crowd. This rambling woman cried out "We want our country back," and proclaimed patriotism by saying her father had fought in World War II, ignoring the fact that Obama's maternal grandfather, the late Stanley Dunham, served in the U.S. Army in Europe during World War II. Furthermore, we'd all sleep better if Memphis officials would fess up to forging Elvis's death certificate to fool us into thinking the King is dead, but this woman did not make such a demand of Castle.

The congressman proved his sanity by snapping at the wackjob rather than her bait. "Well, I don't know what comment that invites. If you're referring to the president, then he is a citizen of the United States." Undeterred by the disruption, Castle reiterated, "You can boo, but he is a citizen of the United States."

There was no word on whether Castle fired the halfwit on his staff who scheduled a town meeting at an insane asylum.

The *Huffington Post* ambushed Republican Congressman Charles Boustany about whether he thought Obama was a native-born American. The response: "I think there are questions. We'll have to see." He retracted the statement three days later on KPEL radio in Lafayette, Louisiana, when he said he believes Obama is a U.S. citizen.

Curiously, Boustany, a surgeon, delivered the Republican response to Obama's September 9, 2009, speech about health care reform, when he condemned "junk lawsuits" against doctors as driving up the cost of health care. He failed, however, to denounce "junk lawsuits" alleging that Obama is not a citizen. Even more peculiar, Boustany was a co-sponsor of the Life Sustaining Treatment Preferences Act of 2009. This legislation required health insurance companies to pay for "end-of-life counseling" with medical professionals. It was this exact clause that right-wingers exploited to scare the bejesus out of seniors with fictive "death panels" that would force the extermination of seniors and the disabled. Boustany did not use his national speech to condemn his fellow Republicans for their "junk" comments that maliciously frightened Americans over his legislation. Isn't that a direct violation of the Hippocratic Oath?

When asked about the birthers, Oklahoma Sen. James Inhofe told the *Tulsa World*, "I believe those people who are concerned about his birth certificate, about whether he is a citizen and qualified, I encourage them to do that."[2]

Newspapers in the heart of Obama-hating country took stands when few elected Republicans resisted the madness.

"Conservatives may harbor legitimate policy differences with Obama, but allowing this off-base attack regarding the president's citizenship to gain any foothold is simply dishonest," the *Dallas Morning News* editorialized.[3]

"Conspiracy idiots . . . will cling to such nonsense despite conclusive evidence to the contrary," the *Honolulu Star-Bulletin* wrote.[4]

"Conspiracy theorists are a stubborn bunch. Facts usually don't deter them," the *Tulsa World* editorialized. It criticized Inhofe: "You could have done the right thing and dismissed the goofiness for what it is, and reminded people that there are far more important issues to worry about. But, instead, you gave them some legitimacy."[5]

"The fundamental fiction is that Obama has refused to release his 'real' birth certificate. This is untrue. The document that Obama has made available is the document that Hawaiian authorities issue when they are asked for a birth certificate. There is no secondary document cloaked in darkness," the online version of the conservative weekly magazine *National Review* editorialized.[6]

Even Ann Coulter for once resisted temptation to side with the liars when she told Fox News on July 26, 2009, "It's just a few cranks out there."

Conservative talk show host Michael Medved told me, "The birther movement represents a toxic combination of dementia and demagoguery. They are altogether the pathetic leaders of this suicidal cult that remains untethered from reality, decency, logic, and their mentally healthy fellow citizens."

On August 1, 2009, Republican strategist Todd Harris told MSNBC's *Hardball*, "I think that this whole issue is ridiculous. Frankly, I think the people who are pushing this issue are not a bit nuts, but a lot nuts." He said Republican strategists and consultants uniformly oppose focusing on the issue.

"I think we can all agree President Obama was born in the United States. President Obama is an American citizen," Ron Christie, an aide in the second Bush White House, said September 13, 2010 on MSNBC's *The Ed Show*.

One elected Republican who had the courage to stand up for sanity was Lindsey Graham of South Carolina. "We [Republicans] have to say that's crazy. So, I'm here to tell you that those who think the president was not born in Hawaii are crazy. He's not a Muslim. He's a good man. Now let's knock this crap off and talk about our real differences," Graham said on October 1, 2009, at the "First Draft of History" conference in Washington, D.C.

When Republican leaders are challenged to take on birthers, they equate it to a fringe view that 9/11 was an "inside job" by the Bush administration. Surveys say at least one-fifth of Americans believe the "inside job" conspiracy. That argument, however, rings hollow. Republican leaders refuse to silence the birthers. When Democrat Cynthia McKinney of Georgia speculated that the Bush administration had advance knowledge of the 9/11 attacks, Democratic leaders condemned her, and she lost the 2002 primary against Democrat Denise Majette. Democrats keep their fringe elements way out in left field, while Republicans aid and abet theirs.

For historical perspective, many people believe that the Roosevelt administration knew the attack on Pearl Harbor was imminent but did nothing so the event would galvanize Americans to declare war on Japan. Seven decades later, with access to written records by President Roosevelt and members of his administration, it's certain something would have leaked out by now if this were true.

I have looked at Obama's birth certificate numerous times. It is posted online. It looks a lot like mine and those of my children. I used my birth certificate to obtain my first driver's license and passport. I am thankful that these weirdoes did not challenge my birth certificate or I might be forced to hitchhike instead.

Because the accusation is so outlandish, most people incorrectly think Obama was the first president accused of not being a natural-born American citizen. Vice President Chester Alan Arthur, who became president upon the assassination of James A. Garfield, was born in northern Vermont to an Irish-born father and American mother. Arthur P. Hinman claimed that Arthur was born in Ireland, then changed his tune and said the twenty-first president was born in Canada.

The difference between then and now is that there was no Internet in Arthur's era to fling the falsehoods far and wide, no unmitigated hatred against Arthur before people knew anything about him, and no racist animosity concerning his ethnicity. Obama will be remembered as a president who broke new ground, for better or worse, and the birthers will be seen as unhinged interlopers typified by the kooks who disrupted Congressman Castle's town hall meeting. Taking the long view, this notoriety will be incredibly sad and shameful for their descendants.

What a difference it would make if the people who waste so much effort promoting the birther movement instead devoted that same time and energy to assisting at homeless shelters, orphanages, or cancer wards. Tragically, these cultists are so overcome by hostility and fear that they find meaning and purpose by tearing down our president and country. As American philosopher Eric Hoffer said, "Passionate hatred can give meaning and purpose to an empty life."

No doubt the birthers will continue to harangue Obama; their beliefs are nestled in a womb of emotion enveloped in stubborn, unshakable contempt for facts.

5

Can You Prove Your Innocence?

No matter what we choose to believe, let us remember that there is no religion whose central tenet is hate.

—Barack Obama

In the heartbreaking 2009 feature film *The Stoning of Soraya M.*, a philandering husband who wants to marry his fourteen-year-old girlfriend enlists the corrupt mullah and mayor of his isolated Iranian village in a scheme to accuse his faithful wife of adultery so she could be stoned to death under Islamic sharia law and free him from paying alimony. The mayor confronts Soraya and asks her, "Can you prove your innocence?"

You can't disprove a negative, which is why our Bill of Rights places the burden of proof squarely on the shoulders of the accuser and prosecutor, not the accused. Numerous nations have patterned their justice system on ours; people around the world envy our liberties.

When it comes to the outlandish accusations made against Barack Obama, the accusers insist, in a very un-American, totalitarian way, that he must prove his innocence. They reject his birth certificate that was issued and authenticated by Hawaii authorities even though they can't prove it to be a forgery. They insist that he prove his acquaintanceship with '60s radical Bill Ayers was nothing more than a passing association, without any substantiation that Ayers was ever a close associate. Some insist that Obama is the Antichrist, even though nobody quite knows who or what the Antichrist is. Others allege he is a Muslim, even though he has attended Protestant churches for more than twenty years and there is no proof that he ever embraced Islam.

Have they, or we, been reduced to the mob mentality of the Ayatollah's Iran, which imposed sharia law? The Obama haters never verified a single accusation while refusing to accept the most basic concept of American justice: innocent until proven guilty.

In *The Stoning of Soraya M.*, based on a true event recounted to a French journalist, the town mullah encourages the mob: "With each stone you throw, your honor will return." When Soraya pleads with her neighbors, "How can you do this to anyone?" they respond, "It is God's law."

Jesus stopped the stoning of an adulteress when he said in John 8:7, "He that is without sin among you, let him first cast a stone at her." Stories from the Bible are as true today as they were 2,000 years ago. So many people refuse to learn such simple truths, even those who claim to be born again in Jesus Christ.

Not surprisingly, the Obama haters sanctimoniously invoke the name of God to justify their shameless actions, just as the Iranian mullahs do. They would feel right at home in theocratic Iran, where they could incite a mob to stone people they don't like but who they can't prove have done wrong.

Obama was variously described in mad mutterings by minuscule minds as a Muslim, a "black liberation theology radical," an atheist, an agnostic, a Jew, and the Antichrist. The single common thread slithering through all these smears is absolute and utter preposterousness.

Obama considers himself a Protestant Christian—as do 51.3 percent of adults in the United States, according to a 2008 survey by the Pew Forum on Religion and Public Life—and has never professed any other religious belief.

Christians in the United States span the political spectrum from left to right and every variation and shade in between, yet the majority of mainstream Protestants and Catholics don't impose their religion or politics on anyone.

Many commentators believe that opposition to Obama is rooted in race. That is a huge factor, but I have found religious fanaticism to be an even more powerful motivation. The Obama-hating bullies view him as "not one of us," whether differentiated by race, religion, national origin or political beliefs. Their fierce enmity is driven by cult-like emotional fervor, not rationality. It is part and parcel of their being, integral to their belief system, to which they cling desperately and blindly.

The Obama haters, indeed, have all the classic markings of a scary cult. Experts define cults through the following characteristics: distressing situation (Obama stealing democracy), problems reduced to one simple explanation (Obama is responsible for all that's wrong), a leader gives affirmation and acceptance to disciples (Sarah Palin, Rush Limbaugh, and Glenn Beck tell them they are picked on or their religious beliefs are in jeopardy), group identity (Tea Party), and severely controlled access to information (Fox News propaganda).

Pointing out these facts, no doubt, will draw their ire, and they will insist that by opposing them, I am opposing God. Like all religious zealots, they have the dangerous habit of confusing their own will with God's. If they oppose contraceptives or sex education or homosexuality or Obama, they find scripture to support a view they impose on others while ignoring anything in that same doctrine which is contradictory. Thankfully, the Constitution, not the Bible, is the law of the land in the United States. Governments that allow a holy book to define the law always twist interpretations. In Europe, popes and kings once controlled the masses through theocracy to the detriment of liberty, science, art, and general well being. That period was called the Dark Ages for good reason.

Obama haters frequently proclaim "Obama says America is no longer a Christian nation." It never was officially a Christian nation, as set forth in the Constitution. But these people are instructed otherwise, and they believe it.

The president clearly separates his own religious views from his official duties. He firmly believes that government should not endorse any religion, as stipulated unequivocally in the Constitution.

Obama's biggest critics tattoo their religiosity on their foreheads. Palin attended an evangelical church where a pastor prayed to protect her from witchcraft. Alan Keyes, the African American who lost the election for the U.S. Senate from Illinois to Obama in 2004 and who was also an insignificant candidate for president in 2008, is a leader in the birther movement. Members of the House and Senate who have trashed Obama most savagely and untruthfully—Jim DeMint, James Inhofe, Pete Sessions, Paul Broun, Trent Franks, Joe Wilson, Tom McClintock, Mike Pence, Tom Price, Steve King, and Michele Bachmann—are all darlings of the Religious Right who defy the Ninth Commandment to traffic in filthy lies about Obama. Political commentators who advertise their religiosity include Beck, Bill O'Reilly and Sean Hannity, among others. Floyd Brown, who smeared Michael Dukakis and Bill Clinton, is president of Excellentia Inc., a company that specializes in marketing to conservatives and Christians. *Quelle coincidence!*

Obama is endowed with the admirable personal qualities conservatives most cherish—Christian faith, marital fidelity, devoted fatherhood, self improvement from humble roots, honesty in business dealings, and treatment of rivals with respect—but, ironically, these cultists hate him while slavishly admiring the most sanctimonious cretins whose actions mock their deeply held convictions.

How in God's name can the Religious Right adore Rudolph Giuliani and Newt Gingrich, thrice-married serial adulterers, but hate the faithful Obama? Obama walks the walk without calling attention to it, while right-wing darlings are worshiped for loudly talking the talk. Why do right-wingers love senators David Vitter of Louisiana and John Ensign of Nevada, who crow about their religiosity, but hate Bill Clinton? All three are adulterers. The sex-crazed senators insisted that Clinton resign over his affair, yet neither quit after committing the exact same offense.

Religious distortions are nonstop. For example, Obama proclaimed May 6, 2009, as the National Day of Prayer, following the tradition of every president since Harry S. Truman. You would not know that if you watched Fox News, where commentators proclaimed breathlessly that Obama "overturned fifty years of tradition" by not holding a public event at the White House. George W. Bush invited leaders of the Religious Right to mark the occasion loudly, but he was not following tradition. Bush invented the "tradition," the only president to ever turn this solemn observance into a spectacle. Every predecessor quietly signed the proclamation, as did Obama. This, however, became one more reason for uninformed religious folk to hate Obama, believing he was single-handedly moving the country "away from God."

The Constitution clearly enumerates the president's powers and duties; it does not mention anything about leading the country toward or away from God.

Reverend James Manning, an African American preacher whose writings appear on Atlah.org, is perhaps the most bizarre of all the Obama haters. He calls Obama a "long-legged mack daddy" (slang for pimp), a "half-breed," and "vice president of genocide." He calls Obama a "freak, homosexual, man-lover," and said "white folk are getting ready to rise up." A fun party game might be to watch Reverend Manning on YouTube, then bet on who can do the best spoof.

MUSLIM

After the terrorist attacks by Islamic militants on September 11, 2001, Muslims became the most loathed group in the United States. People became suspicious of ordinary Muslims or Arabs with no connection to extremists or terrorism. Right-wing bigmouths gave themselves the right to force every Muslim to disavow violence while never demanding that every Christian condemn assassins who target family-planning providers.

In the 2002 and 2004 elections, many Democrats were labeled "soft on terror" or even sympathizers of 9/11 mastermind Osama bin Laden. So it should come as no surprise that the first major smear launched against Obama was to label him a Muslim. In the right-wing playbook, rule number one is to smear the opponent's religious beliefs.

"I think the president's problem is that he was born a Muslim, his father was a Muslim. The seed of Islam is passed through the father like the seed of Judiasm is passed through the mother," preacher Franklin Graham, son of evangelist Billy Graham, told CNN on August 19, 2010. Graham had famously called Islam "evil and wicked."

Sadly, these religious smears are taking hold. The Pew Research Center released a survey on August 19, 2010, which found 18 percent of Americans believe Obama is a Muslim, up from 11 percent in March 2009. Only 34 percent believe him to be a Christian, down from 48 percent in 2009. And 43 percent don't know. Not surprisingly, two-thirds of people who call Obama a Muslim disapprove of his job performance.

From the start, Obama was clear in identifying this distortion as offensive to both himself and to Muslims.

When and where did this absurd rumor start? Anthony Robert Martin-Trigona (Andy Martin)—well known in Chicago for frivolous lawsuits and anti-Semitism—brags about starting the first Muslim rumor in 2004, shortly after Obama became a national figure by delivering his electrifying speech at the Democratic National Convention on July 27. Martin sent out a press release that appeared on August 11 on the right-wing website Free Republic.

"Obama is a Muslim who has concealed his religion. I am a strong supporter of the Muslim community, and I believe Muslims have been scapegoated. Obama has a great opportunity to be forthright. Instead, he has treated his Muslim heritage as a dark secret," Martin said in the press release. "Barack Senior was also a devoted Muslim."

This lie had scant impact on Obama's Senate race that year, which he won with 70 percent of the vote.

The Muslim rumor resurfaced in early 2008 when an e-mail of undetermined origin called "Who is Barack Obama?" began circulating (see chapter 10). This e-mail received an extraordinary amount of attention early in the campaign. It was thoroughly debunked by numerous media outlets, and no evidence showed that Obama had ever been a Muslim.

Some accounts had childhood friends in Indonesia seeing Obama in a mosque with his stepfather. So what? While in junior high school, I belonged to a Boy Scout troop that was sponsored by the Mormon Church. Scout leaders proselytized assiduously, so I attended on occasion. Someone who saw me at church a few times might conclude I was a Mormon, but I never joined. Likewise, there is no evidence that Obama was ever a confirmed Muslim or member of any mosque in Indonesia or elsewhere.

Martin recanted the Muslim smear in an October 27, 2008, interview on CNN. Not surprisingly, nobody has a whit of evidence that Obama is a Muslim. Sane people, in fact, have definitive proof that he is not. Muslims don't partake of pork or alcohol. Obama consumes both publicly, with very un-Islamic gusto. Remember the "beer" summit? It was Vice President Joe Biden who drank near-beer. Does that make the veep a closet Muslim? Case closed. Once again, the Obama haters lose their absurd argument hands down.

REVEREND JEREMIAH WRIGHT

While labeling Obama a Muslim, the same obscure forces stoked fears of his fiery Christian pastor. In March 2008, during the early primaries, a video surfaced of Rev. Jeremiah Wright (did anybody mention he was an "angry" black man?), pastor at Trinity United Church of Christ in Chicago, where Obama worshiped for twenty years. Full disclosure (or lack thereof): this author is not related to Jeremiah Wright.

"The government gives them the drugs, builds bigger prisons, passes a three-strike law and then wants us to sing 'God Bless America.' No, no, no. God damn America, that's in the Bible for killing innocent people," Wright shouted in a now-famous sermon. Wright told his congregation on the Sunday after September 11, 2001, that the United States had brought on al Qaeda's attacks because of its own acts of terrorism toward other countries.

Clips from this sermon were played in an endless loop on twenty-four-hour news channels.

"I reject outright the statements by Reverend Wright that are at issue," Obama said in a press release. He emphasized that he never heard his preacher make such remarks either in sermons or in personal conversations.

This circus dogged Obama for weeks while Wright kept the pot boiling with additional controversial remarks during a book tour. Obama finally quit the church, denounced Reverend Wright, and the issue slowly fizzled.

Throughout the rest of the campaign, Fox News and other critics did everything they could to tie Obama to Wright's shocking utterances. Fox hosts said Obama should have left the church twenty years earlier "after listening to anti-American rhetoric every Sunday," and Hannity raised the issue long after Obama took office. If Reverend Wright made inflammatory remarks "every Sunday," why did only a few videos come out with controversial remarks? Is Reverend Wright, who served in the U.S. Marine Corps, anti-American for criticizing government policies?

If the media were "in the tank for Obama," as Fox News commentators whine, why did they all play the Reverend Wright footage—which hurt Obama's image—over and over again?

While Reverend Wright's comments were over the top, Pat Robertson and Jerry Falwell, progenitors of the Religious Right and guests at George W. Bush's White House, said Americans brought the 9/11 tragedy on themselves by legalizing abortion and being tolerant toward gays. Neither extreme view can be described as mainstream. It's safe to bet that only a fraction of people would agree with Reverend Wright or Robertson and Falwell about blame for the 9/11 disaster. Wright has been pilloried by both left and right, but Robertson and Falwell get a free pass.

Wright has zero influence in the Obama administration. Conversely, the Religious Right dictated social policy in the Bush years, pressuring him to ban federal funding of stem cell research, impeding family planning, and muzzling fact-based sex education in favor of "abstinence-only" sex education, which even Bristol Palin publicly identified as ineffective.

A much odder religious video came to light in which Sarah Palin was blessed in 2005 at her church in Alaska by Pastor Thomas Muthee to free her from the spell of witches. Reverend Muthee prayed over Palin to drive away "in the name of Jesus, every form of witchcraft." A June 2004 survey by Opinion Dynamics showed only 24 percent of Americans believe in witchcraft, so that means 76 percent do not believe in hexes and spells. Does Muthee also invoke God's name to protect parishioners from dragons and vampires? Is Palin, or anyone who participates in such bizarre rituals, even close to the mainstream?

I would gladly accept a blessing from the pope, the Dalai Lama, or the archbishop of Canterbury with grace and humility, but I would not let Pastor Muthee or anyone like him within a mile of my family.

John McCain's campaign debated internally whether they should use the Reverend Wright video against Obama, but the senator, to his credit, believed such tactics would be racially divisive and prohibited their use by the campaign. That did not stop outside groups and opposition media from milking the controversy.

The Obama team must have consulted the Oracle of Delphi before starting its campaign because it understood well in advance that Reverend Wright was poison ivy. Original plans called for Wright to attend Obama's announcement of his presidential candidacy on February 10, 2007, in Springfield, Illinois, but the campaign's wise men decided that the colorful man of the cloth was a liability waiting to explode.

Some religious websites even insist that Obama is an atheist. All presidents live in a fishbowl, but Obama is the first one whose (mainstream) religious practices are subjected to more scrutiny and criticism than his political decisions. Since taking office, Obama—who seeks advice privately from various religious leaders—has been lambasted for praying at the Camp David presidential retreat's chapel instead of ostentatiously worshiping at a church in Washington. After the Reverend Wright kerfuffle, who can blame him for keeping his religious practices private?

THE ANTICHRIST

Religious nutjobs from time to time announce that a public figure or political leader is the Antichrist, foreseen in the Bible as the key figure who will trigger Armageddon, the final cataclysmic battle between the forces of God and Satan. Some Protestants even believe the pope to be the Antichrist, while leaders of non-Christian faiths are also frequent targets. As Obama gained in popularity, he became the focal point for this distinctive breed of nitwits.

This unique form of hatred remained in place after Obama took office. Public Policy Polling said on September 16, 2009, that 14 percent of New Jersey Republicans were sure Obama is the Antichrist, and another 15 percent weren't sure. The same poll also found that an eye-popping one-third of Republicans are birthers (see chapter 4) and 19 percent of all voters believe George W. Bush had prior knowledge of 9/11. This topic is so far out on the fringes that it would not merit inclusion were it not so pervasive. Among those who label Obama the Antichrist, none is a prominent theologian who has studied the Bible or history of the Antichrist or understands what the accusation really means. Theologians and believers vary widely in how they interpret the Antichrist because the biblical passages are shrouded in mystery.

"There really isn't any biblical or other 'test' to determine whether someone is or is not the Antichrist. Usually it is a larger-than-life or even supernatural figure expected in the future, often in the last days. When the tradition or image is applied to a living person, the method is rhetorical, not theological or logical," Adela Yarbro Collins, a theologian at the Yale Divinity School, told me. "The actual term comes from 1 and 2 John, where it is used in a way quite different from its eventual traditional use."

Bernard McGinn wrote in *Antichrist: Two Thousand Years of the Human Fascination with Evil*, "Outside of the Fundamentalist camp, most believing Christians seem puzzled, even slightly embarrassed, by Antichrist, especially given the legend's use in fostering hatred and oppression of groups, such as Jews and Muslims, seen as collective manifestations of Antichrist's power."[1]

McGinn told me, "I'm afraid that these kinds of smears will always be with us."

Frank Schaeffer, author of *Crazy for God: How I Grew Up as One of the Elect, Helped Found the Religious Right, and Lived to Take All (or Almost All) of It Back*, complained that crazies have taken over the Republican Party. "When you see a bunch of people going around thinking that our president is the Antichrist, you have to draw one of two conclusions: either these are racists looking for any excuse to level the next accusation, or they're beyond crazy. And I think beyond crazy is a better explanation," Schaeffer said on September 16, 2009, on MSNBC's *The Rachel Maddow Show*. "You don't work to move them off this position. You move past them. A village cannot reorganize village life to suit the village idiot. . . . This subculture has as its fundamental faith that they distrust facts per se."

Those who claim to know about the Antichrist lean heavily on passages in Revelation, the final book of the New Testament. One well-known indication is a link to 666. Revelation 13:18: "Here is wisdom. Let him that hath understanding count the number of the beast: for it is the number of a man; and his number is six hundred threescore and six."

Obama was born on August 4, 1961. No connection there. So where is a link to the sixes in prophecy? Right-wing prom queen Michele Bachmann displays some of the eerie marks of the beast. She represents the sixth district of Minnesota and was born on April 6, 1956. Bingo. Lots of sixes show up in her life. When will the Antichrist brigade get serious and investigate her?

JEWISH SMEAR

As if it weren't enough to be called a Muslim and all sorts of other misnomers, Osama bin Laden's top deputy came up with another whopper: Obama is a Jew. Tell that to the right-wingers who accuse him of hating and selling out Israel.

"Obama's message to the Muslim world was delivered when he visited the wailing wall, with the Jewish skullcap on his head, when he performed the Jewish prayers despite claiming that he's a Christian," said Ayman al-Zawahiri during Obama's trip to the Middle East.

THE ANTI-OBAMA FATWA

At least three preachers publicly issued "imprecatory prayers" asking God to strike down Obama. They have apparently ripped the page from their Bibles that features Matthew 22:39: "Thou shalt love thy neighbor as thyself."

When Islamic fundamentalists do the same thing under sharia law, it is called a fatwa; clerics who make such statements are called Islamofascists and terrorists. Many on the Right herd all Muslims into the same corral with these incendiary imams.

The dictionary defines fatwa as "a legal opinion or ruling issued by an Islamic scholar; 'bin Laden issued three fatwas calling upon Muslims to take up arms against the United States.'"

Reverend Wiley Drake, pastor at the First Southern Baptist Church in Buena Park, California, told me Obama is a "baby killer," presumably for his stance on legal abortion, before he hurriedly cut off our phone conversation.

"If he [Obama] does not turn to God and does not turn his life around, I am asking God to enforce imprecatory prayers that are throughout the scripture that would cause him death, that's correct," Drake told Alan Colmes on June 3, 2009, on Fox Radio. "That's what God said. Brother, don't get mad at me. Get mad at God. God said it."

The remarks concerning President Obama came during an interview in which Drake was asked about his statement that the murder of Dr. George Tiller, a Kansas physician who performed abortions, was an answer to his imprecatory prayers.

Drake is not just a garden-variety preacher. He was a vice president of the Southern Baptist Convention in 2006–07. The denomination, however, distanced itself from him. In an open letter, Richard Land, president of the Southern Baptist Convention's Ethics and Religious Liberty Commission, urged all pastors to pray for Obama's well-being. Spokesman Roger "Sing" Oldham said, "Wiley Drake is an individual pastor" and does not speak for them all.

If Drake does pastoral counseling to parishioners with marital problems, let's hope he doesn't teach imprecatory prayers to anyone headed for divorce court, or there will be lots of orphans in California.

Drake, in an e-mail sent shortly before Christmas 2008, also threatened the wrath of God on Rick Warren for delivering the invocation at Obama's inauguration.

"God will punish" Warren's "recent plan to invoke the presence of almighty God on this illegal alien." Another warning for Warren: "God will not wink at this." It sounds like Reverend Drake is getting out of his league. From Genesis 1:1 to Revelation 21:21, God never winks. God creates and destroys and guides and warns, but he never winks. By the way, the final verse in the

Bible is Revelation 21:21, which reads, "The grace of our Lord Jesus Christ be with you all. Amen." We might ask Drake if that includes President Obama.

At least two other pastors joined Drake in calling for Obama's early demise. "Here is my sermon, 'Why I Hate Barack Obama,'" Reverend Steven Anderson told the Faithful Word Baptist Church in Tempe, Arizona, two days before Obama's inauguration and again on August 16, 2009. "Nope. I'm not gonna pray for his good. I'm going to pray that he dies and goes to hell."

Reverend Peter Peters, pastor of the LaPorte Church of Christ in Colorado, preached on January 19, 2009, "On those false oath swearers and false oath takers bring destruction. . . . Melt and try with your fiery wrath those who with deceit speak lies and refuse to know you. Bring your vengeance upon them and upon them who have given oaths to Satan and false gods in their practice of divination." Peters also peppered this sermon with biblical justification for white supremacists.

Substitute the word God with Allah, and identical remarks would put right-wingers in a lather. Any Muslim making such remarks would end up on terrorist watch lists or even jail.

What sane person of any religion asks God to bring about someone's death? I have read the gospels—the books of Matthew, Mark, Luke, and John—in their entirety and never saw Jesus sanctioning imprecatory prayers. I was always taught that the words of Christ are paramount for anyone who claims to be his follower.

In fact, Drake appears to be going against God's wishes laid out in Exodus 22:28 ("Thou shalt not revile the gods, nor curse the ruler of thy people") and Acts 23:5 ("Thou shalt not speak evil of the ruler of thy people"). Those pages must be ripped out of the Bibles at his church, which is right down the street from Disneyland. Did Reverend Drake get lost in Fantasyland?

By late 2009, T-shirts and bumper stickers called for Obama's death with the slogan "Pray for Obama. Psalm 109:8"; that Bible verse reads, "Let his days be few; and let another take his office." Obama haters say that means they hope he serves only one term, but the biblical context unequivocally means death. The following verse, Psalm 109:9, reads, "May his children be fatherless and his wife a widow." Will this dangerous talk of praying for Obama's death provoke a psychopath with a weapon to take things upon himself and think he is doing God's work? Has this become part of the Religious Right's official liturgy? When will prominent conservative and Christian leaders take a stand against this? Praying for someone's death sounds more like satanic idolatry or witchcraft than any Christian worship I ever learned.

If a liberal pastor had ever prayed for Bush's death in Wiley Drake fashion, or if folks on the Left had ever called for his death using biblical slogans, it no doubt would have been the only item on Fox News and right-wing radio for weeks. They demonize Jeremiah Wright, who never called for anybody's death, but humor Wiley Drake and the Psalm 109:8 crowd.

There are more than 1,200 mosques in the United States. Not one American imam called for a fatwa on Obama. Apparently, Drake and his buddies snagged the exclusive franchise. Muslims don't hawk shirts or bumper stickers calling for Obama's death with verses from the Koran.

The next time Hannity or Beck rail about Islamofascists who want you dead, gently remind them that those are "imprecatory prayers" in Arabic.

6

The Obama Trifecta: Amazingly a Socialist, Communist, and Fascist Simultaneously

The trouble with the world is not that people know too little,
but that they know so many things that ain't so.

—Mark Twain

When Obama took office on January 21, 2009, the stock market and real estate values had suffered their most precipitous crash since the Great Depression, unemployment was the highest it had been in three decades, and consumer confidence was nearly destroyed. Americans were ready to unite behind their new leader with a mandate to initiate bold endeavors to reinvigorate the economy and their belief in the future.

The new president extended his hand and invited Republicans to offer suggestions. Instead, they ridiculed his every initiative, likening him to Stalin and Hitler. The overheated rhetoric of the campaign was only a warm-up: Republicans not only opposed every plan, but they ambushed Obama at every opportunity.

Obama's first task was to restore confidence. Major banks and investment houses were capsizing. George W. Bush's treasury secretary, Henry Paulson, masterminded a bank bailout in late 2008 that Bush claimed was preventing another Great Depression. But it was not nearly enough. Obama and his economic team scrambled diligently to stabilize the economy.

Before examining whether or not Obama's plans are socialist, communist, or fascist, those terms must first be defined. People should know what labels mean before letting a know-nothing define it for them.

Socialism is "any of various economic and political theories advocating collective or governmental ownership and administration of the means of production and distribution of goods."

Obama is certainly not a socialist. He never advocated collective ownership of business or production. Obama bashers grabbed pitchforks after hearing about his plan to roll back tax cuts for people who earn more than $250,000 per year to 39 percent from 35 percent during the Bush years. The upper-income tax rate approached 91 percent during the administration of Republican Dwight Eisenhower. I like Ike; was he a socialist?

The dictionary defines communism as "a theory advocating elimination of private property; a system in which goods are owned in common and are available to all as needed." Nobody can cite a single instance in which Obama advocates or practices this dogma.

Fascism is "a political philosophy, movement, or regime that exalts nation and often race above the individual and that stands for a centralized autocratic government headed by a dictatorial leader, severe economic and social regimentation, and forcible suppression of opposition." Exalts nation? Don't these same numbskulls complain that every foreign trip by Obama is an "apology tour?"

Obama's running mate, Delaware Senator Joe Biden, was asked in an October 23, 2008, interview, "You may recognize this famous quote: 'From each according to his abilities to each according to his needs.' That's from Karl Marx. How is Senator Obama not being a Marxist if he intends to spread the wealth around?" Biden's response: "Are you joking? Is this a joke?" When Barbara West of ABC affiliate WFTV in Orlando, Florida, said no, Biden asked again, "Or is that a real question?"

When will any Republican explain how it is legitimate to call Obama or Biden a communist but it is a "trick question" to ask Sarah Palin to define the "Bush Doctrine" or which newspapers she reads? Has any Republican presidential nominee or president ever been called a communist, socialist, or fascist in an interview with major media? Was West fed Republican talking points by her husband, a Republican political consultant? Is this "liberal media bias" in overdrive? The right wing always throws out its talking points, seeking to pass them off as fact.

Tom DeLay, the Republican majority leader who resigned under an ethics cloud after he was indicted on conspiracy to violate campaign finance laws, branded Obama a "radical." In an October 29, 2008, interview on MSNBC's *Hardball* he said, "I tagged him as a Marxist months ago."

Political consultant Dick Morris said on Sean Hannity's TV show on March 23, 2009, "This guy [Obama] wants his plan [bank bailouts] to fail. He wants the voluntary private-public partnerships to fail so that he can make the case for bank nationalization and vindicate his dream of a socialist economy." The next day, Hannity said, "In the last two days we know this administration has pushed the idea of the single biggest power grab, a move toward socialism, in the history of the country."

On the March 26 episode of his TV show, Hannity showed a graphic with Obama's face in front of the Soviet hammer and sickle, as he informed viewers of the "very disturbing results" of a poll among right-wing *Investor's Business Daily* readers showing that 39 percent of readers agree that the United States is "evolving into a socialist state" and thirty-six percent disagree.

"The administration is on a mission to hijack capitalism in favor of collectivism," Hannity said on March 30. "The Bolsheviks have already arrived and they're here."

Minnesota Governor Tim Pawlenty on June 3 told Neil Cavuto on Fox News, "This is not the United States of America that we know and love and remember. This looks more like more like some sort of, you know, republic in South America circa 1970s." Does Pawlenty have first-hand knowledge living in Latin America? I do. Would he be willing to debate me on this issue?

On July 22, Nicolle Wallace, who misled the public as Bush's communications director and now does the same thing on Fox News, said, "He is a far-left president."

Obama is "hell-bent" on imposing socialism, according to November 11, 2009, remarks before the Republican Women's Club in Midland, Texas, by Governor Rick Perry, who seems hell-bent on tolerating threats of secession from the United States by his supporters.

Perry's predecessor, George W. Bush, rejected the outrageous rhetoric. "I'm not going to criticize my successor," he said on June 17 at the Manufacturer & Business Association's annual meeting in Erie, Pennsylvania. Asked whether he considered Obama a socialist, Bush responded, "We'll see."

The free market–oriented *Wall Street Journal* reported the findings of a survey of economists in its July 10 issue, which asked, "How much has the fiscal stimulus of 2009 boosted the economy so far?" According to the survey, 53 percent of economists answered "Somewhat, but larger effect to come," 39 percent concluded "Somewhat, and the boost will remain small," 6 percent said "It has harmed the economy," and 2 percent believed the stimulus had helped the economy "a lot."

The guardian of economic conservatism and the business establishment found 94 percent of economists saw benefit in Obama's policies while only a minuscule number found them harmful. If the president were truly radical, wouldn't the economists surveyed be alarmed and describe him as dangerous?

Alan Greenspan, high priest in the church of free markets, backed Obama's plan to reform financial markets. The former Federal Reserve chairman told the *Washington Post* on September 28 that establishing a new Consumer Financial Protection Agency was "probably the right idea." Has the Ayn Rand disciple become a Marxist?

The same newspaper's October 30 headline was "Economy Snaps Long Slump," which reported that the stimulus and bailouts had saved the faltering economy from further losses.

Who can argue credibly that Obama is following economic principles outside the mainstream or that the *Wall Street Journal,* owned by Fox News capo Rupert Murdoch, is "in the tank" for Obama?

Obama's economic approach, in fact, was backed by the world's biggest economies, the G-20, which pledged to maintain emergency economic support—in other words, stimulus plans—at their November 7 meeting in Scotland. Ergo, if Obama's economic approach is communist, so is every major capitalist country in the world.

The free market itself offered a roaring endorsement to Obama and booed Bush on his way out of office. Obama inherited a free-falling economy that plummeted 6.4 percent in the first quarter of 2009 amid the transition of power. Cumulatively, the U.S. economy shrank 14.5 percent during Bush's final three quarters in office. By the fourth quarter of 2009, Obama's policies had reversed the dismal trend: gross domestic product surged 5.9 percent, according to data released February 26, 2010, by the U.S. Commerce Department. The economy continued to grow throughout 2010, shaking off the precipitous decline under Bush.

Even after Obama embraced centrist economic policy during his first year in office, he was called a "committed socialist ideologue" in a February 4, 2010, speech at the National Tea Party Convention in Nashville by Republican former Congressman Tom Tancredo, a right-wing ideologue who advocated bombing Islamic holy sites in Saudi Arabia, likened Hispanic leaders to the Ku Klux Klan and suggested a return to literacy tests as a prerequisite for voting.

ECONOMIC STIMULUS

Obama's signature legislation, the American Recovery and Reinvestment Act of 2009 (better know as the economic stimulus) was introduced days after he took office. Many conservatives objected to the size of the legislation—$787 billion—fearing it might be inflationary or wasteful spending. Republicans instead believed that further tax cuts, which were included in the package, would do more to help the economy than a mammoth spending bill.

"What I proposed is after you complete the contracts that are already committed, the things that are in the pipeline, stop it," Arizona Senator Jon Kyl told ABC News on July 12, 2009.

The Obama administration took the Republican at his word. The next day, Arizona Governor Jan Brewer got letters from five cabinet secretaries pointing out what money was earmarked for projects in Arizona and asking whether they should be eliminated.

"I believe the stimulus has been very effective in creating job opportunities throughout the country. However, if you prefer to forfeit the money we are making available to your state, as Senator Kyl suggests, please let me know," Secretary of Transportation Ray LaHood wrote to Brewer, a fellow Republican.

Kyl accused the Obama administration of "coordinated political attacks" for honoring his own request.

BAILOUTS

The Bush administration spent billions of public dollars to save banks that were deemed "too big to fail," angering Americans who never got a lick of help when their small businesses and personal prospects capsized. The Obama administration then devised another stimulus package to bail out financial institutions a second time.

When the Bush administration, on its way out of town, injected billions of federal dollars into the auto industry and the Obama team expanded that same policy, many people worried it meant a government takeover. That could fit the classical definition of socialism in terms of government ownership of the means of production, a valid concern given the history of free enterprise in which companies and industries rise and fall. Nobody helped buggy manufacturers when automobiles ran over their market a century ago, but General Motors and Chrysler are not buggy makers. Cars will exist for years to come. Team Obama did not want to face the collapse of domestic auto assemblers and parts makers—and the resulting spikes in unemployment—along with total foreign ownership of a vital industry.

The Center for Automotive Research in Ann Arbor, Michigan, released a report in May 2009 that found that failure of the U.S. auto industry would kill 2.5 million to 3 million jobs within a year. It concluded that allowing GM and Chrysler to crater "could have a permanent dampening effect on wealth generation in the U.S. economy." Furthermore, it would put the federal government in a position of guaranteeing pensions and retiree health care, which "would strain the nation's public health care system." No doubt the Obama administration saw this frightening scenario when it decided to yank GM and Chrysler from the Grim Reaper's clutches.

Obama's team emphasized that its assistance was temporary and that it was unwilling to provide long-term life support to comatose enterprises.

"Presidents Bush and Obama both did the right thing in supporting the industry. I do believe that the government will exit quickly at the right time," Dave Cole, chairman of the Center for Automotive Research told me.

Gerald C. Meyers, a professor of organization and management at the University of Michigan and skeptic of federal intervention, confessed to having mixed emotions about the bailout. "As a businessman, I thought you ought to let the company go, particularly Chrysler. But that had to be tempered with a certain amount of social conscience. Unemployment is getting worse and worse. I don't think we as a society can turn our back on a sudden jolt in personal misfortune," he pointed out.

Obama's critics can either step up to the challenge to make the bailout a success and extricate the government as soon as possible, or they can continue to call him names and sabotage the industry by rejecting cars made by fellow citizens.

"I won't buy a socialist car, which means I won't be buying a GM or Chrysler car for as long as the U.S. government owns huge blocks of the companies. . . . Buying a GM or a Chrysler is consenting to a massive leftward lurch in the American form of government," radio talk show host Hugh Hewitt wrote on June 1, 2009, in the *Washington Examiner.* "Buy Ford. Buy Toyota. Buy anything that isn't owned and operated by the federal government."[1]

Do loyal Americans cheer for the destruction of the U.S. economy and jobs?

Restructuring of the auto industry led to another lie by right-wingers, who asserted that Obama was gunning for Republican contributors because 79.6 percent of the 789 dealers ordered closed by Chrysler contributed to the Republican Party and 20.4 percent had donated to Democratic candidates. Fox News host Neil Cavuto accused Obama of exacting political revenge.

Virginia Congressman Eric Cantor, the GOP's House whip, was quoted June 11 by the Associated Press as saying, "you want to reward your political friends" in the bailout. "It's almost like looking at Putin's Russia."

"Evidence appears to be mounting that the Obama administration has systematically targeted for closing Chrysler dealers who contributed to Republicans," the *Washington Examiner* wrote.[2]

There was absolutely no evidence of political meddling. James E. Press, Chrysler's chairman after reorganization, had donated to George W. Bush and other Republican candidates. Would he exact revenge on dealers who gave money to the GOP?

Nate Silver of FiveThirtyEight.com compiled official Federal Election Commission data of donations by auto dealers between 2004 and 2008 and found that 88 percent of the dollars went to the GOP and 12 percent of the total went to Democrats. So, the vast majority of dealers closed by Chrysler are owned by Republicans, and the overwhelming majority of dealerships remaining open are, you guessed it, owned by Republicans.

A majority of Republicans in Congress voted against the bailout. If they had their way, all the GM and Chrysler factories and dealerships and countless suppliers would have closed, not just one-quarter of the retailers.

Bush defended his bailouts after Obama took office and made it clear that he did not want to be remembered as the next Herbert Hoover.

"I firmly believe it was necessary to put money in our banks to make sure our financial system did not collapse . . . I did not want there to be bread lines, to be a great depression," Bush said at the Erie conference. On November 12 he reiterated that the bailout was "a temporary government intervention to unfreeze the credit markets so we could avoid a major global depression."

Smears about the bailout were relentless despite the thumbs-up from Bush; they did not subside when ten banks got approval to repay $68 billion to the Troubled Asset Relief Program (TARP) on June 9. The next day General Motors emerged from bankruptcy protection. A month after that, the government reported a $4 billion profit from repayment of the bank bailout. By the end of 2009, GM began to pay back its $6.7 billion loan to the government, announcing the intention to clear its debt by 2011, four years ahead of schedule. At the same time, the U.S. Treasury Department began selling the warrants (the right to get common stock) in large banks it had acquired as collateral early in the year under the bailout. So, how does this resemble communist economics—even remotely?

"That is unprecedented. I don't know of any company of any size that got out of chapter Eleven in forty days. That's truly remarkable, and it only happened because the federal government, including the president of the United States, was behind it," Meyers said.

SIX-MONTH REPORT CARD

On July 20, 2009, Obama's six-month anniversary, news channels CNN, MSNBC, and CNBC examined Obama's tenure thus far. The networks gave a balanced view of the greatest hits and biggest flops. Not Fox News; it bashed Obama all day.

Hannity played spooky music while showing clips that portrayed Obama as scary. The real world must be frightening to someone with Hannity's cock-eyed tunnel vision.

After playing a clip in which Obama said the United States has made mistakes, Hannity bellowed, "His foreign policy is ashamed of everything this country stands for." If he had played a different clip from this same speech, the audience would have heard Obama elegantly praising the virtues of the United States.

"He's purposely hiding bad economic news," Hannity said. A few hours earlier, Fox News picked apart minute elements in the president's stimulus package; the information was available in fine detail because Obama ordered full disclosure of federal spending, something Bush withheld from the public. Hannity was the one hiding the real facts from his audience with his sweeping statements and rampant distortion.

Glenn Beck said the same day that Obama turned the United States into a "hybrid between France and Venezuela. . . . Obama does not want America to succeed." He offered no examples or proof. If Beck knew anything about Venezuela, as I do, he would know what a scary regime looks like and not make such malicious, asinine comments about Obama.

Amanda Carpenter, a reporter at the *Washington Times* (founded by the Reverend Sun Myung Moon, whose lemming-like followers are called "moonies" but do not include Neil Armstrong), complained bitterly that $100 million worth of stimulus money, or one-tenth of 1 percent, went to providing food to homeless shelters and food pantries. "It doesn't smell like job creation," she sniffed. Her olfactory talents somehow did not whiff out that this spending is one of the most direct and efficient ways to stimulate the economy while accomplishing irrefutable social good.

CZARS

Fox News and right-wing politicians pounded their cudgels daily and protested against Obama's "czars." Fox hosts mocked the concept of special advisers to the president as "the helm of a shadow government" and convinced their audience that Obama invented the practice and borrowed the term to mimic Russian czars and Soviet communist dictators.

Obama appointed "czars" to handle critical areas of government policy, as did his predecessors. "Czar" is journalistic shorthand for "special assistant to the president" with extremely limited authority to analyze information and offer advice. Most czars lack authority to issue policy or orders. Members of Congress, governors, mayors, and other policymakers have special assistants who play identical roles.

Obama did not create "czars." Special assistants to the president have existed since the beginning of our republic. Franklin D. Roosevelt appointed overseers during World War II to make sure the government had all the tools at its disposal to fight the fascists in Europe and Asia. Richard Nixon appointed an energy czar to end dependence on foreign oil (that worked, didn't it?).

The *Washington Post* reported on September 16 that Bush the Younger had thirty-six so-called czar positions filled by forty-six people, accounting for replacements. Obama has thirty-four to forty czar positions, depending on how they were counted and who was counting.

Do Republicans deny that the president should have top-level people devoted exclusively to such overwhelming matters as terrorism, intelligence, Iraq, Afghanistan-Pakistan, U.S. border security, and other crucial areas? They complain about the money spent on economic stimulus. Why don't they want someone overseeing accountability of those massive expenditures? Most Americans, especially conservatives, hate to be overregulated. So, instead of complaining about czars, why don't they offer suggestions to the president's special adviser on regulation to make the regulatory framework more efficient and effective?

Nattering naysayers who would rather grandstand than fix serious problems are nothing new. In *Public Enemies,* the 2009 hit movie about the hunt to capture John Dillinger and other notorious gangsters, FBI director J. Edgar Hoover begged Congress to increase funding for the 1930s "war on crime." A senator derisively accused Hoover of "setting yourself up as a czar." Thankfully, "czar" Hoover's agents got Dillinger, "Baby Face" Nelson, and "Machine Gun" Kelly and ended a wave of terror. Why do right-wingers trash Obama for putting the same attention on solving today's major problems the way Hoover focused on putting bloodthirsty hoodlums out of business? Do they—like Rush Limbaugh and Jim DeMint have said—want our nation to fail in its efforts to combat its overwhelming challenges?

On July 31 Beck said Obama's czars "are evil, wicked, frightening people." Hannity called Obama appointees "a revolving door of radicals."

Republican Congressman Jack Kingston of Georgia introduced the "Czar Accountability and Reform Act of 2009" to withhold funding from any czar's office unless confirmed by the Senate. He and a hundred co-sponsors complained that appointment of czars without confirmation was anti-democratic. If they truly believe this is undemocratic, why did they not forbid the appointment of "czars" or demand controls during the years of unchallenged and unchecked Republican incompetence?

Lamar Alexander, a Republican senator from Tennessee, urged the Senate on September 9 to declare that "these czars are an affront to the Constitution. They're anti-democratic." He failed to mention that six years earlier he had stood on the exact same spot to support a "manufacturing czar in the Commerce Department, which I would welcome," and favored Randall Tobias as the AIDS czar. Don't the people who tell this guy what to say ever check with the people who used to tell this guy what to say?

Republican Congressman Mike Pence of Indiana told the Value Voters Summit on September 19 that "nowhere in here can I find the word czar," waving a copy of the Constitution. "Washington, D.C., must become a no-czar zone." Is it possible to serve five terms in the House and not know that journalists—not Lenin—invented the expression?

Even Karl Rove, Bush's czar for domestic policy without congressional approval, tweeted on Twitter on July 10, 2009, "darned if I can figure out all the czars, except a giant expansion of presidential power." Was Rove snoozing in his White House office when Bush increased the number of czars?

The most preposterous naysayer was Newt Gingrich, who said Congress "should just eliminate" the czars. How many times did Gingrich raise the issue as Speaker of the House when he had the authority to do something about it?

The looniest observation about czars was made by Christine O'Donnell in her campaign for the U.S. Senate in Delaware during a September 21, 2010 candidate forum.

Citing Article 1 Section 9, Clause 8 of the Constitution which prevents the U.S. government from awarding a title of nobility, the pseudo-constitutional scholar blurted out: "I would say to President Obama that czar is certainly a title of nobility, and therefore it is unconstitutional."

Do Americans feel more comfortable with numerous czars dispersed about the government supervising crucial areas, or would they prefer an omnipotent, omnipresent czar like Dick Cheney who can poke his fingers into everything for eight years?

Righties scream that Obama's czars need congressional scrutiny. In fact, it was George W. Bush who flouted constitutional oversight by appointing the undiplomatic John Bolton as the head U.S. diplomat to the United Nations during the congressional break because the Senate would have undiplomatically shot down the right-wing extremist.

In fact, the nation should be thankful that Obama was able to appoint advisers who did not need congressional approval because of unprecedented

Republican foot-dragging. A year after Obama took office, Alabama Senator Richard Shelby was still holding up, without explanation, more than seventy appointments, including numerous top-level officials needed to fight terrorism.

HITLER COMPARISONS

Does anyone in his right mind truly believe that Obama's policies and philosophy have anything in common with Hitler?

No.

Look at anti-Obama websites. Go to right-wing rallies. Pictures of Obama with a sinister moustache are ubiquitous. This did not start after he took office; this fringe element was there from the start.

On his February 11, 2008, broadcast on Fox News Radio, Tom Sullivan made a "side-by-side comparison" of speeches by Hitler and Obama. Ann Coulter made similar remarks.

E-mails of unidentified origin circulated during the campaign calling Obama a "young, black Adolf Hitler" while another one warned Jewish voters about a "second Holocaust" if Obama were elected.

Ezine blog showed a colorful post of Hitler with Obama's "Yes we can" slogan and another of Obama bearing the title "Socialism."

The Republican Women of Anne Arundel County invited members to march in the 2009 Fourth of July parade in Annapolis, Maryland. Joyce E. Thomann, president of the club, compared Obama to Hitler on the group's website:

> Obama and Hitler have a great deal in common in my view. Obama and Hitler use the 'blitzkrieg' method to overwhelm their enemies. FAST, CARPET BOMBING intent on destruction. Hitler's blitzkrieg bombing destroyed many European cities – quickly and effectively. Obama is systematically destroying the American economy and with it AMERICA. First the banking/investment industry, next private enterprise (GM and Chrysler) and now HEALTH CARE. And he is working on grabbing more of the American economy with his environmental extremism!

How could Obama destroy industries that the Republicans reduced to rubble before he even took the oath of office?

The Republican Party of Duval County, Florida, promoted a Tea Party event in Jacksonville on July 2 at which comparisons were made between Obama and Hitler. Tea Party members carried equally offensive signs at numerous rallies nationwide.

Duval County Republican Executive Committee Chairman Lenny Curry, on the party's website, justified the crazies: "I believe Tea Party officials made the right choice in not bringing further attention to those few people in attendance holding inappropriate signs by forcing them to leave or to put their signs away."

Curry can't stop whining: "I regret that a few political opportunists have taken an event with an important message and attempted to muddle that message with lies and false charges." When did denouncing hatred become opportunism?

About 4,000 people attended the "Hands Off Our Health Care!" protest on November 5, called by Minnesota Congresswoman Michele Bachmann and touted by Fox News. Neither Bachmann nor Republican leader John Boehner objected to a huge sign reading "National Socialist Health Care Dachau Germany 1945" alongside an enlarged picture of bodies piled up at the Nazi death camp.

When George W. Bush was in office, there were scattered instances where protesters likened him to Hitler, but Democratic leaders routinely denounced those. Why do such images appear so frequently under the official patronage of the Republican Party with so few complaints by its leaders?

HUGO CHÁVEZ COMPARISONS

"Here are two world leaders that have both, within the last month, nationalized huge private-sector companies. In the case of President Obama, General Motors and Chrysler," Iowa Congressman Steve King said on April 21 on C-SPAN. "And you have Hugo Chávez who nationalized a great American company's facilities, Cargill's rice facilities in Venezuela just about a month ago. Those two have done the same thing to private business."

Michael Savage said on March 5 on his radio show, "Chávez took years to do what Obama is doing in a few months. So in some ways Obama is even more of a terrorist than Chávez is."

Since taking office in 1999, Chávez seized oil joint ventures, power generation, cement factories, steel mills, aluminum smelters, farms, banks, and telecommunications.

Venezuela passed a law that requires the state-owned telecommunications company to monitor all telephone calls and e-mails and report critics to the government. If Republicans bothered to do their homework, they would know that Chávez learned this trick from George W. Bush, not Obama.

In July 2009 the Obama administration approved sending more military aid to Colombia, which angered Chávez. U.S. soldiers in Colombia provide intelligence for fighting Marxist rebels, who have received aid from Chávez in the past. If Obama were enamored of Chávez, as the wingnuts say, why would he militarily back Chávez's *bête noire*, Colombia?

The supposed links between Obama and Chávez are viciously misleading on every single point. Obama bailed out companies begging for money and never expropriated firms against their will. I will debate—in English or Spanish—Congressman King or any other stooge who conflates Obama with Chávez because the facts show conclusively that the two men are as far apart politically as they are geographically.

PRAVDA: WHEN TRUTH IS NOT THE TRUTH

Fox News and the right-wing blogs fell for the latest propaganda ploy from the master of propaganda they had decried in the Soviet era: *Pravda* (meaning "truth"). When a column appeared on the *Pravda* website in April 2009, denizens of the Right hypnotically quoted its anti-Obama screed. The online site is not the same as the printed stalwart of the Communist era, but its accuracy is equally suspect. How utterly comical.

"It must be said, that like the breaking of a great dam, the American descent into Marxism is happening with breathtaking speed, against the backdrop of a passive, hapless sheeple, excuse me dear reader, I meant people," said columnist Stanislav Mishin.

The online version of Pravda is akin to the *National Enquirer*. The same site running this editorial also had numerous articles praising the Russian military (do these *Amerikanski* right-wingers also goose-step?) and pictures of what looked like a Republican convention: grotesque creatures under headlines such as "Dog gives birth to mutant creature that resembles human being," "Russian fishermen catch squeaking alien and eat it," "Baby cyclops born in India," and "Mummified man found in his apartment sitting down for six years."

Would anyone with a brain rely on the Russian version of the *National Enquirer* for political discourse? If Fox News and right-wing bloggers want to repeat material from such illegitimate sources, they should be judged by the company they keep. Glenn Beck, whose greatest talent is attributing meaning to the meaningless, referred to the *Pravda* item twice in late October.

MIRANDA RIGHTS

Right-wingers, in Pavlovian spasmodic reflex, condemn "Miranda rights," which require law enforcement to inform criminal suspects of their legal rights to an attorney and against coercive self-incrimination. Critics call the landmark 1966 Supreme Court ruling on Miranda "judicial activism," ignoring the fact that Miranda rights are in the Fifth Amendment. Did Rush Limbaugh dig in his heels concerning Miranda and waive his right to "plead the Fifth" when he was busted for drugs?

As relates to Obama, this tempest began to form in Bill O'Reilly's imaginary teapot on June 12, 2009, when he shook his head sadly while announcing that "military people" in Afghanistan were compelled to read Miranda rights to detainees. The clear implication was that softheaded liberal extremists like Obama put the nation's security at risk to placate civil libertarians and terrorists. Yet these same boneheads call Obama a fascist or communist without identifying any fascist and communist leader enamored of guaranteeing defendants' rights.

"Four interesting situations, beginning with an accusation by [Republican] Congressman Mike Rogers from Michigan, who says the Obama administration is now ordering military people to read captured Taliban and al Qaeda their rights in Afghanistan. That means they're telling the terrorists that they have a right to remain silent," O'Reilly said.

"Because Barack Obama is changing our approach in the field when it comes to prosecuting or going after terror suspects, and it's a designed change and this is part of it," he slobbered.

Hannity allowed Liz Cheney, daughter of former vice president Dick Cheney, to repeat the same deception. "We're also now capturing guys on the battlefield, and the first thing we say to them is 'You have the right to remain silent.'" Hannity concurred: "It's insane. We're going to Mirandize enemy combatants at a time of war."

The Stepford Foxies apparently got their orders from the *Weekly Standard,* which said, "The Obama Justice Department has quietly ordered FBI agents to read Miranda rights to high value detainees captured and held at U.S. detention facilities in Afghanistan, according to a senior Republican on the House Intelligence Committee."[3]

Neither the wretched *Substandard* nor Fox blabbermouths bothered to check the veracity of Congressman Rogers's prattle. A single phone call or a quick Internet search would have shown that this was not a new Obama directive. The *Washington Post* reported more than a year before that the Bush administration began the policy in which some terrorism suspects were questioned "using time-tested rapport-building techniques" over a sixteen-month period. "The men were read rights similar to a standard U.S. Miranda warning."[4]

General David Petraeus mentioned the matter when answering a reporter's question on June 11 at the third annual Center for a New American Security conference, where he delivered the keynote address. The chief of the U.S. Central Command answered that he had "no concerns at all. This is the FBI doing what the FBI does. . . . The real rumor yesterday is whether our forces were reading Miranda rights to detainees and the answer to that is no."

The U.S. Justice Department issued a statement the same day: "There has been no policy change and no blanket instruction issued for FBI agents to Mirandize detainees oversees. While there have been specific cases in which FBI agents have Mirandized suspects overseas, at both Bagram and in other situations, in order to preserve the quality of evidence obtained, there has been no overall policy change with respect to detainees."

If O'Reilly believed Petraeus and the Justice Department were lying, he must say so. If the *Washington Post* story was shot down (it was not), he needs to mention it. But Fox viewers never knew the Fox version was debunked before it went on the air. Ignoring facts because they contradict an agenda is journalistic malpractice; it is malice toward the intended target and the audience.

When O'Reilly says "Obama is changing our approach" to dealing with terrorists, he is dead wrong on the facts. He is either dreadfully incompetent by not calling the Justice Department and Pentagon for reaction, or he doesn't care that he is wrong and misleads viewers anyway. The Obama administration wants to guarantee that the evidence stands up in court so it can convict these monsters, the way our predecessors did with Nazis at Nuremberg.

Why did Fox hosts not make a phone call to find out: 1) Are Miranda-type rights being read, and if so, to whom and under what circumstances? 2) Is this a new policy under Obama? 3) What is the legal and anti-terror rationale for this policy? 4) What other approaches have been considered, and why were those rejected?

That is standard procedure at any news organization where I have worked. If such information is unavailable, the story must say so clearly.

As a perfect example of the GOP and right-wing media's incestuous relationship, Michigan Congressman Peter Hoekstra repeated the Miranda canard on November 10 on Hannity's show. Hoekstra was the ranking Republican on the Permanent Select Committee on Intelligence. Is that a mouthful of oxymorons or what?

If O'Reilly, Hannity, Hoekstra, and Liz Cheney loathe the Fifth Amendment, their beef is with James Madison, who introduced the Bill of Rights. Did O'Reilly gripe when Ramzi Ahmed Yousef was sentenced to life in prison plus 240 years for planning the 1993 World Trade Center bombing? Did Hannity scoff when Timothy McVeigh was convicted and executed for the Oklahoma City bombing? If Obama haters object so stridently to American legal tradition, a few places spring to mind where they might feel more at home—Cuba, North Korea, Mynamar, Zimbabwe, and Saudi Arabia—where nobody wastes time on legal niceties for accused terrorists.

Next time you watch *The Treasure of the Sierra Madre*, think of a world run by O'Reilly, Hannity, Hoekstra, and Liz Cheney as the *federales* tell Bogie's character Dobbs: "Miranda rights? We don't need no Miranda rights!"

PARAMILITARY ARMY

"How is it possible their candidate (Obama) is seeking to create some kind of massive but secret national police force that will be even bigger than the Army, Navy, Marines, and Air Force put together?" Joseph Farah, founder of the right-wing WorldNetDaily, wrote on the website on July 15, 2008. Fox commentators treated Farah's fantasy as if it were a factual news release and began to trash Obama for imagined Third Reich leanings.

Michele Bachmann ranted that Obama's plans to expand Volunteers in Service to America, or VISTA (also known as AmeriCorps), would establish "reeducation camps for young people" like those in North Korea and Cuba.

"I believe there's a very strong chance we will see that young people will be put into mandatory service and the real concern is that there are provision for what I would call 're-education camps' for young people where young people have to go and get trained in a philosophy that the government put forward and then they have to go work in some of these politically correct forums," Bachmann said in an April 4, 2009, interview with Sue Jeffers on KTLK radio in Minneapolis.

"Obama has a plan to force children into a paramilitary domestic army," Michael Savage said on his radio show on March 23. "Your child will be conscripted by the Obama fascists, put into a uniform and God knows what they're going to be forced to do. This was forced by Hitler with the Hitler youth. This was done by Stalin during the dark days of the Soviet Union under the guise of another volunteer corps."

VISTA is a domestic version of the Peace Corps, which works on public service projects. It is an outgrowth of the Domestic Volunteer Service Act of 1973 signed into law by Republican Richard Nixon. Its members, ages eighteen to twenty-four, earn a stipend while their expenses are covered. VISTA works together with subversive organizations such as Boy Scouts, Boys and Girls Club, Big Brothers, Big Sisters, and Habitat for Humanity.

Since the draft ended following the Vietnam War, Congress has periodically studied various forms of government service for young people. There was minuscule support in Congress, however, for making any such national service mandatory.

A similar conspiracy theory emerged in April 2009 when a RAND Corporation report analyzed the possible creation of a civilian police force that would be used in case of natural disasters and overseas events.

By the end of that year, Beck, Newt Gingrich, and others said Obama was imposing secretive martial law to silence the president's critics. They pointed to Executive Order 12425, which Obama amended to give Interpol immunity from lawsuits and the Freedom of Information Act for law-enforcement activities in the United States. Right-wing paranoids said Obama intended to use

Interpol as his own "secret police" to arrest Americans, even though it does not have such authority. Free Republic and other loopy websites theorized that Obama plotted to use these forces to shut down Fox News or the Tea Party. None of them could explain how Obama persuaded the Bush administration to commission this study in 2007.

WILLIAM AYERS

When Palin said during the presidential campaign that Obama "pals around with terrorists," she was referring to his acquaintance William Ayers.

In the 1970s Ayers was a leader in the Weather Underground radical group, which protested the American role in the Vietnam War. The organization bombed the Capitol, the Pentagon, the State Department building, banks, courthouses, and police stations.

Ayers was never convicted because of prosecutorial misconduct. Many years later he became a professor of education at the University of Illinois at Chicago. His wife, fellow radical Bernardine Dohrn, became a lawyer and professor.

In 1995 Ayers and Dohrn held a coffee event for several candidates for public office in Chicago. Among them was Obama, then running for the Illinois state Senate. Ayers and Obama both served between 1999 and 2002 on the board of directors of the Woods Fund of Chicago, a charitable group devoted to welfare reform and affordable housing; it met four times a year.

Obama and Ayers also crossed paths at the Chicago Annenberg Challenge, a public school reform project, from 1995 to 2001. It was funded by the Annenberg Foundation and matching private donations. Other board members included prominent business and academic leaders, both Republicans and Democrats. The foundation was endowed by the late Walter H. Annenberg, publisher of the *Philadelphia Inquirer*, *TV Guide*, and other publications. In 1969, President Nixon appointed Annenberg as ambassador to the United Kingdom. Annenberg, who died in 2002, was a close friend of President Reagan.

Obama bashers on numerous occasions attempted to describe the Annenberg Challenge as having a radical agenda, and the McCain-Palin campaign tried to make Obama's acquaintance with Ayers the central theme of the campaign.

Hannity broadcast a "documentary" in which discredited anti-Semite Andy Martin was the main source. Talking heads on Fox repeated these alleged Obama-Ayers links every day during the final months of the presidential campaign (see chapter 9).

Martin claimed Obama and Ayers were close for many years. "Is it just coincidence that Obama and Ayers were on the Columbia campus together? Did they meet and make their initial contact at that time?" he wrote in his blog at Obambi.com.

Obama denounced Ayers's radical activities while in the Weather Underground, which took place when Obama was a child. "And the notion that somehow as a consequence of me knowing somebody who engaged in detestable acts forty years ago, when I was eight years old, somehow reflects on me and my values doesn't make much sense," Obama said at the April 16, 2008, debate of Democratic presidential candidates.

Ayers refused to comment during the presidential campaign. Afterward, he wrote an op-ed piece for the *New York Times*. [5]

"Unable to challenge the content of Barack Obama's campaign, his opponents invented a narrative about a young politician who emerged from nowhere, a man of charm, intelligence and skill, but with an exotic background and a strange name," Ayers wrote. "We didn't pal around, and I had nothing to do with his positions. Demonization, guilt by association, and the politics of fear did not triumph this time. Let's hope they never will again. And let's hope we might now assert that in our wildly diverse society, talking and listening to the widest range of people is not a sin, but a virtue."

Ayers played no role in the campaign or the Obama administration. Yet Hannity continued to bring it up. On his TV show on July 7, 2009, Hannity said Obama "never got asked tough questions about his radical friends and associates, except by me and others." Yet we see Obama was asked about Ayers at the Democratic debate quoted previously. After that, the *New York Times* and all the networks raised the question. And the Republicans got uncritical, free propaganda every time Palin accused Obama of "palling around with terrorists."

RASHID KHALIDI

This was another "pals around with terrorists" smear repeated daily by Palin. Obama knew Rashid Khalidi, a fellow instructor at the University of Chicago who left to teach at Columbia University. Khalidi, who is an adviser to the Palestinian Authority government, was described by critics as being an adviser on the Obama campaign. Palin never proved a link between Khalidi and the Obama campaign, though she proved that she could pronounce an exotic name—other than Obama—with three syllables.

Obama said on his website that Khalidi "is not one of my advisers; he's not one of my foreign policy people. . . . To pluck out one person who I know and who I've had a conversation with who has very different views than 900 of my friends and then to suggest that somehow that shows that maybe I'm not sufficiently pro-Israel, I think, is a very problematic stand to take."

Hannity said on October 30, 2008, that Khalidi was a "terrorist spokesman," trying to insinuate a murky tie between Obama and some terrorist. He was referring to Khalidi's acknowledged work for Yasser Arafat. U.S. presidents, secretaries of state, and diplomats "palled around" with Arafat, as did Israeli leaders. George W. Bush actually had closer ties to Khalidi because he allowed the U.S. government to give $300,000 per year to the Middle East Institute, which Khalidi oversees. Why did Bush allow the U.S. government to sponsor a terror cell?

COUP

Newsmax, one of the most insidious Obama-hating websites (see Appendix A), allowed one of its regular contributors, John L. Perry, to post a coup-mongering blog on September 29, 2009, under the headline "Obama Risks a Domestic Military 'Intervention'":

> There is a remote, although gaining, possibility America's military will intervene as a last resort to resolve the Obama problem. Don't dismiss it as unrealistic. . . . Top military officers can see the Constitution they are sworn to defend being trampled as American institutions and enterprises are nationalized. . . . Military intervention is what Obama's exponentially accelerating agenda for 'fundamental change' toward a Marxist state is inviting upon America. A coup is not an ideal option, but Obama's radical ideal is not acceptable or reversible. Unthinkable? Then think up an alternative, non-violent solution to the Obama problem. Just don't shrug and say, 'We can always worry about that later.' In the 2008 election,

that was the wistful, self-indulgent, indifferent reliance on abnegation of personal responsibility that has sunk the nation into this morass.

The morass described by Newsmax is not the Obama administration, but the morass of idiots and traitors engaged in such dangerous talk. There was no unrest in the military and nobody advocating any sort of military takeover.

I lived in Latin America for a decade. I heard furtive whispers by military officers telling me they were discussing "military intervention" with fellow soldiers "for the good of the country." History has shown, tragically, that these chronic interventions by military jackals are an affront to democracy and basic liberties, requiring decades to repair the damage.

To its credit, Newsmax removed the offending item.

Perry was not the first to drop hints about a coup against Obama. Rush Limbaugh on June 29 condemned Obama's criticism of the military coup in Honduras. Limbaugh said, "We learned the Obama administration tried to stop the coup. Now what was—the coup that many of you wish would happen here, without the military."

Every time liberals complain about reckless talk regarding Obama, right-wingers howl that liberals feasted on a non-stop, eight-year hatefest against Bush. Find a single liberal who advocated a military overthrow of Bush. Where are the responsible Republicans lining up to condemn Newsmax and Limbaugh for such dangerous talk? Instead the Republican Party does business with Newsmax, renting its mailing list because GOP leaders know that people who support treasonous trash like coup-mongering against Obama are avid Republican donors.

THE SOCIALIST REPUBLIC OF ALASKA

Palin delighted in labeling Obama a socialist at every campaign stop, but at the same time, she headed one of the world's biggest and most entrenched socialist regimes.

The state of Alaska owns its oil reserves, not private-sector oil companies, and the state budget is based largely on royalties paid by energy extraction. In the socialist state of Alaska, they spread the wealth, in a determinedly socialistic manner. Every year, each resident of Alaska gets a "dividend check" for the exact same amount from the Permanent Fund. Alaskans received a record $2,069 apiece in 2008. In addition, each Alaskan also received $1,200 in a "windfall profits" benefit after Palin gouged the oil companies. When Democrats proposed an identical benefit at the federal level in 2008, they were called socialists. Indeed, Karl Marx would be proud to see his theories in practice in Alaska. If socialism were anathema, why did Palin not use her bully pulpit while she was commissar to run the socialists out of Alaska and turn ownership of energy resources over to the private sector?

In fact, Palin bragged about how the socialist republic of Alaska, under her leadership, strong-armed private-sector oil companies into giving away even more money to Alaskans, the sheiks of the Arctic tundra. You betcha.

Nor did Palin ever mention that she palled around with terrorists when Alaska got free heating oil for low-income native communities from Venezuela's Hugo Chávez. Why did Palin not scotch that deal?

"A share of our oil resource revenue goes back to the people who own the resources. Imagine that," Palin told Sean Hannity in an interview broadcast on June 8, 2009. "We said we want a clear, equitable share of the resources that we own, and the people will share in those resource revenues that are derived." Hannity never asked whether collective ownership of oil was a capitalist or socialist concept.

During the same interview, she lamented the government bailout of the auto industry and federal stimulus legislation. She said, "If Americans aren't paying attention, unfortunately, our country could evolve [doesn't the right wing discourage teaching evolution?] into something we do not even recognize, certainly something that is so far from what the founders of our country had in mind for us."

The ever-objective Hannity chirped, "Socialism?" to which the then-czar of the socialist republic of Alaska happily agreed, saying, "That is where we are headed. And we have to be blunt enough and candid honest enough with Americans to let them know, nationalizing many of our services, our projects, our business, yes, that is where we would head."

In her farewell address as governor on July 26, 2009, Palin bragged that "we sent you the energy rebate" (the socialist windfall profit tax on the oil industry) and a few minutes later warned "be wary of accepting government largesse."

7

Why We Hate: The Many Faces of Loathing Arrayed Against Obama

> If a man say, I love God, and hateth his brother, he is a liar: for he that loveth not his brother whom he hath seen, how can he love God whom he hath not seen?
>
> —1 John 4:20

The most demonstrative expression of hatred against a political leader is the threat of violence. After seeing the Kennedys and Martin Luther King Jr. gunned down and after the foiled attempts to assassinate Ronald Reagan and Gerald Ford, we are wary and hope the Secret Service is doing its job.

The wild rhetoric in the McCain-Palin campaign built to such a thunderous crescendo that when McCain or Palin insulted Obama at their rallies, the sheep would bleat "terrorist," "treason" and "kill him." It was all one-sided, with no reports of threatening language toward McCain or Palin at Obama rallies.

White supremacist websites—Council of Conservative Citizens (cofcc. org) and Stormfront.org—boasted peak traffic around the election and inauguration. The Simon Wiesenthal Center said more than 10,000 hate sites exist on the Internet, their traffic exacerbated by Obama's election. The Southern Poverty Law Center says hate groups "allow people to feel part of a movement."

Law enforcement around the country reported increased threats against Obama. Although the Secret Service never publicly discusses threats against a president, Ronald Kessler, author of the 2009 bestseller *In the President's Secret Service: Behind the Scenes with Agents in the Line of Fire and the Presidents They Protect*, was widely quoted as saying that threats against the president grew 400 percent since Obama took office.

The Secret Service was swamped by unprecedented threats against Obama, a surge in racist hate groups, and anti-government fervor, said an internal report by the Congressional Research Service, according to the *Boston Globe*.[1]

An armed group in Denver made racist threats against Obama and incited assassination fears during the Democratic National Convention in August 2008. Two skinheads in Tennessee were charged with plotting to decapitate blacks around the country and murder Obama while wearing white top hats and tuxedos. Police in Milwaukee found a poster of Obama with a bullet going toward his head.

These incidents intensified after Obama was elected. The Macedonia Church of God in Christ under construction in Springfield, Massachusetts, was torched by men who told police they feared Obama would give minorities more rights.

In Vay, Idaho, someone posted a sign with Obama's name and the offer of a "free public hanging." In Maine a convenience store invited customers to join a betting pool to guess when Obama might be killed.

A classified ad in May in the *Warren Times Observer* in Pennsylvania read, "May Obama follow in the steps of Lincoln, Garfield, McKinley and Kennedy!" the four American presidents who were assassinated in office. The next day, the newspaper issued an apology and helped authorities identify the person who placed the ad.

An anonymous caller reached Randi Rhodes's syndicated radio show on June 18 and said, "If I were Obama I wouldn't worry about health insurance. I'd worry about life insurance."

Fox News announcers are fond of saying that "the Far Left" and "left-wingers"—do they mean liberals?—engaged in "nonstop hate speech against Bush." I listened to lots of talk radio during the Bush debacle, but I never once heard anyone suggest Bush be assassinated. Liberals demanded investigations, impeachment, and trials for Bush and members of his administration, but there was no talk of violence.

In early 2009 the Department of Homeland Security released two separate reports highlighting dangers from extreme-left and extreme-right groups. Right-wingers went into a frenzy, accusing the Obama administration of going after them and threatening their free speech, when it was the Bush administration which commissioned the study.

During the wild and crazy town hall meetings in the summer of 2009, numerous people showed up at Obama appearances toting guns. None threatened overt violence, but their presence complicated the Secret Service's job to protect the president. When people carried guns to appearances by the Kennedys, Gerald Ford, and Ronald Reagan, they used them. How can Secret Service agents tell the difference between a "responsible" gunslinger and a Squeaky Fromme wannabe?

Gun-huggers argue that the Second Amendment is their main issue. They have been whipped into a frenzy by the National Rifle Association's distortions of Obama's position on gun rights (see chapter 2). If they are so devoted to the Second Amendment, why did they never show up to greet previous presidents with firearms? After all, it was the first President Bush who loudly quit the NRA when it sent out a fund-raising pamphlet labeling government agents "jack-booted government thugs." Why didn't they stalk him instead of Obama?

I have never seen a survey about it, but it's reasonable to conclude that the vast majority of Americans reject describing FBI and Secret Service agents as "jack-booted government thugs."

David Frum, a former speechwriter for George W. Bush, wrote about the increase in violent right-wing rhetoric in *The Week*:

> Nobody has been hurt so far. We can all hope that nobody will be. But firearms and politics never mix well. They mix especially badly with a third ingredient: the increasingly angry tone of incitement being heard from right-of-center broadcasters. . . . The Nazi comparisons from Rush Limbaugh; broadcaster Mark Levin asserting that President Obama is 'literally at war with the American people'; former vice presidential candidate Sarah Palin claiming that the president was planning 'death panels' to extirpate the aged and disabled; the charges that the president is a fascist, a socialist, a Marxist, an illegitimate Kenyan fraud, that he 'har-

bors a deep resentment of America,' that he feels a 'deep-seated hatred of white people,' that his government is preparing concentration camps, that it is operating snitch lines, that it is planning to wipe away 'American liberties': All this hysterical and provocative talk invites, incites, and prepares a prefabricated justification for violence. . . . Just yesterday, the radio host Sean Hannity openly contemplated violence—and primly tut-tutted that if it occurs, the president will have only himself to blame. . . . It's not enough for conservatives to repudiate violence, as some are belatedly beginning to do. We have to tone down the militant and accusatory rhetoric. . . . The president can be met and bested on the field of reason—but only by people who are themselves reasonable.[2]

Hatred against Obama is palpable. The never-ending smear about his birth certificate and labeling him a Muslim is not political discourse. It is unabashed loathing. Right-wing hatred of Obama reached a fever pitch leading up to his September 8, 2009, address to school kids.

Some parents, brainwashed by Fox News and right-wing radio, refused to allow Obama to "brainwash" their children with "socialist" ideas. Glenn Beck warned parents to keep their children home from school. Laura Ingraham called it an "underhanded attempt to influence these young people." Monica Crowley said, "This is what Chairman Mao did." Sean Hannity called it "close to indoctrination." Florida GOP leader Jim Greer said Obama was trying to "indoctrinate America's children to his socialist agenda." Oklahoma state Senator Steve Russell warned, "This is something you'd expect to see in North Korea or in Saddam Hussein's Iraq." Michelle Malkin said, "The left has always used kids in public schools as guinea pigs and as junior lobbyists for their social liberal agenda."

This is what the president told students:

"And that's what I want to focus on today: the responsibility each of you has for your education. I want to start with the responsibility you have to yourself. . . . And no matter what you want to do with your life—I guarantee that you'll need an education to do it," Obama said.

"You'll need the knowledge and problem-solving skills you learn in science and math to cure diseases like cancer and AIDS, and to develop new energy technologies and protect our environment. You'll need the insights and critical thinking skills you gain in history and social studies to fight poverty and homelessness, crime and discrimination, and make our nation more fair and more free. You'll need the creativity and ingenuity you develop in all your classes to build new companies that will create new jobs and boost our economy," he added.

How many communists urge children to dream of becoming entrepreneurs?

"You can't drop out of school and just drop into a good job. You've got to work for it and train for it and learn for it," Obama said. "That's no excuse for not trying."

No wonder the parents were in a panic. Personal responsibility . . . how subversive!

After Obama delivered his speech, not one of those liars apologized for the ferocious disinformation. They never do. Fox News danced away from the topic because its commentators were all proven wrong.

Bill O'Reilly made a cogent point the same day of Obama's speech, when he said, "I also think there is a hatred for President Obama as there was for President Bush, and once you get into the hate zone, all thinking is clouded." Fair enough, but one might question the company he keeps at Fox News, where most of the bizarre fearmongering about the speech was made.

Some conservatives rejected the overheated hyperbole.

"I think that there is a place for the president of the United States to talk to schoolchildren and encourage schoolchildren," Laura Bush said in a September 8 interview on CNN. "I also think it's also really important for everyone to respect the president of the United States."

"It's insane when a United States president can't deliver a simple speech to the students of this country without everybody going absolutely berserk and I think it's bad for the country, but I also think it's bad for the Republican Party. It makes us out to be incredibly partisan and out of touch. I think that if anyone actually saw that speech today they'd recognize that this is great for the kids of this country," former Bush and McCain adviser Mark McKinnon said on MSNBC's *The Rachel Maddow Show*. "They shoot at anything that moves, and they shoot before they actually see what they are criticizing."

Obama's speech was totally in sync with stated Republican goals. As for preaching partisan propaganda to schoolkids, leave that to President Reagan in a November 14, 1988, address to kids when he praised his goal of "reducing taxes."

Democrats investigated how much government money was spent when Bush the Elder gave a speech to schoolchildren on October 1, 1991. That was dumb partisan hackery, but how many Democrats ever equated Bush with Chairman Mao?

The real reason why dingbat parents would not allow Obama to speak directly to their kids is simple: it would undermine their authority. They were deathly afraid of the truth, that their children would see Obama as an intelligent man, the leader of the country, and not a monster caricature they had painted. The only brainwashing was by right-wing commentators and parents.

A year later, when Obama planned to address school children once again, Greer had a change of heart when Fox and the Obama haters once again tried to prevent the kids from hearing their president.

"In the year since I issued a prepared statement regarding President Obama speaking to the nation's school children, I have learned a great deal about the party I so deeply loved and served. Unfortunately, I found that many within the GOP have racist views and I apologize to the president for my opposition to his speech last year and my efforts to placate the extremists who dominate our party today. My children and I look forward to the president's speech," Greer told reporters September 14, 2010.

I became curious about how irrational smears take root and decided to explore this terrain. I started a hoax to see how willingly the slime throwers believe and spread the most outrageous fiction and how long it would take to travel from my entry on an anti-Obama blog to acceptance at face value by the right wing.

My blog post unleashed an avalanche of racism, hatred, and schadenfreude by Obama haters, clutching any excuse to justify their hatred.

After living in Latin America for years, I am familiar with African spirit cults. In rural Brazil, I attended an all-night *jarê* ceremony, complete with whirling dervish dancing, chants, spells, puffing on cigars, and avian sacrifice. I settled on a variation of this topic and posted it on Townhall.com with the headline "Witchcraft in the White House" on Saturday, August 15, 2009. Here is the entire text:

The Obama White House is abuzz with talk of witchcraft by first grand-mother, seventy-two-year-old Marian Robinson, who lives in the White House residence. A close friend of Michelle Obama says the president is furious at his mother-in-law after learning that she was practicing Sante-ria, an African spirit cult, in the White House.

"The president is quite upset about this on two different levels. First, he is a committed Christian, no matter what his critics say about Rever-end Wright. He is adamant that Sasha and Malia be raised with Christian influences. He does not want them to be involved with African voodoo. And secondly, he is worried about the political fallout if his enemies get wind of this. Reverend Wright was bad enough, but this would be politi-cal suicide," a close friend of Michelle's confided.

Religion took center stage during the campaign last year when vid-eos showed the Rev. Jeremiah Wright shouting "God damn America." Obama was forced to distance himself from the since-retired pastor at Trinity United Church of Christ in Chicago, where he worshiped for twenty years. Many people were shocked by the videos and questioned Obama's fitness to be president. Since taking office, Obama has avoided worshiping in public and now prefers the chapel at the presidential re-treat at Camp David.

This is how it happened. Marian Robinson became increasingly frustrated as her husband, Fraser Robinson III, was hobbled by multiple sclerosis in the late 1980s. The family pastor prayed with her and coun-seled her, but "she turned to Santeria in a desperate hope," Michelle's friend said. "Michelle put her foot down when she heard that her mother took her dad to ceremonies where they did spells and trances, and sacri-ficed animals, chickens and goats I think. But Marian was desperate and kept going anyway, even when her husband was too sick to go with her. I don't think the president knew anything about this earlier because it was before they met. Michelle and Craig (her brother) wanted to close the book on this and never talked about it again after their father died in 1991."

The first grandma appears to be worried about her health now, even though doctors pronounce her in good shape. "Marian invited an old friend from Chicago to visit her at the White House, and she performed a Santeria ceremony in the residence. When Michelle saw this woman, a voodoo priestess, she recognized her from when her father was sick, and she had a fit. When she told the president about it, he blew up and said, 'No voodoo in the White House. Absolutely. I don't care what you call it.' As far as I know, it only happened once," the friend said.

The president was "totally in favor" when his mother-in-law moved into the White House as a live-in babysitter for eleven-year-old Malia and eight-year-old Sasha. Obama reportedly told Michelle that her mother will have to go back to Chicago if she does not "stop this witchcraft mumbo-jumbo immediately" and ordered the Secret Service to not allow Marian's friend to return to the White House.

The next day my experiment was already number one in Townhall.com's "Top Ten" blogs. It remained there for five consecutive days until the website yanked it. It got copied onto hundreds of other websites and blogs. Many right-wingers made comments such as "I hope it's true." Religious websites took it seriously; racist sites were ecstatic over an excuse to paint Obama as inferior.

Within twenty-four hours, the story went mainstream, appearing in the online versions of *USA Today* and the *Boston Globe*. It showed up in Web versions of the *National Review*, the *Daily Herald* of Provo, Utah; the *Citizen-Times* of Asheville, North Carolina.; the *Napa Valley Register* in northern California; and the *St. Louis Post-Dispatch*. Greta van Susteren's chat room on Fox News's website posted the Townhall.com version, and it was discussed on G. Gordon Liddy's radio show. Daniel Finkelstein, a columnist in *The Times* (London) labeled it "the worst Obama slur yet."

The satirical website Wonkette was the most entertaining. It made a hilarious spoof of my blog, and its readers ridiculed the author without pity as a moron and a fanatic.

Under a pseudonym, I corresponded with fans of the story, but I never gained any real insight into why they hated Obama so intensely. They only spouted off tired slogans, empty rhetoric, and no analytical underpinning. One of them told me "your voodoo blog was a hit with protesters in DC on the twelfth." He was referring to the corporate-sponsored 912 Project promoted by Glenn Beck and Fox News on September 12, 2009.

Organizers boasted on Fox News that up to 2 million showed up and called it the biggest rally ever in the nation's capital. Police and the fire department estimated attendance at about 60,000. Protesters carried signs such as, "We came unarmed (this time)"; a picture of Obama with the caption "undocumented worker"; and "Bury Obama Care with Kennedy" (shortly after Ted Kennedy's death). Others signs depicted Obama alongside Hitler, Stalin, and Fidel Castro, or Obama, Castro, and Hugo Chávez. Those geniuses declaring war on reality must have read that the previous day, Obama signed an extension of the economic embargo against Cuba.

If this rally were attended only by fringe elements, it could be dismissed. But many prominent Republicans were ringleaders. Senator Jim DeMint of South Carolina spoke. Also attending were Republican members of Congress such as Georgians Tom Price and Phil Gingrey, along with Tennessee's Marsha Blackburn.

In a perfect example of Fox's "fair and balanced" approach, a Fox producer whipped up the crowd behind correspondent Griff Jenkins on the air to create the impression of enthusiasm. Fox later apologized for its fakery, but most Fox viewers never saw the apology or knew they had viewed a staged event. Beck neglected to honestly inform viewers that they had not seen a true reflection of events that day.

For years this same right wing painted a target on the back of Congressman Jim McDermott, a Washington state Democrat, after he cited Newt Gingrich for ethics violations and later for challenging the Bush administration's accusations that Saddam Hussein was hiding weapons of mass destruction.

"Ignorance, not knowing what's going on, makes you vulnerable to being misled very easily. And making people afraid is also a very powerful tool, so the combination of fear and ignorance is very easy to manipulate, to make people believe," McDermott told me. "They're in a place where they don't know what's going on, and along comes somebody and tests their fears and their anger."

Jack Levin and Gordana Rabrenovic, professors at Northeastern University in Boston, describe scapegoating and demagoguery in *Why We Hate*.[3]

"In times of economic instability, structural changes or political turmoil, the members of the majority group often react to a real or perceived threat to their position in society by turning against the members of the minority groups in their midst," they wrote. "Certainly economic problems intensify the competition for scarce resources, and political leaders inflame the tension by emphasizing ethnic differences so they can be used as a political weapon."

Kristen Renwick Monroe, a professor of political science and philosophy at the University of California, Irvine, points to "ontological security" in which "threats to our sense of who we are lie at the root of the most extreme political responses." This is "encouraged by politicians who use the hate for those who are 'different.' We saw some of this during the campaign when Sarah Palin exploited fears of Obama."

"Bill Clinton and Obama represent a threat to some people because they feel outmaneuvered and marginalized. If this occurs, people are more willing to strike out and move beyond the parameters of ordinary political discourse," Monroe explained to me.

"Much of the popular base is driven by real grievances, and that though there is plenty of amazing nonsense, instead of ridiculing them we should be asking ourselves why we're not the ones organizing them. They have real problems in their crummy lives, which have been deteriorating for thirty years. And they're not hearing answers, apart from the Limbaughs, etc.," Noam Chomsky, the Massachusetts Institute of Technology expert on linguists and propaganda, told me. "About reality, they don't really know a lot, except for the immediate reality of their lives. That's very dangerous. Has a whiff of late Weimar Germany in my opinion."

Sometimes it boils down to intense fear of change, causing people to lash out. An ancient Indian proverb tells us that when a flower begins to bloom, some people cling blindly to the bud, unwilling to let it transform into a flower.

One basic question perplexed me since I began to conceptualize this project, kept me up sleepless nights and seized me at every turn. I could not shake it loose. Why do people believe a smear—Obama is a Muslim, has a fake birth certificate, pals around with terrorists, is a fascist, or any of the other notions most people find laughable—even when the facts show otherwise?

"Experimental psychologists have found that people form political opinions and THEN look for facts to justify that opinion, a somewhat bizarre experimental finding but one that seems to explain the kind of phenomenon you describe," Monroe said.

Then I asked how and when a fringe viewpoint moves mainstream. In particular I questioned how so many Americans could believe 9/11 was an "inside job." Moral implications aside, that notion is illogical because it would require too many conspirators. Dissenters from within the Bush administration exposed security lapses, missteps in fighting terrorism, and deception in launching the war against Iraq. All of those revelations are horrifying but minuscule compared to the thought of outright complicity in the terrorism. Nobody in a position to know has even hinted such a thing, nor did the non-partisan 9/11 Commission.

"Twenty years ago, psychologists thought emotions and reasoning were separate functions. Now, we know that emotions enter into the cognitive process at many steps along the way, slanting how we view and assess information. My guess is that something like 9/11 taps into the latent cognitive framework we all carry around. People who tend to see conspiracy theories will find that explanation more acceptable because it has a cognitive slot to go into," Monroe explained.

Another question tormented me: who is behind all of this hatred against Obama? I kept looking into the dark forces, the conspiracy described by the Clintons.

The dictionary defines conspiracy as "an evil, unlawful, treacherous, or surreptitious plan formulated in secret by two or more persons; plot."

Some of the suspicious people and shadowy organizations that defamed Clinton emerged as anti-Obama groups, and these same people continue to play a role. The big difference now is that the Republican mainstream has merged with these creepy, secretive groups. Big money and right-wing organizations secretly back the Tea Party and other anti-Obama movements, made to look spontaneous. Instead of buying expensive attack ads, the wildest assertions go out on right-wing blogs and websites. Those flames are then fanned by right-wing radio and Fox News. The disinformation begins to leak into other news organizations, which try to portray "both sides." After that, right-wing politicians quote Fox News or mainstream news outlets, if the lies travel that far. The right-wing propaganda machine has consolidated, the coup has been completed, and the shadowy groups have achieved their goal.

This is a united, cohesive effort to bring down Obama and everything he wants to achieve. DeMint was being boldly honest when he said during a conference call to fellow Republicans—not knowing it would leak out to the public—about the need to make health care Obama's "Waterloo." It's a tag team. One person questions whether Obama is a Muslim or foreigner, the next says he is a fascist, and another charges that the government will "pull the plug on grandma." They do it with a straight face. They are deadly serious. Minnesota's Michele Bachmann calls them "armed and dangerous."

What can we do? The First Amendment does not prohibit well-funded propaganda machines; it is a nightmare the Founding Fathers never imagined. For eight years, the right-wing propaganda machine was an arm of the Bush administration, which had its own network, Fox News, where Bush was made to look heroic, and subsidized columnists to disseminate its lies.

"Obviously, there is a very bright line which one may not cross when it comes to a true threat. But we cut a wide swath for speech in America, even repugnant ideas," Gene Policinski, vice president and executive director of the First Amendment Center, told me. "We provide as a nation a very, very broad protection to speech that even most of us would find absolutely abhorrent, and we do that obviously to preserve the marketplace of ideas in the broadest possible sense."

It's difficult to sue for slander even over the most detestable lies about a president because of the burden of proof. "We set an extremely high standard for public officials in order for them to collect damages against people who say things about them that are negative," Policinski said. "It's not actionable in the sense of neither side can really prove or disprove the allegation."

8

Profiles in Cowardice: A Rancid Collection of Fruits, Nuts, and Psychos

Liars are the cause of all the sins and crimes.

—Epictetus

Although the disgraceful bigmouths on Fox News (see chapter 9) get the most attention for their tirades against Obama, they rarely perform original spadework. Instead of using their journalistic platform and huge staff to perform true investigations or uncover the lies behind nasty smears, they choose instead to multiply and exaggerate the endless parade of falsehoods from every kook on the lunatic fringe.

The denizens who populate this chapter often act as if they are auditioning for a role in the Jim Carrey movie *Dumb and Dumber*. Rush Limbaugh and Michael Savage circulate loathsome chatter to their radio audiences. Savage once said that assassination of President Clinton would have been patriotic. These nitwits might even be comical if they did not cause so much damage by convincing millions of people with outrageous lies.

Limbaugh's most famous remark was, "I hope he fails," uttered January 16, 2009, shortly before the inauguration. Limbaugh said five days later on Sean Hannity's program on Fox News, "We are being told that we have to hope he succeeds, that we have to bend over, grab the ankles, bend over forward, backward, whichever, because his father was black, because this is the first black president." Is that Limbaugh's position when he reaches into the sewer for his material?

Despite crushing unemployment and American soldiers dying overseas, does draft dodger Limbaugh really hope the new president would fail to end two wars and put Americans back to work? Republican political leadership consistently and shamefully groveled to him instead of condemning his lies.

LEE ATWATER

The Obama haters trace their lineage back to Lee Atwater, their inspiration and mentor, the Grand Old Man of the Grand Old Party's modern smear campaign. The political strategist, who died in 1991, masterminded the Agent Orange strategy that guided right-wing campaigns since 1988, when he destroyed the reputation of Massachusetts Governor Michael Dukakis, the Democratic nominee for president, to benefit Vice President George H.W. Bush. This laid the groundwork for master practitioners such as Karl Rove, the chief architect of George W. Bush's campaigns, who was fired by Bush's father for dirty tricks.

"You start out in 1954 by saying, 'Nigger, nigger, nigger.' By 1968 you can't say 'nigger'—that hurts you. Backfires. So you say stuff like forced busing, states' rights and all that stuff," Atwater told Alexander Lamis, a political science professor at Case Western Reserve University, as recounted in his book *Southern Politics in the 1990s*.[1]

"I'm saying that if it is getting that abstract, and that coded, that we are doing away with the racial problem one way or the other," Atwater told Lamis. "You follow me—because obviously sitting around saying, 'We want to cut this,' is much more abstract than even the busing thing, and a hell of a lot more abstract than 'Nigger, nigger.'"

Atwater remained faithful to his sordid mission by finding original ways to fan racial fears. Due largely to Atwater's well-conceived slurs, we never had a President Dukakis. Atwater later recognized the Pandora's box his crowbar had pried opened. He wrote in *Life* magazine shortly before his death, "I used to say that the President might be kinder and gentler, but I wasn't going to be. How wrong I was. There is nothing more important in life than human beings."[2] Legend has it that he apologized to Dukakis, but it never happened, at least not directly.

"If he did [apologize], I don't know what he did and how he did it, I think he deserves a certain amount of credit for that. But in the meantime, unfortunately, he kind of set the standard for these kinds of campaigns," Dukakis told me.

MICHELE BACHMANN

This Far Right publicity monger, a Republican congresswoman from Minnesota, is the Energizer Bunny of right-wing drivel. If a confederacy of dunces were ever formed, she would unanimously be elected its queen bee. She was reelected even after accusing Obama of holding anti-American views. Rambling incoherently in an interview with Chris Matthews on MSNBC, she launched into a McCarthy-like diatribe that news organizations should investigate Congress to "find out if they are pro-America or anti-America." She refused to define what is pro-America or anti-America.

During the October 17, 2008, interview, Bachmann said, "I'm very concerned that he [Obama] may have anti-American views." She later claimed she was tricked into making such wacky remarks.

Bachmann told Fox News on June 25, 2009, "data that was collected by the census bureau was handed over to the FBI and other organizations, at the request of President Roosevelt, and that's how the Japanese were rounded up and put into the internment camps." The census requires no personal information; it is a federal crime for a census taker to violate the confidentiality of a respondent. Congressman Paul Broun and Fox's Glenn Beck also went into overdrive with the same canards that Obama planned domestic internment camps.

On Halloween eve, she gave Sean Hannity a treat—a trick for the rest of the world—by calling health care reform the "crown jewel of socialism." Bachmann is allowed to spout off empty slogans on Fox and right-wing radio without ever explaining what she means. After her rant on MSNBC resulted from Matthews asking logical questions, she now limits her appearances to bootlicking, compliant media organizations. Her behavior begs the question whether Congress should require a sanity test for its members.

MICHAEL BOOS

Michael Boos is vice president and general counsel at Citizens United, which collects money from right-wing fat cats to make propaganda attacks against their targets: Obama, the Clintons, the United Nations, the American Civil Liberties Union, and Michael Moore. This bunch is so extreme that it created ads against John McCain with the comical theme that he was too liberal. The group is so rabid that it was denounced by both presidents Bush; the guys who hired dirty tricksters Lee Atwater and Karl Rove consider Citizens United beyond the pale. Boos gave legal advice to a 527 group called The Real Truth About Obama.

DAVID BOSSIE

The campaign of George H. W. Bush in 1992 referred to David Bossie and his associates at Citizens United as the "lowest forms of life" and branded their tactics "despicable," according to *The Hunting of the President: The Ten-Year Campaign to Destroy Bill and Hillary Clinton.*[3] During the 1992 election, the Bush campaign filed a complaint with the Federal Election Commission against Bossie's group.

Sean Hannity interviewed Bossie for the faux documentary *Obama and Friends: History of Radicalism* on Fox News shortly before the 2008 election, where he spit out a slew of rumors and unproved allegations involving Obama's college years (see chapter 9). He is a talented far-right pimp offering illicit pleasures. When Hillary Clinton denounced the "vast right-wing conspiracy" against her husband, first and foremost among the conspirators was Citizens United, a group headed by Bossie.

Citizens United produced *Hype: The Obama Effect,* a collection of interviews with Republicans who don't like Obama.

PAUL BROUN

The Republican congressman from Georgia on November 11, 2008, reacted to Obama's proposal to expand the Peace Corps and AmeriCorps. "It may sound a bit crazy and off base, but the thing is, he's the one who proposed this national security force," Broun told the Associated Press. "I'm just trying to bring attention to the fact that we may—may not, I hope not—but we may have a problem with that type of philosophy of radical socialism or Marxism.

"That's exactly what Hitler did in Nazi Germany, and it's exactly what the Soviet Union did," Broun said. "When he's proposing to have a national security force that's answering to him, that is as strong as the U.S. military, he's showing me signs of being Marxist."

Broun speculated that the Obama administration might use a pandemic disease or natural disaster as an excuse to declare martial law. "They're trying to develop an environment where they can take over," he told a town hall meeting August 11, 2009, in Athens, Georgia.

FLOYD BROWN

George Stephanopoulos, an aide in the Clinton White House, was quoted as calling Brown "a slimy thug for hire." Brown, the founder and chairman of the board at Citizens United, has been involved in many of the same efforts as David Bossie. He is also president of Excellentia Inc., a company that specializes in marketing to conservatives and Christians.

His National Campaign Fund created the Expose Obama website, which circulated smears against Obama during the 2008 campaign. He authored *Obama Unmasked: Did Slick Hollywood Handlers Create the Perfect Candidate?*, which insists that Obama is a Muslim and socialist. He put out an ad during the campaign blaming Obama for gang-related violence in Chicago. The rest of us seem to have forgotten that gangs and violence did not exist in Chicago until Obama invented them.

Brown plays a prominent role in numerous right-wing groups: the National Campaign Fund, the Legacy Committee, Citizens for a Safe and Prosperous America, and the Policy Issues Institute. He masterminded the infamous, racist Willie Horton ad in the 1988 presidential campaign (see introduction). "Brown earned his status as a political pariah during the final weeks of the 1988 presidential campaign, when the Horton ad was unveiled. Its appeal to white fear was so blatant that even Lee Atwater considered it embarrassing," Joe Conason and Gene Lyons wrote.[4]

CHENEY REDUX

After taking potshots at the Bill of Rights during his eight-year reign of terror, Vice President Dick Cheney couldn't wait to lob cheap shots at the new administration. Ready. Aim. Fire. Cheney, a skilled marksman when shooting friends in the face, took the coward's way out, as usual, by pushing his daughter, Liz, out on stage to bash his successors.

Cheney gave lip service to the Vietnam War but did not put his own life on the line. John Kerry, Al Gore, John McCain, Colin Powell, and Max Cleland all served in Vietnam; Cheney either attacked all these veterans or was allied closely with people who smeared them. This shows an unswerving pattern of cowardice by a man who taught his daughter the bulldog tactics of blindsiding opponents and gnawing on their legs.

Cheney frequently mouths lies about Obama such as "recklessness cloaked in righteousness" and "would make the American people less safe." Cheney never specified what the Obama administration does that is unsafe. If he was so concerned about Obama's policies, why does he not meet privately with Obama or Vice President Joe Biden to offer candid advice, or Defense Secretary Robert Gates, with whom he worked, instead of barking into a megaphone?

As for Liz, she was the first daughter of a vice president in U.S. history to accuse a president of treason. Discussing the potential release, ordered by a federal court, of photos which showed torture of prisoners by U.S. forces, Liz Cheney asked Fox News on May 2, 2009, "When did it become so fashionable for us to side, really, with the terrorists?" She made similar remarks more than twenty times in May and June.

She told CNN's Larry King on July 21, "People are uncomfortable with having for the first time ever, I think, a president who seems so reluctant to defend the nation overseas."

Liz Cheney, who exploited nepotism in a State Department appointment during daddy's regime, bashed Obama for visiting Dover Air Force Base on October 30 to salute the flag-draped coffins of 18 American soldiers and federal agents who died in Afghanistan. "I think that what President Bush used to do is do it without the cameras. And I don't understand sort of showing up with the White House press pool with photographers and asking family members if you can take pictures," she told John Gibson on Fox News Radio. She lied. Bush and Cheney never made fallen soldiers enough of a priority to honor their homecoming or funerals, just as serving in Vietnam was not a priority when it was their turn.

JEROME CORSI

He claims to have earned a PhD from Harvard. That esteemed institution does not offer a program in smears, so it must be assumed he excelled in the art of fiction writing. This master of masquerading fiction as fact established his bona fides in 2004 by writing *Unfit for Command: Swift Boat Veterans Speak Out Against John Kerry*. Corsi, who did not have the courage to serve in Vietnam, was brave enough to attack the proven war heroism of Massachusetts Senator John Kerry. Corsi targeted Obama in *Obama Nation: Leftist Politics and the Cult of Personality*. He repeated every unfounded charge made against Obama by Internet bloggers and wingnuts without proof of anything. He is a staff writer at WorldNetDaily, which has published (or originated) a large number of the many falsities launched against Obama (see Appendix B).

ANN COULTER

Rachel Maddow of MSNBC described Coulter as "one of the most volatile, ruthless, unpredictable, and sometimes flat-out mean people in all of American politics."

"Coulter has made her fortune by generating, fanning, and nurturing hatred and contempt for a variety of people, including liberals, Democrats, gays, foreign nationals, 9/11 widows, feminists, single mothers, Muslims, and any other group she could throw to her disenfranchised readership as shark bait," Michael Rowe wrote on June 11, 2009, on the *Huffington Post*.[5]

After slashing and burning many honorable people, Coulter labeled Obama a Nazi. She wrote about Obama's memoir, *Dreams from My Father*, "Has anybody read this book? Inasmuch as the book reveals Obama to be a flabbergasting lunatic, I gather the answer is no. Obama is about to be our next president: You might want to take a peek. If only people had read [Hitler's] *Mein Kampf*."[6] Coulter offered no basis for comparing Obama and Hitler; she simply peddles one lie after the next without taking responsibility for spewing hatred.

The heartless harpy said John Edwards, the 2004 Democratic vice-presidential nominee, "drives around with a bumper sticker saying 'ASK ME ABOUT MY DEAD SON.'" Edwards's sixteen-year-old son, Wade, died in a traffic accident in 1996. Coulter also called the senior Edwards a "little fag." When Coulter appeared June 25, 2007, on MSNBC's *Hardball*, Elizabeth Edwards asked Coulter to stop the personal attacks against her family. Coulter tersely treated this as a First Amendment issue: "Think we heard all we need to hear. The wife of a presidential candidate is asking me to stop speaking. No."

Nobody ever challenged Coulter's right to speak. Under the First Amendment, Coulter can disgorge filth, Nazis can march in Skokie, and madman Charles Manson can give interviews from prison. The treasure of our Bill of

Rights is that it grants license to the most contemptible forms of speech by the most contemptible people.

FRANK J. GAFFNEY JR.

"There is mounting evidence that the president not only identifies with Muslims, but actually may still be one himself," Gaffney, who worked in the Defense Department during the Reagan and second Bush administrations, wrote in the *Washington Times*.[7]

Gaffney was a signatory to the 1997 Project for the New American Century which published a report entitled *Rebuilding America's Defenses: Strategies, Forces and Resources for a New Century* in 2000. It called for "regime change" in countries seen as a problem, providing the conceptual underpinning for the "Bush Doctrine" which legitimized the unprovoked invasion of Iraq.

He also challenged Obama's birth certificate: "There is evidence Mr. Obama was born in Kenya rather than, as he claims, Hawaii," Gaffney wrote in the *Washington Times* on October 14, 2008. "Curiously, Mr. Obama has, to date, failed to provide an authentic birth certificate which could clear up the matter."[8]

Gaffney belongs to the Center for Security Policy, whose other members pushed for the invasion of Iraq. It's no surprise that cuckoos such as Rush Limbaugh and Michael Savage question Obama's birth certificate. It is downright scary to see the cockeyed logic employed by Gaffney and know that he was formerly a top-level official formulating U.S. defense policy. Knowing that makes it easier to understand how the Bush administration got involved in a war based on faulty evidence.

NEWTON LEROY "NEWT" GINGRICH

Gingrich, as Speaker of the House, was secretly cheating on his second wife while he obstreperously ramrodded the impeachment of Bill Clinton over a sexual peccadillo. He resigned in 1999 after his GOP minions lost seats in midterm elections and being rebuked by the House for ethics violations. Since then, he kept a relatively low profile except occasional Muslim-bashing or racially insensitive comments. That is, until he decided to make racially charged remarks about Obama. As Gingrich prepared for a 2012 presidential run, he positioned himself with the most extreme right wingers.

On September 11, 2010, a day when most Americans unite in memory of our national tragedy, Gingrich instead launched a divisive bouillabaisse marinating every cheap political, racial stereotype foisted on Obama.

"What if [Obama] is so outside our comprehension, that only if you understand Kenyan, anti-colonial behavior, can you begin to piece together [his actions]?" Gingrich charged in an interview with *National Review Online*. "That is the most accurate, predictive model for his behavior."

He even questioned Obama's sanity, as did others (see chapter 2). "I think Obama gets up every morning with a world view that is fundamentally wrong about reality," Gingrich said. "If you look at the continuous denial of reality, there has got to be a point where someone stands up and says that this is just factually insane."

A few days later, at the 2010 Value Voters Summit in Washington, D.C., Gingrich clanged the warning bell against enacting sharia law in the United States. Nobody in the "liberal media" bothered to ask the newt whether his core constituency of pathological fornicators fears that our flagrantly Muslim president might impose death by stoning.

JAMES INHOFE

The Republican senator from Oklahoma questioned Obama's patriotism during the 2008 election. "Do you really want to have a guy as commander in chief of this country when you can question whether or not he really loves his country?" he asked in an interview with the *Tulsa World*. "That's the big question."[9]

Then he took umbrage with Obama's June 2009 remarks in Cairo that George W. Bush's invasion of Iraq was a "war of choice." Is that basic information not available in Oklahoma yet? "I just don't know whose side he [Obama] is on," Inhofe told the *Oklahoman* newspaper, adding that Obama's views were "un-American."[10]

STEVE KING

Words spoken by Steve King, the Republican congressman from Iowa, are more frightening than those written by Stephen King, the author of horror novels.

"I will tell you that, if he is elected president, then the radical Islamists, the al Qaeda, the radical Islamists and their supporters, will be dancing in the streets in greater numbers than they did on September 11 because they will declare victory in this War on Terror," King said in a March 7, 2008, interview with KICD radio in Spencer, Iowa.

"Additionally, his middle name [Hussein] does matter," the congressman said. "It matters because they read a meaning into that in the rest of the world. That has a special meaning to them. They will be dancing in the streets because of his middle name."

The name Hussein does not have any political connotation or possess any links to terrorism or Islamic fundamentalism. The name means "good, small, handsome one." Jordan's late King Hussein enjoyed warm relations with successive American presidents. Yet Obama haters persist in trying to make a common name in Arabic into a pejorative.

THE KOCH BROTHERS

Charles and David Koch, the billionaire owners of energy giant Koch Industries, have funneled millions of dollars into anti-Obama organizations. They are the twenty-first-century version of their late father, Fred Koch, who funded the paranoid hallucinations of the John Birch Society in the 1950s and 1960s.

Think Progress titled a December 8, 2009 research report about the Koch brothers' influence, "The Billionaires Behind the Hate," which detailed their stealth support for groups which oppose Obama's initiatives such as clean energy and health care reform.

Jane Mayer wrote in the August 30, 2010 edition of *The New Yorker* that the Koch brothers are not mere ideologues. The owners of refineries and oil pipelines have a massive economic stake in blocking Obama's effort to turn the United States away from reliance on fossil fuels in favor of "clean energy" sources.

The Koch brothers founded and financed dozens of right-wing publications, "think tanks" and attack groups. For instance, David Koch sponsored Americans for Prosperity, which organized Tea Party rallies and disrupted town hall meetings by Democratic politicians, all the while disguised as a "grassroots" organization. These activities—stocked by overheated rhetoric, racist signs and actively promoted by Fox News and right-wing radio—undermined Obama's agenda and helped turn public opinion against him.

RUSH LIMBAUGH

"Giving away Rush's daily radio programs for free to rural radio stations is brilliant. It's like delivering the garbage directly to the hungry rats in an effort to get them fatter. Or in this case, more bigoted and ignorant of the facts," a reader called "applescruff" posted on April 30, 2009, on the *Huffington Post.*

"He could be in a lot better taste on a daily basis in which he's delivering misinformation, lies, to a large audience in America," *Time* columnist Joe Klein said in a May 10 interview on CNN.

An NBC/*Wall Street Journal* poll conducted in June 2009 showed only 23 percent of respondents had a favorable impression of the tubby trash talker and 50 percent had an unfavorable view. His negatives would be much higher if the fence-sitters heard more of his hateful filth (see chapter 3).

It's no surprise that Limbaugh ascended to captain on the Obama haters' ship of fools. Like the Bush-Cheney administration, Limbaugh exploits the 9/11 tragedy. "Obama is eager to paralyze our ability to defend ourselves, which is what our enemies want," he said on April 27, 2009. "Obama is terrorist attack number two; Obama is the follow-up to 9/11."

When Obama went to the Middle East, Limbaugh said on June 3 on Sean Hannity's show on Fox News, "If al Qaeda wants to demolish the America we know and love, then they'd better hurry because Obama's beating them to it."

Limbaugh frequently accuses Obama of dictatorial tendencies. "Adolf Hitler, like Barack Obama, also ruled by dictate," he said August 6, 2009.

"It's the most dangerous time in my life for freedom and liberty in this country. . . . This man is systematically dismantling our ability to collect intelligence to protect ourselves against an attack. He is purposely using his attorney general to make the United States the villain of the world," Limbaugh said on August 26, 2009, on Glenn Beck's show on Fox News. "This is statism, totalitarianism versus freedom."

Limbaugh imagined the most direct link between Obama and bin Laden during his show on January 29, 2010: "It gets harder and harder to tell bin Laden's complaints from those of the average, run-of-the-mill leftist, like Obama or Harry Reid or Nancy Pelosi or the entire Democrat Party. I mean, every time Obama releases—Osama releases a tape, it's just Democrat talking points. Or maybe they're getting their talking points from him."

On August 16, 2010, Limbaugh called Obama "our first anti-American president."

MICHELLE MALKIN

Close your eyes and imagine . . . Michelle Malkin is Glenn Beck with more estrogen. If you watched Beck's show every day and took copious notes, then did Web searches about making connections between unrelated events and people, then invented a sinister motive for Obama and everybody in his administration and every action each one takes, you would have Malkin. Beck and Malkin could swap places and there would be little change in substance.

This right-wing columnist is a mixed bag. She continuously connected anti-Palin attacks to Obama, even after Obama publicly and vehemently denounced any such tactics. Yet to her credit, Malkin pooh-poohed the Michelle Obama "whitey" video smear (see chapter 2), saying, "Larry Johnson, the main source of the rumors is not, not, not to be trusted." As a contributor at Fox News, she is mentioned prominently in chapter 9.

ANDY MARTIN (ANTHONY ROBERT MARTIN-TRIGONA)

The big kahuna among anti-Obama conspirators, he was a principal source for anti-Obama books and baseless attacks. He filed a lawsuit in Hawaii claiming that Obama's birth certificate was a fake. Despite his staggering lack of credentials and numerous red flags about his reliability, Martin was a "guest journalist" on Sean Hannity's show on Fox News (see chapter 9).

Martin accused Obama of hiding his grandmother, eighty-six-year-old Madelyn Dunham, from the press because she was white. Dunham, who succumbed to cancer the weekend before Obama's election, did not grant interviews because she was dying. Martin also perpetrated the lie that Obama was educated in a Muslim madrassa. He has been widely condemned for making anti-Semitic and racist remarks as well as blatant lies.

In 1973 the Illinois Supreme Court refused to grant Martin a license to practice law. It cited several instances of troubling conduct on Martin's part, including an attempt to have a parking violation thrown out because it had been "entered by an insane judge" and his description of an attorney as "shaking and tottering and drooling like an idiot."[11]

In a 1983 bankruptcy case, he referred to a federal judge as a "crooked, slimy Jew, who has a history of lying and thieving common to members of his race." The U.S. Court of Appeals for the Eleventh Circuit in Atlanta described him in 1993 as a "notoriously vexatious and vindictive litigator who has long abused the American legal system."[12]

When Martin ran for Congress in Connecticut in 1986, he listed the purpose of one of his political committees as "to exterminate Jew power in America and to impeach the judges of the U.S. Court of Appeals in New York City."[13]

When asked about the various Muslim smears against Obama, Martin bragged, "They are all my children."[14]

"GUNNY" BOB NEWMAN

The host of a show on Denver radio station KOA, Newman accused Obama of saying, "If that sumbitch even tries to get into my [Democratic National] convention, I'll have him disappeared like Jimmy Hoffa." Newman alleged that Obama, seeing Newman approach, warned him, "If you come any closer, I'll have the Secret Service shoot and then waterboard you, you fascist Marine capitalist bastard!" Radio professionals carry recording devices at all times. Why did Newman not record these encounters? When were Obama and Newman ever in a vacuum, with no other human being within listening range to corroborate these fictions?

On his website, Newman has a drawing of Obama wearing a beret with the caption CHE OBAMA. A doctored photo on the same website shows Obama with Osama bin Laden.

SARAH PALIN

The Alaska governor was a star waiting to be born, the twenty-first-century version of Norma Desmond primping herself for her starring role in *Sunset Boulevard,* waiting for the screenwriter to tell her what to say and flunkies to feed her delusions. Palin was the first politician to adopt a "reality TV show" persona as she played the victim masterfully to people who feel victimized.

Palin doesn't simply talk. She screeches and wheedles and whines. She badgers and moans. Her incessant, specious remarks as John McCain's running mate in 2008 are displayed throughout this book. Palin must be addicted to smears because she continued the vicious sniping long after Americans rejected her decisively. Following the election, most losing candidates go home and resume their lives. But the "reality show" consumed Palin's life, so she stayed in the limelight, playing to her vacuous base, winking and cajoling, smearing and lying.

"We need to be aware of the creation of a fearful population and fearful lawmakers being led to believe that big government is the answer to bail out the private sector," Palin told an audience in Anchorage on June 3, 2009. "Then government gets to get in there and controls the people."

There is nothing wrong with criticizing federal bailouts, but Palin never bashed the Bush administration for rescuing Wall Street. Most troubling is the use of "fear."

The right wing hatched the idea that citizens should fear the Obama administration after it ignored the reasons to fear the government during the Bush-Cheney years: torture, wiretaps, gutting the right of habeas corpus, and denying the right to a fair trial. Palin was never asked why she employs such harsh, loaded words.

Upon announcing her resignation as governor of Alaska on July 3, Palin made this bizarre statement: "You can choose to engage in things that tear down, or build up." Did Palin build up our government when she accused the Obama administration of creating "a fearful population?" When she said Obama "pals around with terrorists?" When she called Obama a socialist? When did she ever "build up" the United States rather than tear it down with empty anti-Obama slogans?

Despite her nonstop Obama bashing, neither Obama nor anyone on his campaign or staff ever treated Palin the same way she has treated him, both as a candidate and as president.

Palin told NBC's Andrea Mitchell in an interview broadcast on July 7, 2009, that she got fed up with having to "fend off these frivolous, ridiculous, wasteful ethics violations." Mitchell failed to remind Palin about the two instances in which Alaska state officials found that the governor had broken ethics rules. The veteran journalist also declined to question Palin about her anti-Obama smears.

Fox correspondent Carl Cameron said on July 6, "These ethics investigations were all dismissed by the legislature." Why did he ignore both instances where Palin was found in violation of Alaska's ethics rules?

On October 10, 2008, Stephen Branchflower, chief investigator for a state legislative panel, issued a report that found Palin violated Alaska Statute

39.52.110(a) of the Alaska Executive Branch Ethics Act for her dismissal of Public Safety Commissioner Walter Monegan after he resisted Palin's pressure to fire her estranged brother-in-law as a state trooper. However, there was no penalty for violating the ethics code, and it found Palin had the legal authority to fire Monegan.

Then on June 19, 2009, Palin paid back to the state of Alaska $8,143.62 after ethical complaints concerning nine trips in which her children accompanied the governor to events where they had no official role. A report by Timothy Petumenos, an investigator for the Alaska Personnel Board, found that the state should pay for such travel only when the presence of family members serves the state's interests. Palin attorney Thomas van Flein grumbled that her predecessors were not subjected to such scrutiny for their travels.

No evidence exists that Palin's predecessors billed the state for children's travel. "There was no valid reason for the children to be along on state business," former Alaska Governor Tony Knowles, a Democrat, told the Associated Press on October 21, 2008. "I cannot recall any instance during my eight years as governor where it would have been appropriate to claim they performed state business."

When she resigned, Palin alleged that she was forced to pay $500,000 in legal expenses due to criticism from bloggers. It was not bloggers who conducted investigations; it was state agencies. She incurred legal expenses to defend herself after she broke state ethics rules. Why do right-wingers, who react like jumping beans about government spending, defend Palin billing the state for travel expenses of her children when they were not invited and had no official role? Why didn't she just do the right thing and reimburse the $8,000 for her freeloading family's travel expenses instead of paying lawyers to fight it?

Hannity smeared the frosting on the cake when he said the departing governor's critics suffer from "Palin Derangement Syndrome." He was making a play on "Bush Derangement Syndrome," coined by Charles Krauthammer, a columnist and Fox commentator, referring to the former president's critics. By the time Bush left office, more than two-thirds of the population believed Bush's attempts to justify the war were wrong, so does Krauthammer truly believe that an overwhelming majority of the population is deranged? Public opinion polls show consistently that a huge margin of Americans believe Palin is unqualified to be president. Does that fit into the standard medical definition of derangement?

Palin burst on the scene to high approval, but her ratings dropped as people got to know her better. Through 2009 and 2010, she was liked by only one-quarter to one-third of Americans, depending on the poll.

O'Reilly said on September 28, 2009, that critics "are never going to give Sarah Palin a break," and are "always going to portray her as a dunderhead." He never mentioned that numerous Republican insiders, not liberals, fed this image.

Why was Fox in a tizzy over criticism of Palin while ignoring the smears against Obama, in which it gladly participates and even organizes? She is criticized for ethical lapses pointed out by Republican officials, not Democrats, in Alaska.

Palin and her family have been poked and prodded by comedians. David Letterman apologized profusely after making a tasteless joke involving Palin's daughter Bristol for bearing a child out of wedlock. Had Chelsea Clinton or the Bush twins behaved in a similar way, does anyone doubt that they would have been the butt of similar jokes? Letterman and other comedians made far more jokes about Bill Clinton's sex life than any other politician in history. Did Palin or any conservatives object? Comedians' remarks might be in poor taste, but this is not the same as a political smear.

The Foxies had another chance to froth at the mouth when Carl Cannon wrote an opinion piece, "Sarah 'Barracuda' Palin and the Piranhas of the Press," that appeared on the Politics Daily website on July 8, 2009. This was seen as evidence of so-called "media bias" against Palin. Cannon, who earlier penned "Three Cheers for Dick Cheney" for the same site, is hardly an unbiased observer. What is objective about writing rah-rah accounts about the reviled Cheney? The levers of power were pried from Cheney's cold hands with less than one-third of Americans approving of him and six out of ten strongly disapproving.

An inexcusably nasty piece published on August 31, 2008, on the Daily Kos website alleged that Palin was unfaithful to her husband, bashed her for bearing a disabled child (which would cost taxpayers), and for having a pregnant unwed teenage daughter. The only part of this hit piece that got traction in the mainstream media was Bristol's pregnancy. Palin's screeching about this piece gave it far more publicity that it would have gotten otherwise. Obama himself condemned this story. Equally significant is that fact that the Daily Kos removed the item when it was proven wrong. That is in sharp contrast to the Obama haters, who continue to repeat every debunked lie ad infinitum.

If there was any "Et tu, Brute?" moment for Palin, the knife was thrust by the McCain campaign, not the media or Democrats. The postmortem on the campaign unleashed a bloodbath, with unidentified campaign staffers calling her an erratic "diva" who "takes no advice from anyone." They also complained about her "going rogue," called her a loose cannon who spent more time shopping for clothing than getting adequately coached before interviews, said "her lack of fundamental understanding of key issues is dramatic," and concluded that she was "unqualified to be vice president." No Obama staff member ever spoke harshly about Palin, before or after the election. Significantly, McCain himself did not deny the off-the-record comments.

Another source for saucy anti-Palin babble is Levi Johnston, the father of Palin's grandson. Johnston said that Palin sought to hide Bristol's pregnancy from the public, was an absentee mother, and complained that her job as governor was "too hard." Johnston, who lived at the Palin home in Wasilla when he was engaged to Bristol, also said Palin acted as if she, not McCain, was running for president and that she intended to quit her job as governor so she could "triple the money" she was earning.

Palin accomplished the rhetorical trifecta of wrapping herself in the flag, attacking her enemies, and bashing the media during her farewell address July 26, 2009, when she said, "How about, in honor of the American soldier, you quit makin' things up?" Palin, however, did not live by that motto when she was "makin' things up" with unfounded accusations against Obama.

Another remark at her *adieu* in Fairbanks: "Our new governor has a very nice family too, so leave his kids alone," she said, to energetic whoops and hollers from the audience. Did she ever return the courtesy to Obama—who pointedly defended the Palin clan—by defending the Obama kids when they were attacked by racist bloggers?

After Palin lost the moxie to face her critics as governor, she did not relent in her obnoxious lies about Obama and his administration. When right-wing talking heads contrived and stoked fears about Obama's health care plan as being a euthanasia plot, Palin wrote on her Facebook blog on August

7, 2009, "The America I know and love is not one in which my parents or my baby with Down Syndrome will have to stand in front of Obama's 'death panel' so his bureaucrats can decide, based on a subjective judgment of their 'level of productivity in society,' whether they are worthy of health care. Such a system is downright evil." It is lies such as this, which weak-minded people somehow believe, that are downright evil. Palin lacks any sense of class or shame when she trots out her family as props for her sick-minded inventions.

No health care legislation ever even hinted at "death panels."

The only death panels in recent memory were those convened by the Bush administration, which signed death warrants for hundreds of thousands of innocent Iraqi civilians, and heartless bureaucrats at private health insurance companies, which drop paying customers when they file expensive claims. While condemning fictive panels that do not exist, Palin never had the courage to take on the real death panels, which Obama not only condemned but also set out to dismantle.

Republican House leader John Boehner and Iowa Republican Senator Charles Grassley parroted Palin's death panel lie, but some fellow conservatives took a principled stand.

"I just had a phone call where someone said Sarah Palin's website had talked about the House bill having death panels on it where people would be euthanized. How someone could take an end-of-life directive or a living will as that is nuts," Johnny Isakson, a Republican senator from Georgia, told the *Washington Post*.[15]

"It does us no good to incite fear in people by saying that there's these end-of-life provisions, these death panels," Senator Lisa Murkowski, a fellow Alaska Republican, told constituents. "Quite honestly, I'm so offended at that terminology because it absolutely isn't [in the bill]. There is no reason to gin up fear in the American public by saying things that are not included in the bill."

Neil Cavuto of Fox News condemned Palin's rhetoric as way over the top. "That's a stretch," he said on August 10, 2009. "It disrupts the debate."

During the campaign, conservative columnist Kathleen Parker questioned Palin's readiness to be vice president or president. After the election, Parker wrote that Palin had effectively tapped into Southern anger about race and social issues, which Richard Nixon used effectively to win the 1968 election.

"That same rage was on display again in the fall of 2008, but this time the frenzy was stimulated by a pretty gal with a mocking little wink. Sarah Palin may not have realized what she was doing, but Southerners weaned on Harper Lee heard the dog whistle," Parker wrote in the *Washington Post*.[16]

"My honest view is that she would not be a winning [presidential] candidate for the Republican Party in 2012, and in fact, were she the nominee, we could have a catastrophic election result," Steve Schmidt, who managed John McCain's presidential campaign, said on October 2 at the "First Draft of History" conference in Washington, D.C.

John Weaver, McCain's closest political adviser for the past decade, told the *Washington Post* in the October 5 edition that he did not believe Palin would be the Republican nominee but if she were, "it would surely mean a political apocalypse is upon us."[17]

Even George W. Bush questioned Palin's readiness for national office. "This woman is being put into a position she is not even remotely prepared for. She hasn't spent one day on the national level," Bush was quoted by Matt Latimer, a White House aide, as saying in his 2009 memoir *Speech-less: Tales of a White House Survivor.*

If right-wingers want to blame liberals for bashing Palin, they should wait until opposing candidates get a hold of her in the 2012 election (if she runs). If Obama and Hillary ripped each other to shreds, imagine how savvy Republican candidates will treat Palin if she enters the next race. As Bette Davis once said, "Fasten your seatbelts, it's going to be a bumpy night."

KARL ROVE

In 1988 Rove earned his reputation as the master smasher of reputations but was fired by Bush's reelection campaign four years later for dirty tricks.

Rove helped Bush the Younger get elected governor of Texas in 1994 by smearing Democratic Governor Ann Richards as a lesbian. When Bush ran for president six years later, Rove was ready. Bush had an engaging personality but few accomplishments, so he looked like a midget next to John McCain for the 2000 Republican nomination. After the war hero won the New Hampshire primary, Bush was on the ropes. Next came the South Carolina primary, where Rove had a winning scheme: "inform" voters that McCain fathered a child with a black prostitute and that he had turned on his fellow prisoners of war in Vietnam for special favors.

During the Bush administration, Rove crafted a propaganda blitz in which anyone who questioned Bush's misguided Iraq policy was branded as a traitor.

Currently, as a commentator on Fox News, Rove plants frequent nasty comments about Obama and members of his administration.

RICK SANTELLI

As a business journalist and regular CNBC viewer for many years, it pains me to include Santelli on this list. His market reports from the Chicago Board of Trade are energetic and witty. I always imagined that if I were a business reporter in Chicago, I'd toss back beers with him after work in Mike Royko's favorite hangouts. Santelli, however, crossed all journalistic boundaries of objectivity and fair play on February 19, 2009, with his famous anti-Obama rant that many credit with igniting the Tea Party movement. This frantic outburst grabbed attention because it was so uncharacteristic of CNBC reporters.

"How many of you people want to pay for your neighbor's mortgage that has an extra bathroom and can't pay their bills?" Santelli asked, as pit traders at the Chicago Board of Trade displayed thumbs-down to demonstrate disapproval for government initiatives to help homeowners threatened with foreclosure. "President Obama, are you listening?" he continued, to scattered cheers.

"Cuba used to have mansions and a relatively decent economy. They moved from the individual to the collective. Now they're driving '54 Chevys," he emphasized.

How does preventing foreclosures resemble Cuba? Indeed, it is the polar opposite. The Obama administration preserved individual home ownership for some debt-strapped families, while Cubans are prevented outright from title to their dwellings. Whether Americans blame rapacious lenders, stupid politicians, asleep-at-the-wheel regulators, or uninformed borrowers for the housing crisis, nearly everyone agrees that promoting individual home ownership is essential.

Does Santelli really want to make pre-Castro Cuba, a brutal dictatorship where organized crime was given unfettered control and ordinary people had no chance for upward mobility and home ownership, his economic model?

I'd be willing to give Santelli a pass if he recognized his mistakes, both factually and journalistically, but rather than apologizing for his petulant tantrum, Santelli labeled the incident "the best five minutes of my life" in an interview with the *Chicago Sun-Times,* published September 19, 2010. That's inexcusable. CNBC viewers need simple facts, not his out-of-kilter opinions which flout the irrefutable truth.

MICHAEL SAVAGE

The Napoleon complex–afflicted host of the syndicated radio show *The Savage Nation,* whose real name is Michael Alan Weiner, frequently makes scathing, racist remarks about Obama, such as, "The only people who don't seem to vote based on race are white people of European origin." On another broadcast, this monstrous moron mumbled that "Senator Barack *Madrassa* Obama" was "indoctrinated" by a "Muslim madrassa in Indonesia." Many Savage remarks resemble mutterings in a mental hospital.

"He's a fascist. I know that you don't want to hear this, but the man is a neo-Marxist, fascist dictator in the making. He is not using his fascism yet because he doesn't have enough power to wield the fascist instruments of power. But he is aggrandizing enough power to become a very dangerous president," Savage said on March 6, 2009.

"The American people are sitting like a bunch of schmucks watching a dictatorship emerge in front of their eyes . . . he's out of control," Savage yelled on March 10. Obama has never screamed in public, while Savage yells regularly on his show. Who is in control and who shows himself to be out of control?

Obama was planning a "Maoist revolution that they dream of with death camps . . . arresting people for being patriotic . . . virtually anything that's happened in China and the ex-Soviet Union can happen here," Savage said on March 16.

"We're living through a Stalinist revolution in the United States of America," he said on March 23.

After the British government put Savage on a list of people banned from the country, along with other hatemongers across the political spectrum, Savage's first step was to get his lawyers to insist that Secretary of State Hillary Clinton appeal personally to Britain on his behalf. This demand came after calling her "a very dangerous human being," "fraudulent huckster," "the most godless woman in the Senate," and claiming that she engaged in "Hitler dialogue."

Then Savage turned on his fellow coterie of right-wing filth spewers on May 19: "And yet here in America, I've had some people come to my aid. They see the bigger picture. They're not like [Bill] O'Reilly; they're not like Limbaugh, who's the biggest disappointment of all. Limbaugh has turned out to be the biggest phony of them all, all of them. Amongst all of them, he is the biggest fraud. Rush Limbaugh is a fraud. When he was accused of the drug abuse, I supported him. But that man is a one-way street. It's all about him. He's in it for nobody but himself."

Amen.

PETE SESSIONS

The Republican congressman from Texas told the *New York Times* on May 11, 2009, that President Obama's agenda was "to inflict damage and hardship on the free enterprise system, if not to kill it" and "diminish employment and diminish stock prices" as part of a "divide and conquer" strategy. If that was Obama's goal, he failed miserably, since the Dow Jones Industrial Average had gained 7.8 percent from his inauguration through the day Sessions's comment was published. Later in the year, the Dow passed 10,000 for the first time in more than a year, more than 20 percent higher than the day Obama took over. U.S. stocks leaped 31.2 percent from Inauguration Day through the end of 2009.

Sessions's model for free market excellence appears to be Obama's predecessor, under whose tenure the Dow plunged 24.9 percent from Inauguration Day 2001 to the day he was run out of town. According to the U.S. Bureau of Labor statistics, Bush inherited a jobless rate of 4 percent and left his successor with quickly worsening 7.6 percent unemployment. Under whose watch did the economy crumble? The Conference Board Leading Economic Index was sideswiped into a deep gulley during Bush's watch but improved measurably after Obama took over. Sessions should explain how a rising stock market and improved economic indicators hurt free enterprise and how the economy was better served by Bush.

LARRY SINCLAIR

Among all the Obama haters, Larry Sinclair is the most reviled, even by other Obama haters. He is a pariah among pariahs. Accusations about Obama's birth certificate, alleged ties to leftists, and racist smears bounce freely through the right-wing echo chamber with no concern about veracity. But few are willing to repeat Sinclair's pornographic ramblings.

The convicted felon is the lowest of the lowlife Obama haters. His self-published book of lies called *Barack Obama and Larry Sinclair: Cocaine, Sex, Lies & Murder,* alleges a 1999 drug-induced homosexual tryst inside a limousine with Obama.

Sinclair's detailed description of the alleged sexual encounter was crude and offensive. It has never been corroborated by anyone else. By 1999 Obama was well known in Chicago as a state senator. Other people would have surely noticed any erratic behavior. Reality check: wouldn't a person in Obama's position use an alias if he engaged in behavior that could haunt him later? Wouldn't the limo driver sell his story to the *National Enquirer* for a million dollars?

CRAIG SHIRLEY

Craig Shirley is the president of Shirley & Banister Public Affairs, a public relations company that represents numerous right-wing individuals and groups such as Ann Coulter, Citizens United, the National Rifle Association, and Richard Viguerie. He ran the Stop Him Now website, which circulated rumors and distorted Obama's positions. In 1988, he produced the Willie Horton smears against Michael Dukakis. Shirley was forced to leave his official role in McCain's 2008 campaign when it was disclosed that he was also a consultant for a 527 independent group called "Stop Her Now," which attacked Hillary Clinton. The group later changed its name to "Stop Him Now" and smeared Obama.

ORLY TAITZ

A casual observer could easily confuse her irrational rants for an amateur, dimwit stand-up comedian. This California-based lawyer, the mascot of the birther movement, might go down in *Guinness World Records* as filing the most outrageous frivolous lawsuits. She represents plaintiffs who seek to disqualify Obama from the presidency by alleging that his birth certificate is fake (see chapter 4). She carried things a step further by introducing forgeries into evidence, claiming that they proved Obama was born in Kenya. Taitz, who runs the Defend our Freedoms Foundation, is too fringy for even the fringiest birther elements.

Born in Moldova when it was part of the Soviet Union, Taitz immigrated in 1981 to Israel, where she studied dentistry. After meeting her husband, Yosef, she moved to the United States, where she studied law online at Taft Law School, which is not accredited by the American Bar Association. California is the only state which allows Taft graduates to take the bar exam.

Here are her other noble achievements: she brought a lawsuit asserting that Obama has used a "multitude of Social Security numbers" to perpetrate fraud, claims Obama was supported in law school by the Saudi royal family, asserts that Obama was involved in the deaths of gays at his former church in Chicago, says Obama had someone killed who was cooperating with the FBI to expose alleged fraud involving his passport, and argues that Obama is building internment camps to house political adversaries.

9

Fox News: The Anger Machine Gushing Out Nonstop Propaganda

After they give their opinions, which is fine with me, they then
state as facts things that aren't facts at all.

—Bernard Goldberg

If Fox News were a person, it would be Sarah Palin: lots of flash, dash, and
trash; vain; saucy; treacly; boastful; insecure; insincere; mean-spirited; prone
to twisting facts and exploiting emotion; loved by supporters; despised by
the other side; and unsure why it is not universally adored.

The raison d'être of Fox News is to deliver a singular message to
make its side look good and the other side look bad. If it wants to incite anger
toward the other side, by all accounts, it succeeds wildly at that goal. Right-
wingers who watch Fox News get madder by the minute at every news report
that justifies their hatred for Obama and its other targets. Fox is highly successful at its real mission: to serve as a propaganda machine, a free infomercial, for the hatemongering right-wing cult.

The dictionary defines propaganda as "the spreading of ideas, information, or rumor for the purpose of helping or injuring an institution, a cause
or a person; ideas, facts or allegations spread deliberately to further one's case
or to damage an opposing cause."

Scott McClellan, Bush's former press secretary, admitted that Fox News
served as a lackey for the Bush administration. He said on July 25, 2008, on
MSNBC's *Hardball*, "Certainly there were commentators and other pundits at

Fox News that were helpful to the White House." MSNBC's Keith Olbermann that same day quoted McClellan as telling him that the White House sent talking points to Fox News, whose commentators served as spokespeople with a script that gave the Bush administration "its desired results." Former Fox employees have said that they must adhere to the "message of the day."

David Brock, a former right-wing hit man, said in the 2004 documentary *Outfoxed: Rupert Murdoch's War on Journalism* that the network puts out "false, distorted caricaturing" in which "wrong pieces of information are repeated through an echo chamber."

Conservative columnist Jonah Goldberg wrote on March 16, 2007, on the website RealClearPolitics, "Look, I think liberals have reasonable gripes with Fox News. It does lean to the right, primarily in its opinion programming but also in its story selection (which is fine by me) and elsewhere."[1]

Jeffrey Lord, a former political director in the Reagan White House, acknowledged Fox's rightward tilt: "Rupert Murdoch's invention of Fox News was a television network waiting to happen. Suddenly, beaming into American living rooms through satellite and cable was a different world view altogether, a conservative world view," he wrote in *The American Spectator*.[2]

Even the *New York Post*, also owned by Murdoch, began calling Fox a "conservative network" in November 2009.

Liberals are invited to speak on Fox News, but many don't return after being shouted down.

"People come on the air and they insult them as they did me, they cut off their mics as they did me, they shout at them and they interrupt them as they did me, and they even curse at them as they did me," Alan Grayson, a Democratic congressman from Florida, said on October 21, 2009, on MSNBC's *The Ed Show*.

If Fox's news reports were submitted as college term papers, they would get an F for lack of research, absence of critical thinking, and utter disdain for facts.

Fox News operates on the assumption that every other news organization is "in the tank for Obama." They won't admit that the mainstream media were in the tank for Bush until his second term began to crumble. Serious, unresolved questions about the Supreme Court order to stop the 2000 vote count in Florida vanished as soon as Bush took office. After September 11,

2001, Bush was portrayed as a leader; news organizations hesitated in probing whether lapses in leadership and judgment contributed to the worst terrorist attack in U.S. history. When Bush waged unprovoked war on Iraq, the *New York Times* and almost everyone else beat the drum. Bush's image turned negative only after his reasons for the Iraq war were proved false; after nonpartisan commissions showed serious gaps in leadership leading up to the 9/11 attacks; after ineptitude during Hurricane Katrina; and after Americans became outraged by the gutting of constitutional guarantees against torture, spying by the government, and denial of habeas corpus.

Fox News transforms news reports into Manichean morality plays. There is a bad guy: the Obama administration, a bureaucrat, an "activist judge," a Democratic politician, a Muslim, "a radical environmentalist," a union, or a civil rights organization. Then there is a good guy: "the little guy," a Republican, or a "persecuted Christian." All the elements are set into motion, and Fox viewers are clearly the Davids standing up to the godless liberal Goliaths.

Any day there is bad economic news, whether a decline in the stock market or negative indicator such as higher unemployment, Fox runs banners across the screen that reflect poorly on Obama. On the days the stock market is higher or the economy grows, Fox never runs a banner showing confidence in Obama. Why not? Wouldn't that be fair and balanced?

Headlines such as "So Long to the Free Market?" or "War on Prosperity" or "Catastrophe for the Country" or "Health Care Plan: Scarier Than Cancer?" or "Why Liz Cheney Says Obama's Radical Policies Are Putting Us at Risk" roll across the TV screens or slide off an announcer's tongue every day.

It would come as no surprise if mental illnesses got named after Fox News and its hosts. Here are some suggestions:

- Fox News Disorder: the delusion that "fair and balanced" really means unbiased.
- Glenn Beck Derangement: incoherently babbling unrelated events thinking they are intertwined.
- Hannity Insanity: Repeating the same lies over and over as if they were facts.
- O'Reilly Syndrome: Yelling at everyone you disagree with, calling them "warped," a left-wing extremist or a pinhead.

The Project for Excellence in Journalism report in 2006 said 68 percent of Fox stories contained personal opinions, compared with 27 percent at MS-NBC and 4 percent at CNN. Their 2005 report concluded that "Fox was measurably more one-sided than the other networks, and Fox journalists were more opinionated on the air."

Fairness and Accuracy in Reporting (FAIR) said that in a nineteen-week period it studied from January to May 2001, the evening news program *Special Report with Brit Hume,* featured fifty conservative guests versus six liberal ones.

Like the Bush administration, Fox presents an alternate reality devoid of facts when the facts don't reflect well on its agenda at a time the public needs unbiased news more than ever.

"When society seems to be entering the 'post-factual' era, in which only opinions exist, independent of reality, the existence of anchors of objectivity, the systematic compilation of verifiable data according to recognized methods becomes essential for citizens to reach confident conclusions about what is going on around them," Carlos Eduardo Lins da Silva wrote on May 31, 2009, in his ombudsman's column in *Folha de São Paulo.* Lins da Silva was formerly a U.S.-based correspondent for Brazil's largest-circulation newspaper.

Bill Sammon, Fox's Washington bureau chief, said on June 18 that Obama "takes gratuitous swipes at his predecessor every chance he gets." This was the person reporting from the nation's capital upon whose shoulders the curse of "fair and balanced" falls.

Obama has said that he was bequeathed a record budget deficit, economic catastrophe, high unemployment, and two wars from the previous administration. Is he incorrect to state these basic facts? Obama acknowledged on February 3, days after taking office, that even though he was dealt a lousy hand, it was up to him to make wine from the sour grapes left over from his predecessors.

Sammon should recite at least one gratuitous statement Obama made about his predecessor. Otherwise, we must conclude that Sammon is taking gratuitous swipes at Obama. On another occasion, Sammon described Obama's "agenda toward socialism."

Sean Hannity called Fox host Martha MacCallum on July 16 to kvetch about Obama's health care plan. "Does America want a cradle-to-the-grave, a womb-to-the-tomb nanny state with Soviet-style government-run health care, or does America believe in freedom and liberty and risk and reward?" he asked. "They want to take over the car companies, they want to run financial institutions, they want the banks."

Hannity, apparently reading a script written by Republican consultants pitching the newest catchphrases tested in focus groups, was wrong on everything. Obama did not propose anything resembling Soviet-style health care. He did not seize banks or car companies. General Motors exited from bankruptcy six days earlier, and by this point, numerous banks had repaid billions of dollars in Troubled Asset Relief Program (TARP) loans.

MacCallum agreed with Hannity, saying, "But they also want somebody to pay for it. And that somebody is people like you and people who make a lot less money than you do."

On other occasions, Steve Doocy and Gretchen Carlson slavishly repeated the lie from Obama-hating blogs that Obama is a Muslim.

These are only a few examples of how Fox News lets opinion contaminate its news coverage on a daily basis.

President Obama has also noticed the Fox bias against him.

"First of all, I've got one television station entirely devoted to attacking my administration. And you'd be hard pressed if you watched the entire day to find a positive story about me on that front," he told John Harwood in a June 16 interview on CNBC.

The next day, columnist and Fox commentator Charles Krauthammer said, "What's really interesting, the president yesterday has said, he complained about Fox, and he said, I think accurately, that it is the one, only voice of opposition in the media . . . the rest of the media are entirely in the tank, and it's embarrassing."

Does officially positioning a network as "opposition" to the administration qualify as "fair and balanced?" Shouldn't a news organization be neutral rather than pro or con? When will Fox be embarrassed as Krauthammer suggests?

Rush Limbaugh, appearing on *The Glenn Beck Program* on August 26, also punctured the "fair and balanced" facade when he said, "His [Obama's] number one opposition is on radio and Fox News."

Bernard Goldberg, who is the Chicken Little of alleging liberal media bias, also barbecues Fox on occasion. He said on September 29 on *The O'Reilly*

Factor that the network's promotion of anti-Obama Tea Party protests was wrong, and that Fox hosts "don't cover rallies, they cheerlead." He pointed out that Tea Party activists "are not a cross-section of America."

Even more damning, he said some Fox commentators call themselves journalists when it is convenient and commentators when it fits. "The commentary part of it is legitimate, but to give false information, just because you're a commentator, is unacceptable," Goldberg said. "After they give their opinions, which is fine with me, they then state as facts things that aren't facts at all."

Fox News actively organizes and participates in anti-Obama crusades on a regular basis. Besides the Tea Party, it also promoted Beck's 912 protest; the "Hands Off Our Health Care!" protest on November 5, 2009; "Restoring Honor" event on August 28, 2010; and the Beck-Palin political rally in Anchorage that exploited September 11, 2010, for profit. Contributor Dick Morris plugged his website, which told readers "how to defeat" health care legislation and provided "talking points" to include in form letters to Congress.

Fox viewers were disoriented on August 26, when the death of Edward M. "Ted" Kennedy was announced. They were perplexed at the mourning and heartfelt respect pouring in for Kennedy from around the world and from politicians of all stripes, a shock for people who tune in to see sewage sprayed on Democrats and liberals nonstop. One anchor admitted the confusion, saying that viewers were sending e-mails asking why Fox was not focusing on Kennedy's misdeeds; she explained that there was plenty of time for that later, but this was the right time to honor and respect the late senator.

Americans are fortunate to have Fox News to supplant inefficient, government-run trials and investigations. When army psychiatrist Maj. Nidal Malik Hasan reportedly gunned down thirteen fellow soldiers on October 5 at Fort Hood in Killeen, Texas, the right wing identified the culprit immediately: Obama. They also showed their blood lust when exploiting the tragedies of others. Dick Morris said it was "a consequence of the unilateral disarmament Barack Obama has brought to the intelligence community." Hannity concluded, "There is a chance our government knew all about" the events about to unfold. "What does it say about Barack Obama and our government?" Jerome Corsi's story at WorldNetDaily incorrectly said, "Shooter Advised Obama Transition." Limbaugh added, "We could almost say that this is Obama's fault."

When Obama spoke to the House Republican Conference in Baltimore on January 29, 2010, all of the news networks carried the ninety-minute event as he pointed out that his health care program, criticized as imposing Soviet-style dictatorship, is similar to those proposed by former Republican leaders Bob Dole and Howard Baker. Obama effectively showed the arguments against him to be shallow and the accusations to be hollow. When it became clear that Obama was eloquently and factually punching holes in the unending lies against his plan—such as "You'd think this was some sort of Bolshevik plot"—Fox pulled the plug on the truth and reverted to what it does best: right-wing commentators puking out false, mindless attacks on the president.

Frum, a former speechwriter for George W. Bush, told ABC's *Nightline* on March 22, 2010: "Republicans originally thought that Fox worked for us, and now we're discovering that we work for Fox."

Republican Tom Coburn, one of the most conservative members of the Senate, told a town hall meeting in Oklahoma City on March 31, 2010: "Don't catch yourself being biased by Fox News," and that some of its news reports are "so disconnected from what I know to be the facts."

The merger of Fox News and the GOP became official in early 2010 when empty-headed Sarah Palin became a talking head for the network and Hannity accepted an invitation to deliver the keynote address at the National Republican Congressional Committee's annual fund-raising dinner in March, an honor usually bestowed on elected Republican officials.

BIASED COMMENTATORS

Fox executives freely admit that Bill O'Reilly, Sean Hannity, and Glenn Beck spout off opinion rather than facts. But they never acknowledge that numerous other personalities in front of the camera are biased and have been discredited in the real world.

Among the worse offenders are George Allen, David Freddoso, Judith Miller, Dick Morris, Col. Oliver North, Chip Saltsman, and Don Imus, as well as Karl Rove, Nicolle Wallace and Dana Perino, who all worked in the Bush White House.

Allen was a Republican senator from Virginia who in 2006 revealed his lack of character when he mocked a dark-skinned young man of Indian ancestry at a rally by calling him "macaca." Allen denied knowing the term was a slur until journalists learned his mother grew up in Tunisia, where "macaca" was a pejorative used by French colonials to describe dark-skinned natives. Allen lost his seat in a squeaker to Democrat Jim Webb. Since his Freudian slip, Allen has been a pariah to serious news networks, but he fits in snugly in the Land of Fox as a guest.

Freddoso, who wrote *The Case Against Barack Obama: The Unlikely Rise and Unexamined Agenda of the Media's Favorite Candidate*—a collection of gossip that wasn't quite reliable enough to make the cut at *National Enquirer*—is a contributor for Fox News (see Appendix B). In a July 16, 2009, discussion about tax rates, Freddoso described people earning above $250,000 per year as "so-called higher income." U.S. government agencies categorize $250,000 income in the top 2 percent of earners. Why does Fox News invite guests who spout such incorrect drivel on its airwaves without correcting them?

Miller left the *New York Times* in disgrace after the newspaper discovered that she had served as an unquestioning lackey for Bush-Cheney administration officials to plant false stories in the media to justify the invasion of Iraq.

Morris is a fixture on Fox News. He was fired from his job as an adviser in the Clinton White House after allowing a prostitute to listen to his conversation with the president. He was resurrected as a critic on Fox News, where he supplies the most outrageous fabrications.

Remember when fanatics got rudimentary weapons and cruelly butchered thousands of people? Americans would think of Osama bin Laden and September 11. Nicaraguans would point to the Contras. In the 1980s Col. Oliver North provided weapons to the mullahs of Iran, fanatic enemies of the United States. Did Fox investigate whether Iranian thugs butchered Neda Soltani in June 2009 with weapons or ammunition supplied by North? Instead, Fox blamed Obama, who never sold weapons to America's enemies. The profits from North's illegal weapons sales were funneled to Contras, who killed government officials in Nicaragua along with many innocent civilians. The U.S. Senate's subcommittee on terrorism, narcotics, and international operations found references about narcotrafficking by the Contras in North's own notebooks.

If bin Laden is considered a terrorist, then North, by the same definition, is also a terrorist. This unrepentant terrorist is a darling of Fox News.

Rove filled his Boy Scout sash with merit badges in sleaze-mongering. His famous tricks were whisper campaigns to smear Ann Richards, the Democratic governor of Texas, as a lesbian, and accusing John McCain of fathering a child out of wedlock with a black prostitute, branding him as a traitor, when he is actually a prisoner of war in Vietnam (where cowards Bush, Cheney and Rove never served). He is a perfect match for Fox's ethics.

Chip Saltsman lost his race for chair of the Republican National Committee in early 2009, despite a valiant effort to curry favor by sending the racist spoof "Barack the Magic Negro" to members (see chapter 3). This raised his stature at Fox News, where he gets invited to comment about topics such as Palin: "She's had a target on her back since the election was over." Why do they not ask Saltsman why he and Palin both targeted Obama so unfairly and distastefully?

Wallace, a veteran of the White House and McCain campaign, was the strategist behind Palin's accusations that Obama "pals around with terrorists" (see Introduction). Neither the ventriloquist Wallace nor her dummy Palin ever apologized for using such filthy un-American tactics and rhetoric.

Perino said on August 13 on Fox News that Obama has "vilified the free-enterprise system." This is coming from the press secretary to George W. Bush, who left America's free-enterprise economy in tatters.

And in the irony to end all ironies, Don Imus got a job with Fox after being booted from MSNBC and CBS Radio for making racist remarks.

FOX'S ON-AIR PERSONALITIES
Glenn Beck

Beck is the guy most likely burst an artery on live TV. Like a doddering old crazy uncle who is slowly overcome by senility, he is sometimes amusing and increasingly annoying, but he always tries our patience. Beck is such a caricature that one is forced to ponder whether he is simply playing a cartoonish role or willfully making a mockery of mockery.

Exactly four months to the day after the president put his hand on Lincoln's Bible to take his oath of office (remember the muttonheads who said that Obama would put his hand on the Koran?), Beck unleashed this tirade: President Obama has "shredded the Constitution." Beck did not provide a single example of what he was saying, just a blanket statement.

I immediately sent an e-mail to Beck's show that read, "You just said that Obama has shredded the Constitution. I challenge you to tell your audience one freedom in the Constitution that we have lost under Obama. Of course you can't because you just made it up."

He never responded to my e-mail and never explained on air that day or on subsequent days what Obama has done to shred the Constitution.

Beck can't appreciate, much less fathom, the irony of making this statement on the same day that President Obama spoke at the National Archives to reinstate the Constitution (by releasing documents Bush had concealed) after its shredding by the Bush gang.

If Beck were simply somebody's crazy uncle stashed away from view, his mumblings and humbugs would be moot. Unfortunately, millions of people watch Fox News and then go around repeating the slogans they hear without the faintest inkling about what they mean. And these people have just as much right to vote as thinking people.

On June 1, 2009, Beck described a meeting of health care reform advocates as a "rogue's list of people dismantling capitalism." On July 13 he said Americans couldn't sit by idly "as our country burns to the ground."

Beck blurted out July 22, "We are not capitalists any more." Within hours Obama proved Beck to be either a fool or a liar, when answering a question about bank profits at his press conference. "Now banks are making profits. Some paid back TARP. That's a good thing, good thing they are profitable. This is America. If you are profitable, you benefit," Obama told a reporter from Bloomberg News.

Obama, of course, has not only paid lip service to bank profits but also pursued policies which encourage a financially sound banking system, the cornerstone of capitalism, that became moribund on Bush's watch.

Beck said the government is "turning us into slaves" that day. He greeted viewers with "*Wie gehts comrades*" (German for "How are you, comrades?") in an obvious attempt to link Obama with Hitler. Instead, Beck showed himself more in league with Sergeant Schultz from *Hogan's Heroes*, who regularly stammered, "I know nothing!"

Then Beck made a bizarre confession: "This is not the same country I grew up in. If it was, more people on TV would be telling you the truth." It was unclear whether he was speaking for himself alone or referring to Fox News in general.

Beck devoted the week of August 24 to breathlessly accusing numerous Obama appointees of being communists. This was the same week Obama reappointed (Bush nominee) Ben Bernanke to another term as chairman of the Board of Governors of the United States Federal Reserve, yet Beck strangely failed to investigate the Fed chief's lifelong Stalinist ties.

While accusing Obama appointees of being radicals or communists, Beck and other Fox hosts never mention his designation of Republicans and officials from the Bush administration. Those included Secretary of Transportation Ray LaHood and Secretary of the Army John McHugh (both former congressmen), Secretary of Defense Robert Gates (a Bush holdover), Secretary of Veterans Affairs Eric K. Shinseki (Army chief of staff under Bush), and Ambassador to China Jon Huntsman Jr. (former Utah governor). Would Republicans serve a president leading the nation on a radical trajectory? Would Gates and high-level military officers work for an administration hell-bent on destroying the nation's defenses?

The amazing thing is that so many people can watch Beck's show without realizing it is truly a circus freak show—with geeks and clowns—but instead take seriously what he says. To say Beck has a screw loose would defame screws unfairly.

Beck went on a binge on July 30, claiming that the Big Brother government was taking over computers of car dealers because of a disclaimer the dealers had to agree with when enrolling in the Cash for Clunkers program. It turned out that the wording was a leftover from Bush's USA PATRIOT ACT.

On August 5, Beck said, "We are entering the most frightening time I can remember in my life." I'd be willing to bet that September 11, 2001, was the most frightening time for 99.9 percent of Americans. That same day he alleged that the Obama administration was fomenting unrest so "they can use an iron fist and crush people." He asked, "When will someone stand up and say 'traitor?' When will someone stand up and say 'thieves?'" and said, "The American way of life is being systematically dismantled and destroyed! The republic is in danger!"

South Carolina Republican Congressman Bob Inglis had enough. When asked by a constituent about Beck at an August 6 town hall meeting, Inglis retorted, "Turn that television off when he comes on." When the audience booed, he responded, "You want to know why? Because he's trading on fear. And you know what? Here's what I think: I think if you trade on fear, what you're doing is, you're not leading, you're just following fearful people."

After that event, Inglis said, "If Walter Cronkite said something like Glenn Beck said recently on the air, about the president being a racist, Cronkite would've been fired on the spot . . . But I guess the executives of these cable news shows are more enamored with the profits that come from selling this negative message than they are with undermining the faith of people in this wonderful constitutional republic."[3]

"What are Beck's viewers responding to? On air, Beck promotes sinister conspiracy theories," Frum wrote March 16 at the New Majority website. "There's always been a market for this junk of course. Once that market was reached via mimeographed newsletters. Now it's being tapped by Fox News."[4]

Frum emphasized that "big parts of it seem almost self-consciously copied from Peter Finch's legendary declamation in the movie *Network* . . . .Of course, Finch was only pretending to be crazy. He was an actor performing a role. Then again—so probably is Glenn Beck. But what about Fox News? What's their excuse?"

Peter Wehner wrote on September 21, 2009, at *Commentary Magazine*'s website that Beck "should worry the conservative movement. . . . His interest in conspiracy theories is disquieting." Calling Beck "a rolling mix of fear, resentment, and anger—the antithesis of Ronald Reagan," Wehner labeled Beck's statement that Obama has a "deep-seated hatred for white people" as "quite unfair and not good for the country." He emphasized that Beck "is not the kind of figure conservatives should embrace or cheer on."[5]

The website Salon said on October 12, 2009, "Republicans parrot Beck's crackpot notions and pet issues routinely—sometimes running with his manias the morning after he first airs them."[6]

Sean Hannity

The most insidious thing about Hannity is that he prefaces questions with false premises—typically remarks such as "Obama wants to Mirandize enemy combatants" or "He wants to sit down with a Holocaust denier" or "He believes in one-world government"—as if they were facts, with all the class and subtlety of a lawyer badgering, "When did you stop beating your wife?"

When American soldiers are killed in Iraq or Afghanistan, Hannity blames Obama for "lack of decisiveness" or "emboldening the enemy" or "putting troops in jeopardy." When U.S. forces have a good day routing the enemy,

Hannity never praises Obama. When Bush was in office, Hannity said anyone who did not march in lockstep with the commander-in-chief was unpatriotic.

Responding to Colin Powell's criticism of Limbaugh, Hannity said on May 6, "He attacks Rush Limbaugh, he talked about the nastiness of Rush on the radio, which I don't hear, ever." Hannity apparently agrees with Limbaugh referring to Obama as "Halfrican American" (See chapters 3 and 8).

Hannity hinted at outright rebellion against Obama on August 13 when he said, "The seeds of a revolution against the president's radical agenda have been planted."

Obama spoke to Congress about health care reform on September 9. The president mentioned people who get dropped by their insurance carriers for pre-existing conditions. "Insurance executives don't do this because they're bad people; they do it because it is profitable."

That same night, Hannity blatantly lied: "He said that insurance executives are bad people."

After Obama spoke to the United Nations General Assembly on September 23, Hannity and his guests made remarks that meet the dictionary's definition of schizophrenic ("a state characterized by the coexistence of contradictory or incompatible elements"), saying Obama displayed "jaw-dropping arrogance" and "policies of retreat and surrender." How on earth can a single person show unmitigated arrogance at the same time he is surrendering?

Obama, in fact, showed the opposite of arrogance when he said, "I am well aware of the expectations that accompany my presidency around the world. These expectations are not about me. Rather, they are rooted, I believe, in a discontent with a status quo that has allowed us to be increasingly defined by our differences, and outpaced by our problems. But they are also rooted in hope—the hope that real change is possible, and the hope that America will be a leader in bringing about such change." Hannity said Obama abandoned American exceptionalism, but the president proved Hannity dead wrong.

Instead of surrender and engaging in an "apology tour" as right-wingers describe every foreign policy pronouncement, Obama flexed U.S. muscle: "Now, like all of you, my responsibility is to act in the interest of my nation and my people, and I will never apologize for defending those interests."

The UN speech echoed Obama's April 4 remarks in Strasbourg, France: "I believe in American exceptionalism."

Michelle Malkin said Obama's UN speech kowtowed to "hard-left ideological friends and allies" and showed him to be "the weakest of weak leaders." Perhaps she meant this "weak" Obama comment: "We have set a clear and focused goal: to work with all members of this body to disrupt, dismantle, and defeat al Qaeda and its extremist allies, a network that has killed thousands of people of many faiths and nations, and that plotted to blow up this very building."

When Malkin mentioned "hard-left ideological friends and allies," she must have been talking about Britain and France, because two days later Obama, Gordon Brown, and Nicolas Sarkozy together announced a united tough stance against Iran's nuclear program. Germany, Russia, and China also blasted the Persian regime.

Wallace said the Obama speech was "detached and insulated from the values of the American people." He told the General Assembly, "On my first day in office, I prohibited—without exception or equivocation—the use of torture by the United States of America." The Eighth Amendment in the Bill of Rights bans "cruel and unusual punishments." Does Wallace truly think the American people object to upholding the Constitution?

Malkin said Obama's foreign policy has thrown friends under the bus "along with what's left of our allies" and described Obama as "a laughingstock," while data prove the opposite. Were the leaders of Britain, France, Germany, Russia, and China laughing at Obama when they united in opposing Iran?

The Pew Research Center's Global Attitudes Project report, released on July 23, found that attitudes toward the United States surged in the twenty-five nations surveyed, with 71 percent having confidence in Obama's handling of world affairs versus 17 percent confidence under Bush. Attitudes toward the United States improved in Europe, Latin America, Africa, and Asia, while suspicions lingered in most Muslim majority countries.

GfK Group on October 5 released its annual report, which showed the United States as the most-admired country worldwide, up from seventh place in 2008.

"The results suggest that the new U.S. administration has been well received abroad and the American electorate's decision to vote in President Obama has given the United States the status of the world's most admired country," said Simon Anholt, founder of the Nation Brands Index.

The other most prestigious nations are France, Germany, the United Kingdom, Japan, Italy, Canada, Switzerland, Australia, Spain, and Sweden. Should we assume that Michelle Malkin knows more than the thousands of people surveyed in these polls?

Do Malkin and these other Fox jesters believe the U.S. government can have a positive influence when the vast majority of people around the world hate us? These right-wingers say Obama "grovels" in front of dictators but can't identify a single concession he has granted any despot. Why do they have such a pathological aversion to the truth?

Hannity said Obama "weakens the country" while federal agents closed in on domestic terrorists who were plotting real attacks around the United States, not fictional attacks in Hannity's empty head.

On the same day that Obama and the allies took a unified stance against Iran, Hannity nearly piddled his pants over a video posted on YouTube a week earlier showing schoolchildren in New Jersey singing about Obama. The lyrics included words such as "Hooray Mr. President, you are number one." Hannity said this constituted "worship and idolizing" and even "kidnapping." Hannity and his guests made comparisons to dictatorships. The White House had no involvement with this video. The school said it sent home the lyrics to parents in advance and none complained.

O'Reilly said that this "never happened" when Bush was president but did not mention schoolkids singing Bush's praises during the 2006 Easter Egg Roll. Nobody on Fox corrected themselves after the "propaganda" video of children serenading Bush came out because they would rather exploit children to make their point, truth be damned.

This video isn't a national issue. Hannity avoided mentioning serious progress regarding Iran—which affects everybody on the planet, not just sixteen cherub-faced kids—because he refuses to credit Obama for doing anything good.

Bill O'Reilly

"I don't care about the Constitution," O'Reilly acknowledged, at long last, on November 17, 2009. It would be fitting if he made this confession the motto of his program, because so few of his viewers understand the supreme irony of calling it "the no-spin zone."

The next night he asked Lou Dobbs if Obama is "the devil." No, I'm not making this up.

If Joe Biden is a blowhard, as right-wingers love to call him, then O'Reilly is *Blowhard: The Prequel*. Like Ann Coulter, he has no compunction about going after families of 9/11 victims. In a February 4, 2003, interview, he told Jeremy Glick, whose father died in the terrorist attacks, that the young man was mouthing a "far-left position" over his opposition to the U.S. invasion of Afghanistan. When Glick began to explain his position calmly, O'Reilly wagged his finger in Glick's face and said, "You keep your mouth shut. . . . You have a warped view of this world and a warped view of this country." Glick, unruffled, challenged O'Reilly to explain that remark, to which the bigmouth responded, "I'm not going to debate this with you," twice ordered Glick to "shut up" and ordered his staff to "cut his mic." O'Reilly later described Glick as "out of control." Anybody who watches this interview on YouTube can see that O'Reilly clearly lost his cool while Glick was calm and patient despite the host's badgering and bullying.

O'Reilly labels anyone with whom he disagrees—or anyone who debunks his patently false statements—as "far-left" or "left wing" or "loony" or "quasi-socialist." He said Obama "used a far-left path to assume power" and calls the *New York Times* "a far-left operation" and a "loony paper."

On August 3, 2009, O'Reilly called the *St. Petersburg Times* of Florida a "far-left newspaper" when columnist Eric Deggans mistakenly said O'Reilly, Beck, and Rush Limbaugh had called President Obama a racist. The next day, the newspaper ran a front-page correction in which the columnist apologized. Beck and Limbaugh had made such a statement; O'Reilly had not.

The newspaper formed the Pulitzer Prize–winning PolitiFact.com, which investigates claims made in the media (see Appendix C). It tracks Obama's campaign promises and has a "Truth-O-Meter" to separate fact from fiction in public remarks by politicians, journalists, and pundits. If this publication were "far-left," why would it show where Obama has fallen short as well as inaccuracies by both Democrats and Republicans?

O'Reilly said on September 8 that NBC and its sister networks were involved in a "coordinated effort to promote Obama" after parent company GE said in a memo that it had worked with legislators to craft climate change legislation. GE manufactures meters that measure pollution and stands to profit from tighter environmental controls. Nothing about the GE memo even hinted that NBC or its sister networks were involved in this effort. Has O'Reilly ever seen CNBC, where Rick Santelli famously blew an anti-Obama fuse (see chapter 8)? Larry Kudlow would sneer at anyone who said he promotes Obama. Anybody who says on-air hosts such as Jim Cramer, Charlie Gasparino, Michelle Caruso-Cabrera, and "money honey" Maria Bartiromo shill for Obama either has never seen the network or is delusional.

O'Reilly occasionally challenges crackpot views espoused by guests, but not often enough. "That fact that seems to me is that he [Obama] has some malevolence toward this country that is unabated," guest Tammy Bruce said on September 17. O'Reilly is willing to beat up 9/11 families as "far-left" over a difference of opinion over war but is afraid to challenge such an untrue, malicious assertion for which his guest did not provide a single example?

POLLS

Fox News emphasizes polls that support its worldview while it downplays or ignores those that contradict it.

A so-called poll by the right-wing *Investor's Business Daily (IBD)* on September 16 said that 65 percent of doctors oppose health care reform and 45 percent would consider quitting if Obama's health reforms passed. *IBD* has a bad track record measuring public opinion. Its poll before the 2008 election had John McCain winning the youth vote by 74 to 22 percent.

Fox dismissed the *New England Journal of Medicine*'s survey of members of the American Medical Association, the largest physician group in the United States, with startlingly contrary results. That poll found 63 percent of doctors preferred a blend of public and private insurance and only 27 percent opposed. Nor did Fox mention a few weeks later that a National Public Radio poll of doctors found the same results as the AMA survey; this poll was taken by researchers at Mount Sinai School of Medicine in New York.

That didn't stop the Foxies from touting the bogus data. On October 7 Hannity and Malkin pointed to this *IBD* phony poll in an attempt to discredit Obama's invitation to physicians to the White House to promote health care reforms.

Would a responsible news organization ignore credible polls while allowing its hosts to repeat ad infinitum surveys with no credibility?

Obama Vs. Fox

In mid-October 2009, White House Chief of Staff Rahm Emanuel and Senior Adviser David Axelrod jabbed back at Fox News, saying, "It's not really news. It's pushing a point of view."

Hannity whimpered on October 19 that Obama was trying to "bully this news organization." Then he bragged. "We were way ahead of the curve on issues like Jeremiah Wright, Bill Ayers" and that Fox was relentless on "the controversy surrounding the czars in the administration."

When almost 130 million Americans voted in November 2008, were Reverend Wright or Bill Ayers on the ballot? All the polls showed voters were concerned about the economy, the wars in Iraq and Afghanistan, health care, and education, not Fox's slavish attention to wedge issues to make Obama look bad. Hannity isn't smart enough to realize that he proved Obama's argument by boasting that Fox made a big deal about the so-called czars. He neglected to mention that Bush had a similar number of presidential assistants (nicknamed 'czars') and that Fox never complained about it before.

Bernard Goldberg also admitted in a backhanded way that Obama was correct to challenge the network's reporting by saying, "Fox is part of the reason it's rising," referring to Obama's disapproval rate. An unbiased news organization should not try to influence the president's approval or disapproval rate.

The next day Tennessee Senator Lamar Alexander said Obama was veering toward the creation of an "enemies list" à la Nixon.

Nixon spied on political opponents, broke into Democratic Party headquarters, and audited the taxes of pesky journalists, while his henchmen plotted to kill columnist Jack Anderson. Bush the Second spied on reporters and liberal organizations. Obama did not censor his critics or take action against groups that opposed him. Denying Fox pool coverage to a Treasury Department official on one occasion was wrongheaded, and Obama the administration, fortunately, backtracked quickly. Perino confessed on Fox that the Bush White House blocked access to MSNBC, but that does not excuse the Obama White House from committing the same mistake.

Fox News showed its bias again that week. When Obama gave a speech about clean energy at the Massachusetts Institute of Technology on October 23, all the other news networks carried it. Fox, instead, ran a story about some anonymous guy complaining to police about a nude neighbor. Fox News nakedly shows its disdain for Obama and news judgment. I report, you decide.

INSIDE THE BELLY OF THE BEAST

For one brief moment, as a guest on Fox News's sister network Fox Business News, I got to see the anti-Obama machine from the inside looking out. I saw how the unrelenting propaganda machine twists events to cast a sinister aura around the president. Hosts and the other guest used a completely unsubstantiated, hackneyed theory to attack the president.

My fleeting stint as a "talking head" came in 2009, shortly after Obama returned from the Fifth Summit of the Americas in Trinidad and Tobago, where Venezuelan president Hugo Chávez foisted himself on the new popular leader for a photo op. Chávez behaved like a fawning schoolboy rushing for the autograph of a movie star.

I was invited to appear on April 20 to discuss Chávez because of my three decades of journalistic experience covering Latin America. The topic was, "Is there any way Obama's visit will make Latin America a more attractive place?" and whether the United States should do business with enemies. Fair enough. Chávez is an antagonist to the U.S. government, and how to deal with him is a strategic topic.

I had no idea what to expect. My TV cable does not carry the network, so I knew nothing about it and went into the "Street Meat" segment of the *Fox Business Happy Hour* with an open mind. I expected to describe how Chávez ruined the oil company and the nation. Unfortunately, the topic became entirely devoted to the handshake between Chávez and Obama at the summit, so I spent my time defending Obama from guilt by association with Chávez over a brief photo op.

Host Rebecca Diamond led off with Chávez's incendiary remarks: "The U.S. government is the most savage, cruel, and murderous empire that has existed in the history of the world. *Wow.* The U.S. is a devil that represents capitalism. *Double wow.* Chávez has also said in the past every day, U.S. imperialism is surpassed by its own immorality. Let us examine Mr. Obama's belief that we can indeed change that hatred by being seen as a force for good and reaching out to our enemies, basically, essentially turn them to friend from foe. Will these overtures to Cuba and Venezuela be good for American business, or will those countries still see China and Russia as their natural friends?"

It's fair to question U.S. policy toward a bellicose leader. But Diamond's next question whisked me straight into the Outer Limits. She asked me, "What do you say? People are debating whether the president should have been so welcoming and warm to the Venezuelan president, or did that make him look weak in some way? Some people say it hurt us strategically somehow."

Chávez is unfriendly to American political and economic interests. Characterizing Obama as expressing an affinity for Chávez was incorrect. Anyone who watched the summit could see that Obama was taken aback by Chávez's lunge in his direction.

I offered no defense of Chávez: "One thing you've got to keep in mind with President Chávez is that he is very colorful, he's very erratic and boy oh boy, he sure loves to talk. Keep in mind that he's also insulted the pope and King Juan Carlos of Spain. So, it's not just the *gringos* he's picking on. He's an equal-opportunity insulter. And, whether or not President Obama extending his hand to him gives him more power, I don't think so. I think it diminishes his power."

Another host, Eric Bolling, exploded in his sharp disagreement.

"How in the world can it diminish his power? You have the world leader, the number one head honcho there shaking hands with a terrorist thug dictator like Chávez. Let me take you to the bouncing ball. [Mahmoud] Ahmadinejad in Iran today said Israel racist regime [referring to an address by the Iranian president at a U.N. forum]. Ahmadinejad buddies with Chávez. Chávez now shakes hands with our president. Not good, so I don't know how it does anything other than to legitimize a thug," Bolling exclaimed while waving his arms excitedly.

Using this logic, one could argue that Franklin Roosevelt legitimized Stalin, Dwight Eisenhower legitimized Khrushchev, Richard Nixon legitimized Mao, and every U.S. president legitimizes Stone Age Saudi royalty. No one blamed our former presidents for the tragedies perpetrated by these dictators, and nobody said they weakened the presidential office by meeting with brutal tyrants. So from the get-go, I rejected this flimsy straw man argument to pin guilt on Obama because of a ten-second association—which he did not seek—with Chávez.

The "bouncing ball" from Ahmadinejad to Chávez to Obama was so far-fetched and absurd that I had to deflate that fictive ball immediately. "I don't think there are very many people in the world who believe anything that Mr. Ahmadinejad says, so I don't think he's a very credible source for information on much of anything," I answered.

Host Cody Willard asked the other guest, Republican Congressman Thaddeus McCotter of Michigan, whether the United States should in principle do business with Venezuela.

"The reality is that the president of the United States represents the greatest force for moral good the world has ever known, which is our free republic. Our consistent support for the freedom of other individuals undergirds the free market and our very own liberty at home. And to think that Mr. Chávez is simply a clown that can be dealt with when he's antithetically opposed to the very concepts that make us a free people is a very gross mischaracterization and a very dangerous one," McCotter recited his memorized right-wing talking points at a rapid clip.

Diamond asked him whether President Reagan's meetings with Soviet leader Gorbachev weren't the same thing as Obama shaking hands with Chávez.

When Ronald Reagan took office he was considered a nuclear cowboy. The rejection of détente with the Soviet Union, the rejection of moral equivalency. Gorbachev was brought to the table in a position to negotiate the Soviet Union's surrender to the United States and the forces of freedom. This wasn't just two guys chumming it up in Reykjavik, McCotter said.

I was up next, and Bolling tried to thrust me into the Obama-Chávez vortex again, saying that Chávez could not have shaken Obama's hand without his approval.

I deflected with the facts, saying, "We also have to keep in mind that the very first Latin American leaders that President Obama met with were Lula of Brazil and Calderón of Mexico. Those weren't just handshakes. Those were real meetings, and those were very substantive issues that he discussed with leaders that are much more pragmatic and much more centrist."

Then I took the opportunity to focus on the topic I went there to discuss, Venezuelan oil.

"Venezuela is a country that is hurt more from the way they are turning away from the United States than the United States is hurt because the United

States buys oil from other countries. Chávez, with his fiery rhetoric, ends up selling oil to places like China, which end up losing a lot of money for him." That was it. This was a short segment, and, at this point, they cut me off.

Given another half minute, I would have said next that Obama has been tougher toward Venezuela than the Bush administration had been. Immediately upon taking office, Obama shifted official U.S. policy to wean itself off Venezuelan oil completely within ten years. This is policy, not rhetoric or idle name-calling. But I was not allowed time to make my point. I spun off facts and figures while the congressman hissed rhetoric that had been soundly defeated in the 2008 election. I had to think on the fly, pulling myriad facts and figures out of my head. I went on the air prepared to talk about a subject I know intimately, Latin America, but never dreamed I would have to pronounce 'Ahmadinejad' (which I mangled) on live TV.

Chávez burst on the scene for two reasons. He became the anti-Bush in Latin America and won fans by opposing Bush's policies, which were despised throughout the region. Then, Chávez used his astounding earnings from rocketing oil prices to buy influence around the region with free and discounted oil. When Bush left office and oil prices collapsed, Chávez was relegated to the sidelines as the buffoon described by McCotter, while failing to realize that he was now living in the sixteenth minute of his fifteen minutes of fame. Where McCotter got it wrong was seeing Chávez as a continuing strategic threat after the strongman lost his muscle and become little more than a boil on the butt of U.S. policy.

This confluence of events gave Obama a unique opportunity to exploit the vacuum left by the gaping failures of Bush and Chávez and improve relations with Latin America, thereby marginalizing and isolating Chávez and Cuba. The Obama haters are so myopic that they refuse to seize opportunities to mend relations abroad, instead aiming all their narrow efforts at trying to debilitate the president.

This brief encounter showed how the right-wing smear machine doesn't care a whit about facts that negate their preconceptions and how Fox is a loud partisan sound machine.

An amusing footnote about McCotter. He represents the eleventh district in Michigan with a 90 percent white constituency that borders districts in Detroit with equally lopsided black constituents represented by liberal Democrats such as John Conyers and John Dingell. As a toddler, I lived in the Detroit suburb of Inkster, abutting what is now McCotter's congressional district. I dare anybody to link me to McCotter's retrograde drivel through dint of geographic proximity or our fleeting association on TV.

The congressman needs to be reminded that his hero, Reagan, willingly embraced Deng Xiaoping, the tyrant of Tiananmen who was "antithetically opposed to the very concepts that make us a free people." This was not just a momentary photo op. Would McCotter deny that Reagan legitimized Deng by chumming it up in Beijing with the man who let the Chinese Army mow down peaceful protesters in Tiananmen Square?

As for Fox Business News, I was not invited to return despite the fact that Chávez pops up in the news frequently. Go figure.

SPECIAL REPORTS: "OBAMA AND FRIENDS: THE HISTORY OF RADICALISM"

Fox broadcast a special report on the October 5, 2008, edition of Hannity's program called "Obama and Friends: History of Radicalism" based on speculation, Internet rumors, and smears. It prominently featured Anthony Robert Martin-Trigona, known as Andy Martin (see chapter 8), whose every utterance had been debunked. This blatant propaganda was repeated myriad times before the election. Not only did Hannity whitewash Martin's credentials, he did not question a single assertion made by the man who was refused admittance to the Illinois bar for "moral defect."

David Bossie (see chapter 8) said, "Barack Obama definitely has something to hide" but did not say what. Hannity repeated the rumor that Obama was hiding his "senior thesis" from Columbia. That rumor was torn apart by Obama's former professor in chapter 2.

Hannity made illusory connections to radicals Obama never met.

Martin said Obama was "training for radical overthrow of the government" and that he had "probably" met William Ayers during his years in New York. Martin made a wacky connection between Obama and communist leaders in Latin America.

Hannity interviewed victims of Weather Underground attacks against judges, police, and military recruiters, as well as an FBI agent who infiltrated the radical group. He depicted Ayers as a bad guy in the 1960s and unfairly tried to link Obama closely to Ayers.

He said Obama was "heavily influenced by the radical pastor," referring to Reverend Jeremiah Wright, quoting a sermon in which the preacher decried apartheid and apathy. Does Hannity disagree with this conclusion?

Hannity tied Obama to Rashid Khalidi, whom Obama knew as a fellow professor at the University of Chicago (see chapter 2). He quoted a *Los Angeles Times* article about Obama hosting a farewell dinner for Khalidi in which he said Khalidi and his wife "challenged his thinking" and recognition of "my own blind spots and my own biases." That sounds more like intellectual discourse and open-mindedness than brainwashing or adherence to radical ideology.

Hannity failed in his attempt to scare Jewish voters away from Obama, who got 78 percent of the Jewish vote in the election. That's better than John Kerry, who won 74 percent in 2004, and on a par with Al Gore, who took 79 percent in 2000.

"Hannity's program on Sunday was notable in presenting partisan accusations against Mr. Obama in a journalistic, documentary format in prime time," said the *New York Times*.[7]

THE ACORN NON-CONNECTION

For several consecutive days in mid-September 2009, Fox played tapes recorded by an undercover filmmaker who posed as a pimp with a woman pretending to be a prostitute looking for advice at various Association of Community Organizations for Reform Now (ACORN) offices. Fox had been bashing ACORN since early in the presidential campaign.

In the Baltimore office, two ACORN employees were seen agreeing to go along with the scam and giving advice about how to avoid taxes. Fox anchors were giddy, nearly rapturous all day, over the brief "gotcha" film. ACORN promptly fired the two offending women.

The next day Fox showed another tape of a similar occurrence in Washington, DC. ACORN dismissed two more employees over that incident. Glenn Beck said, "They were doing the bidding of people way up above." How does he know this? Absolutely nothing substantiated such a reckless, defamatory statement.

Fox's real motive was to hurt Obama. Old footage of candidate Obama speaking to ACORN was shown in order to make a spurious connection between Obama and the people trapped in the sting. Tapes showing Obama talking to ACORN were cleverly edited to show people in the audience, who bore a resemblance to the women filmed in the Fox sting, cheering Obama. Thus viewers saw ACORN employees recorded in a sting, saw Obama speaking to ACORN, then saw cheering women in the audience who looked like the women in the sting. Why did Fox keep showing unrelated images of Obama while it ran this story unless it wanted to associate him with the stupid behavior depicted in the taped sting? This was identical to Republican campaign ads in 2002 and 2004 that interspersed the faces of Democrats with those of Saddam Hussein and Osama bin Laden. This powerful imagery creates guilt by association, no matter how flimsy the connection.

On other days Fox showed two ACORN offices in California. A man in San Diego said he was willing to help smuggle underage prostitutes from Mexico. A woman in San Bernardino confessed to having killed her husband. The Foxies were orgasmic over that claim. Only one problem: it wasn't true. Local law enforcement agencies said the woman's former husbands were very much alive, and she later said that she was spoofing the gonzo filmmakers. Of course, Fox did not follow up with these facts.

Fox never bothered to call the police to substantiate this claim; its hosts simply accused her of murder. This violates the very first rule in journalism about checking facts, as well as basic ethics. No legitimate news organization would allow such a report to be aired without asking police about the alleged murder. There was no rush; these films were broadcast months after being recorded.

California's then–attorney general, Edmund G. Brown Jr., ordered his office to study the unedited tapes to see whether any ACORN employees had broken the law. In a report released April 1, 2010, Brown said "things are not always as partisan zealots portray them through highly selective editing of reality. Sometimes a fuller truth is found on the cutting room floor." Brown's report found that undercover videographer James O'Keefe III was not dressed up like a pimp as shown in the broadcasts and that the ACORN worker in San Diego, instead of going along with the scheme as depicted, called the police to report the incident.

What if someone did a story about renegade Mormon polygamists in Utah—those crazies with multiple wives, some of them girls in their early teens—and interspersed shots of Glenn Beck? After all, Beck is a Mormon. No proof exists that Beck has any involvement with polygamist pedophiles, just as there is no evidence that Obama sanctions activities of ACORN employees who broke the law. ACORN, which had thousands of employees, fired those who broke the law. Likewise, the Mormon Church expels polygamists. Linking Obama with abuses by ACORN employees is equally as valid as blaming Beck for polygamy.

Fox howled for the government to sever all contracts with ACORN but never worried about military contractors and Republican contributors who bilk taxpayers for far more money. I report; you decide.

In January 2010 O'Keefe was arrested along with three other men for plotting to tamper with the telephone system in the New Orleans office of Democratic Senator Mary Landrieu. In May, he entered a guilty plea to a lesser charge.

WATER SHORTAGE

Fox in general, and Hannity in particular, relentlessly blamed Obama for the lack of water for farms in California's Central Valley. In a special broadcast on September 17, 2009, Hannity showed parched acreage and intoned that this was "right out of *The Grapes of Wrath*," comparing it with the dust bowl of the 1930s that drove millions of farmers from their land into squatter camps during the Great Depression. He alleged that "radical environmentalists threaten the American dream." The program showed people losing their jobs and crying, all because of Obama and his cohorts.

Hannity proclaimed that farmers lost their water so "wacko environmentalists" could save "a two-inch minnow." Every time Zeke Grader of the Pacific Coast Federation of Fishermen's Associations spoke, he was drowned out by boos in the audience. Grader said farmers had sold water for $77 million to Southern California; he said drought was the main reason for the water shortage. Hannity never asked other guests about these statements.

Mighty dramatic stuff. Quite convincing. No doubt, millions of viewers were driven to tears as well as rage at the president for allowing "radical environmentalists" to pull his strings. What the viewers don't know, because Hannity never told them, is that on June 30, the federal government did turn the water back on. But it was diverted to other users under byzantine California water-use laws and the state's hopelessly outdated water supply infrastructure.

The Foxies always claim that Obama is making an unprecedented power grab but have never shown a single example of where he overreaches. This time, however, they condemned him because he was reluctant to usurp the authority of California officials and federal courts, which ordered a 5 to 7 percent cut in water flows to save salmon, sole, sturgeon, smelt, bass, and whales.

It would be damning evidence against Obama if all of this were true. Yes, the impact of parched land was all true. Yes, these farms are not getting water they badly need. But what portion of the agricultural land in the vast Central Valley was affected by this water shortage? Hannity never said, so there was no perspective about the extent of the crisis. Did farmers sell water to Southern California? Who sold it? When? Was there really a drought? How are water rights divided in this area? Was some group or individual hogging more than its fair share?

Local news reports said the valley got 80 percent of normal water flows, but the problem resulted from distribution by water districts. Hannity also "forgot" to mention that Republican Governor Arnold Schwarzenegger refused to sign 700 pieces of water legislation passed by the state legislature in 2009 and that U.S. Secretary of the Interior Ken Salazar and Commissioner of the Bureau of Reclamation Michael Connor spent a lot of time twisting arms in California to resolve the problem.

Hannity asserted that there would be almond shortages and tomato prices would skyrocket, forcing the United States to import tomatoes from countries with questionable sanitation. Yet the California Tomato Growers Association said the 2009 harvest was up 15 percent over 2008, and the almond industry reported a bumper crop. Hannity did not report this.

If Hannity wanted to inform the public about ALL the issues surrounding the water shortage in this region, he would have asked such questions. After working in journalism for 35 years, I have learned that issues of this type are complicated, with overlapping responsibility and numerous culprits. But informing the public was not Hannity's goal. His objective was to do a hit piece to make Obama look bad no matter where the facts and truth led.

Seeking to mimic Ronald Reagan's famous "Mr. Gorbachev, tear down this wall," Hannity concluded, "Turn the water back on, Mr. President." Imagining himself Reaganesque, Hannity instead came off as Daffy Duck whiffing a helium balloon.

At the same time that Hannity accused Obama of being under the spell of environmental extremists, the Union of Concerned Scientists complained about loopholes in the Environmental Protection Agency's greenhouse-gas emissions standards for 2012 to 2016. When a political leader gets blasted by both sides, that usually indicates policies somewhere in the middle, certainly not extremist by any measure.

Fox's special reports are Republican attack ads' Siamese twin. That's no surprise, since Fox president Roger Ailes was an adviser to the 1988 Bush campaign when the toxic Willie Horton ads fouled the airwaves. "You look at Fox News and some of the compadres there, it's sort of Willie Horton 24/7," Pulitzer Prize–winning author Ron Suskind said on October 16, 2009, on MS-NBC's *The Rachel Maddow Show*.

I paid my dues in the trenches of journalism at modest-paying jobs where I made rookie mistakes while learning about the most accurate ways to report complex information. Nowhere I ever worked would have allowed such propaganda to reach the public.

Now go back to the beginning of this chapter and reread the definition of "propaganda." You will see that these many examples prove beyond a shadow of a doubt, in courtroom parlance, that Fox serves as a propaganda machine to destroy Obama's reputation.

SETTING THE RECORD STRAIGHT

Fox News, to its credit, occasionally gets things right. The network saw fit to distance itself from Hannity's outrageous fictions in the *History of Radicalism* special.

Bill Shine, Fox News senior vice president of programming, told the *Washington Post* he disagreed with Martin's remarks. "Having that guy on was a mistake," Shine said. "We obviously didn't do enough research on who the guest was."[8] Hannity never acknowledged that he concocted this horrible smear by legitimizing Martin, who is shunned by respectable news organizations. Martin wasn't simply one person in the so-called report; his lies comprised the entire framework. Without Martin, the report would not have existed.

Shine has a talent for devouring crow on behalf of nitwits. After a racist caption said "Outraged liberals: Stop picking on Obama's baby mama," referring to Michelle Obama, Shine admitted "a producer on the program exercised poor judgment in using this chyron during the segment."[9] "Baby mama" refers to a woman who has a baby with a man who is not her partner.

Shine also distanced himself from Beck's "Obama is racist" rant. "During *Fox & Friends* this morning, Glenn Beck expressed a personal opinion which represented his own views, not those of the Fox News Channel. And as with all commentators in the cable news arena, he is given the freedom to express his opinions," Shine told TVNewser website on July 28, 2009.

Hannity apologized on air on November 12 after Jon Stewart pointed out on *The Daily Show* that Hannity showed footage from the 912 rally to depict the sparsely attended "Hands Off Our Health Care!" event. MSNBC and impartial media critics point out Hannity's errors regularly, but it took a comedian to force him to be honest, at least once.

These occasional apologies are a half step in the right direction, but instead of a guy in a suit issuing a bureaucratic statement to news organizations that will never be seen by most Fox News viewers, Ailes instead should require that the offending host issue an unequivocal correction straight into the camera. That's the way CNN and MSNBC do things. Rachel Maddow regularly asks guests, "Did I get anything wrong?" while hosts Chris Matthews, Ed Schultz, and Keith Olbermann put out corrections during the same broadcast when they or any of their guests make a factual error. Or they correct themselves the next day. If Fox News did the same, they might begin to move in the direction of their cheap, hollow slogan, "Fair and balanced."

There was no apology after Hannity's blatant lie about Obama's health care speech, the rampant distortions in his hit piece about California's water shortage or blatant lies about ACORN. All this begs a simple question: why does this continue?

In 2004 Dan Rather interviewed someone who claimed George W. Bush had been AWOL from his Air National Guard unit during the Vietnam War. Even though statements by the base commander questioned Bush's attendance, documents to support the AWOL claim were later proved to be forgeries. CBS fired four people who worked on the project, and Rather's retirement was hastened.

Rather had no prior knowledge that he was using faked information but was jettisoned because he did not do a better job of confirmation. The mishandling of facts at Fox in these instances is the opposite. Andy Martin's accusations had been toppled long before Hannity put him on the air. Millions of people saw Obama say the exact opposite of what Hannity accused him of saying on numerous occasions. Beck was never forced to apologize after accusing Obama of racism.

Fox always talks about a double standard in the media, and they are living proof that it exists. When people at other networks make an egregious error of fact, they must apologize and run the risk of losing their job. At Fox, it's all in a day's work.

Even Ailes admits that Fox News hosts are irrational. The *Washington Post* reported an alleged agreement between Ailes and Jeffrey Immelt, CEO of General Electric (NBC's parent company), to tone down the bitter feud between MSNBC's Keith Olbermann and O'Reilly: "Ailes offered a blunt, if slightly jocular, diagnosis of the problem. He could control his nutcases, Ailes said, but Immelt couldn't control his."[10] There was no evidence that Immelt considers MSNBC's salty-tongued editorialists "nutcases." Olbermann regularly pokes fun of Fox personalities and relishes in pointing out their frequent factual errors, which go uncorrected. When Fox hosts bash Olbermann or Maddow, they can never identify erroneous facts, so the rival hosts are merely called pinheads, hatemongers, or leftists.

The only other broadcast I have ever seen in my life in a league with Fox's bias was a program in New York City in the 1990s. A vile smutmeister named Al Goldstein, who published the pornographic magazine *Screw*, got free airtime on a public access channel, where he broadcast a porn show called *Midnight Blue* and pocketed the money from ads he sold to escort services. I watched the show with friends for the hilarious "Fuck You" segment, where a slovenly, foul-mouthed Goldstein would spit venom at cab drivers, doormen, or restaurant waiters and then majestically salute the offender with his middle finger. Likewise, Fox shows its collective middle finger to Obama, and to all of us, but with much more subtlety. While nobody took Goldstein seriously, millions of people, unfortunately, slurp up what Fox dumps in their trough.

10

Fight the Smears: Obama and His Allies Build an Effective Truth Squad

We were very careful to have good factual underpinnings and good documentation for our rebuttals.

—Ed Rendell

When Barack Obama declared his candidacy for president on February 10, 2007, in Springfield, Illinois, where Abraham Lincoln began his political career, he was a long shot. All of the cognoscenti believed the election was Hillary Clinton's to lose. At this point, he had completed only two years in the U.S. Senate following eight years as a state legislator in Illinois. Many people, including African Americans, wondered whether the United States was ready to elect a black man as president.

The role of underdog is much easier than that of frontrunner, who has to deflect potshots from other candidates in the same party, the opposition party, and freelance mudslingers. Senator Clinton started the race with her husband's enemies all lined up against her.

One might expect that Hillary would have taken all the flak in the early days. There were no organized smear campaigns directed against other Democratic candidates—2004 vice-presidential nominee John Edwards, New Mexico Governor Bill Richardson, or senators Joe Biden and Christopher Dodd. These were political heavyweights, but no major organizations or big money lined up to smear them. Perhaps it was assumed that, due to his slender résumé, only a handful of racists would bother slurring Obama.

In their infancies, most campaigns hire experts at "opposition research," who examine past statements and votes by opposing candidates to unearth something embarrassing, hypocritical, or just plain stupid. The Obama campaign, however, was forced to go on the defensive early on. Among the earliest campaign hires were people to deflect nasty e-mails of undetermined origin.

The first hit piece to be debunked was the "Who is Barack Obama?" e-mail, which surfaced in early January 2007:

Who is Barack Obama?

Very interesting and something that should be considered in your choice.

If you do not ever forward anything else, please forward this to all your contacts . . . this is very scary to think of what lies ahead of us here in our own United States . . . better heed this and pray about it and share it.

We checked this out on 'snopes.com'. It is factual. Check for yourself.

Who is Barack Obama?

Probable U.S. presidential candidate, Barack Hussein Obama was born in Honolulu, Hawaii, to Barack Hussein Obama, Sr., a black MUSLIM from Nyangoma-Kogel, Kenya and Ann Dunham, a white ATHEIST from Wichita, Kansas.

Obama's parents met at the University of Hawaii. When Obama was two years old, his parents divorced. His father returned to Kenya. His mother then married Lolo Soetoro, a RADICAL Muslim from Indonesia. When Obama was six years old, the family relocated to Indonesia. Obama attended a MUSLIM school in Jakarta. He also spent two years in a Catholic school.

Obama takes great care to conceal the fact that he is a Muslim. He is quick to point out that, 'He was once a Muslim, but that he also attended Catholic school.'

Obama's political handlers are attempting to make it appear that he is not a radical.

Obama's introduction to Islam came via his father, and that this influence was temporary at best. In reality, the senior Obama returned to Kenya soon after the divorce, and never again had any direct influence over his son's education.

Lolo Soetoro, the second husband of Obama's mother, Ann Dunham, introduced his stepson to Islam. Obama was enrolled in a Wahabi school in Jakarta.

Wahabism is the RADICAL teaching that is followed by the Muslim terrorists who are now waging Jihad against the western world. Since it is politically expedient to be a CHRISTIAN when seeking major public office in the United States, Barack Hussein Obama has joined the United Church of Christ in an attempt to downplay his Muslim background. ALSO, keep in mind that when he was sworn into office he DID NOT use the Holy Bible, but instead the Koran.

Barack Hussein Obama will NOT recite the Pledge of Allegiance nor will he show any reverence for our flag. While others place their hands over their hearts, Obama turns his back to the flag and slouches.

Let us all remain alert concerning Obama's expected presidential candidacy. The Muslims have said they plan on destroying the US from the inside out, what better way to start than at the highest level - through the President of the United States, one of their own!!!!

Please forward to everyone you know. Would you want this man leading our country? . . . NOT ME!!!

There are numerous variations of this e-mail, which is stuffed fatter than a Thanksgiving turkey with brazen falsehoods. Anyone who took one minute to research it would have learned that Snopes, instead of blessing it, shot it down.

Obama was sworn into the Senate by then–Vice President Dick Cheney with his left hand on a family Bible, as depicted in photographs of the event.

The other e-mail from the early days was titled "Can a good Muslim become a good American?" and concluded, "And Barack Hussein Obama, a Muslim, wants to be our president!!!"

Because they were anonymous, there was no way of determining the origin. Unidentified people use fake e-mail addresses and falsify anything without paying the price. These are not Tom Paines proudly affixing their names to a noble manifesto. Rather they are cowardly, hidden snipers seeking to destroy a candidate under the cover of darkness.

Right-wingers blamed Hillary Clinton's campaign for the anti-Obama e-mail, but Obama staffers never believed her team was involved.

In the early days, the Obama campaign handled smears on a case-by-case basis, not wanting to attract attention or give the accusations wider circulation. But the campaign was forced to act decisively when campaign workers in Iowa, where the first caucuses were scheduled for early January, became concerned that too many voters fell for the lies.

The Fight the Smears website was born. In mid-November 2007, the Obama campaign put extensively researched information on its website to debunk the many unfounded assertions sprouting everywhere. At campaign headquarters an experienced team headed by Devorah Adler performed research and responded quickly to the smears. Campaign staffers held conference calls to decide how to deal with any smear, whether to ignore it, answer it on Fight the Smears, issue a press release, release a reaction by a campaign spokesperson, request a response from a high-profile surrogate, or provide an answer from the candidate himself.

"The first research document that I put together was a response to the 'Who is Barack Obama?' e-mail," Adler told the *Huffington Post* on January 26, 2008. When I contacted Adler by telephone in 2009 to discuss Fight the Smears, she refused comment.

On January 17, 2007, Insight Magazine's online version alleged that Obama was educated in an Islamic madrassa in Indonesia. The magazine is published by the Reverend Sun Myung Moon's News World Communications, which also owns the conservative *Washington Times*. Within two days, Fox News repeated the same accusations, quoting Insight as its source.

CNN, instead of picking up the scurrilous report from Insight, did its own spadework and debunked the story. CNN correspondent John Vause spoke to teachers and administrators at the Basuki school that Obama attended in Jakarta. "This is a public school. We don't focus on religion," deputy head-master Hardi Priyono told CNN in an interview broadcast on January 22. Fox never bothered to speak to anyone who could confirm or deny the *Insight* charges, nor did the network retract earlier statements after they were proven wrong.

Another equally false e-mail made the rounds in the early days, but it did not get the same attention as the first attack e-mail:

Subject: Obama's church
Obama mentioned his church during his appearance with Oprah. It's the Trinity Church of Christ. I found this interesting.

Obama's church:
Please read and go to this church's website and read what is written there. It is very alarming.

Barack Obama is a member of this church and is running for President of the U.S. If you look at the first page of their website, you will learn that this congregation has a non-negotiable commitment to Africa. No where is AMERICA even mentioned. Notice too, what color you will need to be if you should want to join Obama's church . . . _ B-L-A-C-K!!!_ Doesn't look like his choice of religion has improved much over his (former?) Muslim upbringing. Are you aware that Obama's middle name is Mo-hammed? Strip away his nice looks, the big smile and smooth talk and what do you get? Certainly a racist, as plainly defined by the stated posi-tion of his church! And possibly a covert worshiper of the Muslim faith, even today. This guy desires to rule over America while his loyalty is to-tally vested in a Black Africa!

I cannot believe this has not been all over the TV and newspapers. This is why it is so important to pass this message along to all of our fam-ily & friends. To think that Obama has even the slightest chance in the run for the presidency, is really scary.

Click on the link below:

This is the web page for the church Barack Obama belongs to: www.tucc.
org/about.htm

This was a blatant appeal to racism, and racists probably believed it. Although Rev. Jeremiah Wright made many controversial statements during
his years as head pastor at Trinity, and a majority of members are black, the
congregation has non-black members. Another lie in this e-mail is Obama's
middle name, which is Hussein, not Mohammed.

Trinity describes itself as "a congregation which is Unashamedly Black
and Unapologetically Christian" and which "does not apologize for its African roots." But nowhere did the church state or practice a blacks-only policy.
Ironically, Obama haters link him to remarks made at Trinity by a guest pastor, Father Michael Pfleger, who is white.

Obama was asked about viral e-mails during a January 15, 2008, debate
sponsored by MSNBC. He answered, "The American people are I think smart-
er than folks give them credit for."

A week later he addressed the subject in an interview with the Christian
Broadcasting Network. "This is obviously a systematic political strategy by
somebody because these e-mails don't just keep coming out the way they have
without somebody being behind it," he said in the January 22, 2008, interview
with David Brody. "I want to make sure that your viewers understand that I
am a Christian who has belonged to the same church for almost twenty years
now." Obama also made it clear that while he is not, nor has he ever been,
a Muslim, people who practice Islam "are deserving of respect and dignity."

Asked whether he believed the Muslim smear came from another campaign, he said, "We have no way of tracing where these e-mails come from, but
what I know is they come in waves, and they somehow appear magically wher-
ever the next primary or caucus is, although they're also being distributed
all across the country. But the volume increases as we get closer to particular
elections. That indicates to me that this is something that is being used to try
to raise doubts or suspicions about my candidacy."

On numerous occasions, Obama has professed his Christian beliefs,
saying, "We worship an awesome God," and identified his membership at
Trinity.

The smears multiplied in direct proportion to Obama's growing popularity. Soon people would begin to hear that Obama was not a U.S. citizen, was a black nationalist, harbored secret ambitions to erect a communist or fascist state, and was involved with nefarious characters. Obama had personally deflected the Muslim smear enough that it did not derail or injure his candidacy significantly, but new smears were now rocketing at warp speed. Obama had to get out his message about fixing the deteriorating economy, wars in Iraq and Afghanistan, heath care, education, and a bevy of other real issues Americans worried about every day.

The campaign decided to let surrogates do most of the heavy hitting when it came to knocking down new and recurring smears.

Pennsylvania Governor Ed Rendell, who had backed Hillary Clinton in the primaries, signed on as an enthusiastic Obama surrogate once the nomination was sealed.

"We developed a truth squad. Every time someone made an incorrect statement about Senator Obama's position or anything that would get into a personal smear, we would send somebody out to refute it the next day. We had to do as quick a response as we could. And in most cases when it was Senator McCain or Governor Palin, I would try to be their respondent," Rendell told me.

"We used third-party validators whenever we could, so it wasn't just Obama surrogates refuting what McCain or Palin had said, but that we had third-party surrogates, whether that be newspapers, magazines, or policy centers or FactCheck.org. We used a lot of FactCheck.org," he emphasized. "So, we were very careful to have good factual underpinnings and good documentation for our rebuttals."

Rendell lamented the Muslim smear. "The lowest blow was the continued inference, not by Senator McCain, but by McCain surrogates, that Senator Obama was a Muslim. To me that was patently and blatantly incorrect, an outright lie, and yet it was perpetuated at many rallies," he recounted. "At a presidential level, it was the worst [smear] I've seen in the modern era."

Other key surrogates included both Clintons, Bill Richardson, Ohio Governor Ted Strickland, Michigan Governor Jennifer Granholm, Kansas Governor Kathleen Sibelius, Virginia Governor Tim Kaine, and Illinois Senator Dick Durbin.

Kip Tew, who served as the Obama campaign's state chair and senior adviser in Indiana, said it was tough to fight irrational smears using logic and reason.

"They don't care about reality. They just care about their grievance. In the end that's what it is, grievance," Tew told me.

"There was a rumor du jour, then people would receive the information at the rapid response group, and before long we would see Senator [John] Kerry or Howard Dean or somebody with a good bit of influence make a statement about it," Molly Hanchey, an organizer at grassroots volunteer group Obama Dallas, told me.

"There were regular conference calls to the surrogate team through the country," she added. "Whenever one of those kind of things would come up then there would be communication to the surrogates so they could begin to disseminate information back down at the local level because not everything was national."

Besides the surrogates speaking to national media organizations, local efforts, such as phone banks, worked to counter misinformation. The Obama campaign, however, gave up on Oklahoma because it was unable to dissuade people who believed the smears.

"I pulled the plug on it after a while because every third call was someone who said, and I love this, 'but he's a Mooslim,' that's 'Moo-slim.' I had everyone trained to say the following, 'Well sir or ma'am, we have an independent set of facts on that that were provided by independent sources, and it's two pages of resources if you'd like to have that e-mailed to you, we'll be happy to do so.' Well, of course, no they didn't. They didn't want to know the facts," Hanchey told me. "So I pulled the plug on calling Oklahoma because I just felt like it was like watering bricks, it made no sense for us to put our efforts there."

While the Muslim smear did not sway the majority of Americans or a significant number of states, it was particularly effective in some places. McCain won his biggest margin of any state, with 66 percent of the vote, in Oklahoma, where Obama failed to garner a majority in a single county.

The Obama team effectively fought back the smears elsewhere and won the election. But the smears did not stop. Once he took office, Obama was still forced to contend with all the smears from the campaign, as well as new ones lurking around every corner. The White House ignored most of those, but found it needed to push back against lies in its first year in office.

In 2009 Glenn Beck campaigned against the Olympics once the White House announced that Obama would go to Copenhagen to advocate on behalf of Chicago. Beck alleged that Obama wanted the Olympics in Chicago only to reward cronies and that the effort would be a huge money loser. Beck asserted that the Vancouver Olympics lost $1 billion. The White House punched back.

"Last night Fox News continued its disregard for the facts in an attempt to smear the Administration's efforts to win the Olympics for the United States. In the past, hosting the Olympics has been a source of pride and unity for the country, but once again, Fox News' Glenn Beck program has shown that nothing is worthy of respect if it can be used as part of a partisan attack to boost ratings," the White House shot back on September 30.

It corrected Beck by pointing out that the Winter Olympics in Vancouver would take place in the future, in February 2010.

The United States hosted the Summer Olympics four times between 1904 (St. Louis) and 1996 (Atlanta). It hosted the Winter Olympics the same number of times between 1932 (Lake Placid, New York) and 2002 (Salt Lake City). New York lost its bid in 2005 to host the 2012 Summer Olympics. Democrats and liberals did not gloat nor did they condemn George W. Bush over the loss.

The right wing, however, clapped when Obama's charms did not win over the Olympics committee. The Club for Growth, Rush Limbaugh, Glenn Beck, and Michelle Malkin all cheered loudly. Laura Ingraham chanted "R-I-O, R-I-O" to celebrate Brazil's victory. The Drudge Report bragged "World Rejects Obama." Do they applaud when unemployment worsens or when people lose their health insurance because this weakens Obama? Will they cheer or gloat the next time terrorists hit a U.S. target, just to prove their contention that Obama is soft on terrorism?

Sean Hannity and guest Dick Morris were still trashing Obama over the Olympics three days later; Bill O'Reilly, to his credit, disagreed with the right wing's shrill anti-Americanism.

On October 1 the White House shot down misinformation floated by Republican Congresswoman Michele Bachmann. After falsely asserting that the Obama administration was planning concentration camps to detain Americans and that the AmeriCorps program—which her own son later joined—was the domestic equivalent of Hitler's brownshirts, the maxi-moron of Minnesota topped even herself with a doozy.

Bachmann said on the floor of Congress that a provision of legislation to fund health clinics in schools would instead create a "sex clinic": "Does that mean that someone's 13-year-old daughter could walk into a sex clinic, have a pregnancy test done, be taken away to the local Planned Parenthood abortion clinic, have their abortion, be back, and go home on the school bus that night? Mom and dad are never the wiser."

Instead of denying the absurdity of Bachmann's claim, the White House website linked to independent PolitiFact.com, which said, "We see no language in the three main versions of the bill that would allow school-based clinics, which have a long history of providing basic health services to underprivileged students, to provide abortions. Nor would the clinics even be new—they have been around for three decades."

Obama himself rarely joined the fray, but occasionally got fed up with the nonsense. "Surely you can question my policies without questioning my faith or, for that matter, my citizenship," he said February 4, 2010, at the National Prayer Breakfast.

11

Conservatives with a Conscience: Lonely Voices of Reason in the Republican Wilderness

I support the president, and I just think we shouldn't look back on the past and look forward. We should all move on.

—Meghan McCain

Some Republicans—though, sadly, far too few—recognize when the Rubicon has been crossed, when attacks on Obama far exceed the bounds of political rhetoric and posturing, and when their side has completely abandoned the truth and common sense.

We can only hope more of them wake up to the traditional give and take of democracy. This means they must reject gutter politics and far-fetched conspiracies and denounce their own ranks for shameful behavior. They have precedent. William F. Buckley condemned the far-right John Birch Society as the founder of *National Review* in 1965. Republican President Dwight Eisenhower fought off the Birch crazies and Senator Joseph McCarthy after both accused Eisenhower—the man who saved democracy for millions of people in World War II—of being a Communist dupe. The sensible Republicans mentioned in this chapter are roundly skewered by extreme elements of the right wing, which is threatened by thoughtful critical analysis. Then again, any leader who summons up the courage to challenge weak-minded zealots— be it Winston Churchill or Abraham Lincoln—faces the enduring wrath of those willing to lead their fellow man off a cliff as well as the lemmings that can't function without their controller.

Many historians now consider Eisenhower among our ten greatest presidents. Why isn't a single Republican leader willing to honor Ike's memory by standing up to the extremists in the Republican Party and Tea Party? Instead, they appease today's equivalent of Joe McCarthy and the Birchers.

Conservative David Horowitz, whose critiques of liberalism are harsh and unforgiving, nonetheless broke with the right wing's excesses. So did David Frum, who worked in the second Bush administration.

Horowitz said people display "over-the-top hysteria" when they compare Obama to Joseph Stalin, David Koresh, Charles Manson, and Saddam Hussein. He labeled such unrestrained assertions as "Obama Derangement Syndrome," adapting a label from conservative columnist Charles Krauthammer who in 2003 said critics of the then-president suffered from "Bush Derangement Syndrome."

"Conservatives, please. Let's not duplicate the manias of the left as we figure out how to deal with Mr. Obama. He is not exactly the Antichrist, although a disturbing number of people on the right are convinced he is," Horowtiz wrote on the FrontPage Magazine website. "As for Obama's speeches, they are hardly in the Huey Long, Louis Farrakhan, Fidel Castro vein. They are in fact eloquently and cleverly centrist and sober."[1]

"This is bad, but it doesn't make Obama a closet Mussolini, however deplorable the conservatives among us may regard it," Horowitz continued, referring to federal spending in Obama's economic stimulus package. "The American system, the one the Founders created, is still in place."

"This is lunatic stuff," Horowitz wrote in a subsequent article for FrontPage Magazine.[2] "Obama is better compared to [former British Prime Minister] Neville Chamberlain than to Adolf Hitler," he insisted. "Obama is a machine politician and whatever dangers he represents (and as I see it there are many) are dangers because they reflect the heart and soul of today's Democratic Party, not because he is a Manchurian candidate or a closet Islamist, as more than a few conservatives seem to think."

Horowitz laid out his orderly, sharp rebuke of Obama's foreign policy, then concluded, "These facts add up to a worrisome prospect but a revival of the Third Reich is not one of them, and those who think it is and say so discredit only themselves."

In a *Newsweek* cover story, Frum, a wordmeister for Bush the Second, came out against the over-the-top Obama demonizing.[3] He carefully and thoughtfully dissected Rush Limbaugh's famous "I hope he fails" remark better than anyone else:

> Notice that Limbaugh did not say: 'I hope the administration's liberal plans fail.' Or (better): 'I know the administration's liberal plans will fail.' Or (best): 'I fear that this administration's liberal plans will fail, as liberal plans usually do.' If it had been phrased that way, nobody could have used Limbaugh's words to misrepresent conservatives as clueless, indifferent, or gleeful in the face of the most painful economic crisis in a generation. But then, if it had been phrased that way, nobody would have quoted his words at all—and as Limbaugh himself said, being 'headlined' was the point of the exercise. If it had been phrased that way, Limbaugh's face would not now be adorning the covers of magazines. He phrased his hope in a way that drew maximum attention to himself, offered maximum benefit to the administration and did maximum harm to the party he claims to support.

Frum recounted becoming a target after speaking out against the hate speech: "Most of these e-mails say some version of the same thing: if you don't agree with Rush, quit calling yourself a conservative and get out of the Republican Party. There's the perfect culmination of the outlook Rush Limbaugh has taught his fans and followers: we want to transform the party of Lincoln, Eisenhower and Reagan into a party of unanimous dittoheads—and we don't care how much the party has to shrink to do it. That's not the language of politics. It's the language of a cult."[4]

Most Americans, I suspect, would agree wholeheartedly with Frum: "When you use extreme language, you're much more likely to push away the audience."[5]

After the death of Senator Edward Kennedy, Frum reminded readers that some young people who support Obama today will become conservatives later in life, thus criticism of the president should be sober and respectful. "As we struggle to defeat that Obama agenda, let's never forget that we are also playing to capture his supporters—and let's try to refrain from doing things for short-term gain that will impede that larger long-term project."[6]

Like a reformed drunk tumbling off the wagon, Horowitz made an abrupt U-turn and joined the Obama crazies after such thoughtful analysis of their odiousness. A September article on FrontPage Magazine referred to Obama as the Manchurian Candidate. In his appearance on Glenn Beck's September 4, 2009, show on Fox News, he referred to Obama as a "radical" and "socialist." It is a puzzling turnabout because Obama did not change. Meanwhile, I won't invite Horowitz to a party until I know which David would show up: the thoughtful one who described muting the wild rhetoric or the zombie who got sucked into that same rhetorical black hole.

Besides Frum and Horowitz, very few elected Republicans took on the loudmouth liars.

"Well, Mr. President, welcome to Fort Myers, Florida," Republican Governor Charlie Crist said on February 10 at a town hall meeting alongside Obama. Crist, who appointed Democrats to key positions in his administration, said, "This issue of helping our country is about helping our country. This is not about partisan politics." Crist later quit the Republican Party and became an independent.

Washington state congresswoman and vice chair of the House Republican Conference Cathy McMorris Rodgers, the fifth-ranking Republican in the House, had enough after town hall meetings descended into donnybrooks during the summer of 2009.

"I think the purpose of the town halls is for people to be able to express their views in an orderly and respectful manner, and that needs to take place on both sides," she told *The Hill*, a nonpartisan newspaper that covers the federal government. "I certainly don't condone violence, I don't condone calling President Obama Hitler and painting swastikas on signs at town halls."[7]

Why do Senate Minority Leader Mitch McConnell and House Speaker John Boehner not have McMorris Rodgers's mettle? They've had ample opportunity to digest the distortions, and yet are willing to appease the irrational forces among their constituency. That is not leadership. They, not Obama, are the ineffectual Neville Chamberlains of our generation because of their unwillingness to stand up to the lunatics they allowed to hijack their own party.

Boehner is one of the leaders of the party that gave our country Lincoln, Eisenhower, and Reagan, but instead of harkening back to those presidents, he instead channeled the nuttiest of the nuts when he told the Value Voters Summit in Washington on September 19, 2009, "They want their country back. And we can take our country back," parroting the zany birthers who disrupted a town hall meeting of Delaware Republican Congressman Mike Castle in June (see chapter 4).

The Obama haters have never defined what they mean when they say, "We want our country back." Back to what? A time when a president used false information to start a war? When a president unilaterally decided that he could have anyone in the world captured and jailed? When a president ignored our own treaties and laws to torture? When a president ordered spying on people without a court order? Do they want to go back to Bush's legal, ethical, and constitutional violations? Their "country" died when Strom Thurmond and Jesse Helms were buried.

True leadership by a living Republican is embodied by Colin Powell, who led U.S. forces in the first Gulf War against Saddam Hussein's army in Kuwait. Powell could have been a formidable contender for the presidential nomination of either party in 2000.

Following the millennial election, Powell joined the Bush administration as secretary of state, the first black person to hold that high-power office. He gave a famous speech to the United Nations in February 2003 that laid out the case against Saddam Hussein. After Powell left office and the "evidence" was later debunked, Powell apologized for his unknowing role in the scheme. Fast forward to 2008: Powell endorsed Obama for president, praised his friend McCain, but took no active role in the campaign.

After Limbaugh made his "I hope he fails" remark, Powell was one of few high-profile Republicans to publicly denounce the radio dilettante: "I think what Rush does as an entertainer diminishes the party and intrudes or inserts into our public life a kind of nastiness that we would be better to do without," Powell said in a May 4 speech at a software conference in Washington.

Former Vice President Dick Cheney, however, sided instead with Limbaugh. Asked who is a better Republican between Powell and Limbaugh, he sniffed on CBS's *Face the Nation* on May 10, "If I had to choose in terms of being a Republican, I'd go with Rush Limbaugh. My take on it was Colin had already left the party. I didn't know he was still a Republican."

When did the definition of a good Republican and a patriotic American sadly diverge? Powell served the nation with distinction in Vietnam and the first Gulf War, while Cheney and Limbaugh artfully evaded military service.

Michelle Laxalt, a political consultant who is the daughter of former Nevada Senator Paul Laxalt (a close confidante of President Reagan), had the pluck to challenge Limbaugh.

"I couldn't disagree more with Rush Limbaugh, excuse me very much. I don't think he has been elected even dogcatcher as of yet. And, as a Republican, I don't want him as part of my party," she told MSNBC's *Hardball* on June 8.

Tom Ridge, a rare moderate Republican and the former governor of Pennsylvania and director of homeland security (a Bush "czar"), spoke out against extremism. "We have to reshape our message, reduce the decibel level—we're too doggone shrill – and be less judgmental about the people in the party that may disagree with us," he told MSNBC's *Hardball* on May 7. Ridge's own problem with the right wing came after suggesting in his 2009 book, *The Test for Our Times*, that the Bush-Cheney administration used terror alerts for political advantage during the 2004 election, as liberals long suspected.

One might expect the offspring of a losing presidential candidate to be embittered. Meghan McCain, the daughter of the 2008 Republican nominee, however, was astoundingly gracious after her father's defeat. Furthermore, one might expect members of that candidate's own party to give his daughter a pass to speak her mind without retribution. Think again. Meghan suffered ridicule and vile personal attacks. From Democrats? Not really. They leave her in peace. Liberals, by the way, didn't bother the Bush daughters either, other than good-natured wisecracks when their penchant for heavy-duty partying became a police matter. The right wing, nonetheless, criticized Meghan for daring to preach moderation and fairness, concepts alien to the Far Right.

"I straight up don't understand this woman [Ann Coulter] or her popularity. I find her offensive, radical, insulting, and confusing all the time. But no matter how much you or I disagree with her, the cult that follows Coulter cannot be denied," Meghan wrote on The Daily Beast. "Coulter could be the poster woman for the most extreme side of the Republican Party."[8]

Meghan continued: "More so than my ideological differences with Ann Coulter, I don't like her demeanor. I have never been a person who was attracted to hate or negativity. I don't believe in scare tactics and would never condone or encourage anyone calling President Obama a Muslim. But controversy sells and Coulter is nothing if not controversial. Everything about her is extreme: her voice, her interview tactics, and especially the public statements she makes about liberals. Maybe her popularity stems from the fact that watching her is sometimes like watching a train wreck."

In subsequent broadcast interviews, Meghan emphasized that some Democrats swing too far left and some Republicans push too far right, and that she rejects both extremes. Not a single liberal blasted that evenhanded remark.

Coulter, uncharacteristically, passed up a chance to spew toilet water. Instead, Barbie look-alike Laura Ingraham splashed through the sewer. Instead of engaging the McCain *fille* in a healthy debate about a vital topic, Ingraham sought to dethrone Coulter as the most hateful harebrain by showing off her finest talent: an ability to simultaneously open her mouth and unplug her pea-size brain.

"Maybe if they all talk like you maybe we'll get all the dumb people to vote for us," Laura Ingraham mocked on her radio show March 12 in a nasally, valley-girl voice. "They don't like 'plus-size' models, they only like the women who look a certain way. And on this 50th anniversary of Barbie, I really have something to say." Meghan shot back that women especially should not feed the sexist stereotype about another woman's weight.

Instead of apologizing for her own offensive remarks, Ingraham, as guest host of Bill O'Reilly's show March 18 on Fox News, charged that the "left-wing smear machine is using Meghan McCain to demonize conservatives." What conservative other than Ingraham herself was criticized? She did not identify any others because there were none.

Ingraham said her point was that Republican candidates do best when they adhere to bedrock conservative principle. That is a fair, though debatable, point. But that was not the thrust of her radio diatribe. Her intent was to ridicule Meghan, not expound conservative ideology. Her remarks would have gone unnoticed if reasoned debate had been her real point instead of bashing Meghan so tastelessly.

She said, "To suggest that I judge the merit of a political argument based on physical appearance is patently absurd. This contrite flap isn't about me or Ms. McCain. It's just another left-wing attempt to silence any criticism of the liberal agenda." It was Ingraham, not liberals, who brought up physical appearance.

Ingraham said, "Left-wing groups scour conservative media for snippets to take out of context, which they then disseminate to create a diversion" so they don't have to defend "failed policies and stale ideas."

Liberals "gin up a phony catfight to distract you from the truth," according to Ingraham, so people will ignore government debt and "the fact that America's enemies are suddenly emboldened." What "phony catfight?" Meghan was truly offended by Ingraham's cruel remarks. What enemies are emboldened? In a so-called defense of her honor, Ingraham, like a skunk, spewed malodorous lies in all directions.

In her postscript, Ingraham said, "The Obama attack dogs can twist my words, engage in emotional exploitation and distort my intentions, but they will never, ever silence me." Attack dogs? Who attacked whom? In her whimpering defense, she never cites one example of her words being distorted, because it did not happen. Ingraham's words speak loudly and clearly without interpretation.

Ingraham is quite aware of what smears are. She surrounds herself every day with people who routinely make untrue, ferocious statements about Obama and any Democrat or liberal they feel like targeting. Criticism of Ingraham for belittling Meghan's plea for civility was not a smear. Ingraham mocked Meghan's weight. She ridiculed the way Meghan talks. She trivialized Meghan's serious message. Nobody took Ingraham's words out of context or twisted her vile message.

Bernard Goldberg, the former CBS reporter who has made a cottage industry of accusing the mainstream media of unquestioningly supporting Democrats and liberals and unfairly bashing Republicans and conservatives, finally grew himself a pair late in life when he challenged one of the worst liars on his own turf.

Goldberg appeared with Sean Hannity on Fox News on April 13, 2009, shortly after brave U.S. Navy SEALs rescued Capt. Richard Phillips from Somali pirates. Hannity declared, "There was an orchestrated effort for them [the Obama administration] to go out there and take credit for this" after Obama authorized shoot-to-kill orders that won Phillips's freedom.

"I don't want to put Barack Obama on Mount Rushmore for simply being the commander-in-chief, but we have to stop going out of our way to find fault with every single thing he does . . . But I'm not going to be like the Left was with George Bush and criticize everything he does," Goldberg responded. "Look, Sean, the good guy is alive and well. The bad guys are dead. That's all good. It happened on Barack Obama's watch. He gets the credit."

Another prominent conservative stood up for reason in the Obama birth certificate smear. "The news story is nonsense. Those who dwell on it are distracting us from today's real issues," R. Emmett Tyrrell Jr. wrote in an opinion piece in the *Washington Times*.[9] He lamented that an unidentified TV show withdrew its invitation when the booker discovered that he debunked this birth certificate rumor.

"Alas, the show's producers did not want me to set the record straight. They had wanted me to defend the false story. But I reminded the booker that I knew the story to be false. In fact, I had provided the show with irrefutable proof that the story is false. Mr. Obama is American-born," Tyrrell wrote. "The show proceeded to find a guest who would repeat the false story, either knowingly or out of ignorance—so much for getting to the truth of issues on television. As for me, I would never knowingly publish anything I knew to be untrue, not in this column or in the *American Spectator*."

Tyrrell never identified the TV show, but it is pretty easy to guess which TV network refused to debunk a lie about Obama.

Joe Scarborough, a former Republican congressman from Florida and current host of MSNBC's *Morning Joe*, also pleaded for moderation on the June 14 episode of NBC's *Meet the Press*, when he said, "I also don't think that we win the middle of America again by being intemperate by calling Barack Obama a communist."

When many Republicans, in particular Cheney, were breathing fire over Obama's decision to close the Guantanamo Bay prison and release information detailing torture by U.S. forces, Ed Rollins begged to differ. "I don't think we lost one iota," the erstwhile adviser in the Reagan White House told CNN on April 24. "He's put a very strong national security team around him and I think he's made some correct decisions early on here that are keeping us safe."

Two Republican senators, Georgia's Johnny Isakson and Alaska's Lisa Murkowski, stood up to Sarah Palin's fearmongering, as did Neil Cavuto of Fox News and conservative columnist Kathleen Parker. They are quoted in the Sarah Palin entry in chapter 8.

Another Republican senator stood up to the bullies and know-nothings in her party. Maine Senator Olympia Snowe was asked by John Harwood of the *New York Times* for her reaction to chatter that Obama is a socialist.

"In fact, I sense the opposite. He's been very realistic in his views on health care," Snowe said. She described Obama as "more a moderate than a liberal" and "flexible." Snowe said in the interview broadcast on September 17 on NBC that Obama "understands different views" and "solicits contrarian views."

Idaho is among the most conservative states where elected Republicans could get a pass for suffering fools gladly, but they don't. Republican senators Mike Crapo and Jim Risch, along with Congressman Mike Simpson, condemned a Republican gubernatorial candidate for saying he would buy a license to hunt Obama. Rex Rammell was talking about tags for hunting wolves when a member of the audience in Twin Falls on August 25 asked about tags to hunt Obama. Rammell responded, "The Obama tags? We'd buy some of those." When asked by the Associated Press about his remarks, Rammell refused to apologize because it was a joke.

Jonathan Henke, who runs the conservative blog The Next Right, blasted mainstream Republicans for not condemning the lunatic fringe, in particular WorldNetDaily, known as WND and published by Joseph Farah. This was one of the first websites to peddle the "birther" nonsense, as well as every right-wing conspiracy in existence.

"They traffic in the paranoid conspiracy theories that take away from our ability to discuss more important issues. They feed people with perhaps what they want to hear instead of actual facts. And they justify it by saying we're just reporting what people are saying," Henke said on September 8 on MSNBC's *The Rachel Maddow Show.*

"They tear down the intellectual foundations of the right," he added. "What we need to argue with are the credible organizations, the credible people or the people who should be respected who are associating with them and urge them not to be associated with the disgraceful organizations." He accused the Republican Party of turning to "people who sell conspiracy theories and fear and frankly, the fevered swamps." Henke also said the Republican National Committee has purchased WND's e-mail list for marketing to its readers.

Conservative radio host Michael Medved analyzed the inflated influence of extremist media figures. "This odd development reflects the different standards of popularity in media and politics. A radio host who reaches just 5 percent of listeners wins huge success, earning great fame and wealth. A candidate who gets 5 percent of the electorate, however, is a fringe figure with scant clout. Cable TV and radio figures only need to cultivate a niche audience, but successful politicians need to assemble big, broad coalitions."[10]

Even Ari Fleischer, George W. Bush's press secretary, gave a balanced appraisal of Obama's national security credentials. "When it comes to counterterrorism, Barack Obama is pretty strong," he told Fox News on October 6.

Other Republicans doubtless have argued for sanity. I can't read each news article and watch every TV show. But the scarcity of statements is truly remarkable.

The sultans of smear may order their staffs to sift through every page of this book seeking this discrepancy or that inconsistency; I would expect they may find a handful of minor items to which they will point and charge that the whole book is riddled with errors, that Mr. Wright is really Mr. Wrong. Sorry guys, but I heard that one in third grade.

Some will argue I took their quotes out of context. I don't need to bend their words; they torture the English language enough already. They might say I hate conservatives. Not true. I love and respect family members and close friends who lean to my right, I voted for Gerald Ford, and I embrace fellow Americans who speak the truth.

I have double-checked the offensive, offending quotes, which I heard myself in either live broadcasts or replays. My research has been meticulous, so if there are any discrepancies or inconsistencies, I accept full responsibility and apologize in advance. Nevertheless, the major thrust remains irrefutable: these so-called critics have stepped way over the line and gone far beyond the pale in their criticism of Obama. Their comments and accusations are unconscionable.

Some conservatives criticize Obama in a dignified, respectful way, without stooping to name calling or fictive accusations, and I agree with some of what they say. Whether or not criticism is valid, whether or not criticism is dignified, the First Amendment of our Constitution guarantees that right, even to sleazebags like Ann Coulter, Don Imus, or Larry Flynt.

Many Obama haters labeled people on the other side traitors when they disagreed with President Bush. Still, nearly all the criticism of Bush was proven to be valid. His shaky rationale for invading Iraq, assaults on constitutional rights, and numerous other offenses were shown to be improper.

David Horowitz, before jumping back to the dark side again, offered conservatives a rational prescription for dealing with Obama or any other political leader, an approach with which most Americans could certainly agree: "Obama faces increasingly tough choices . . . Hopefully, he will make the right choices, and should he do so conservatives will need to be there to support him. If he makes the wrong choices, conservatives will need to be there to oppose him. But neither our support nor our opposition should be based on hysterical responses to policies that we just don't like."[11]

Amen.

POSTSCRIPT

The Next Step—It's Up to Us to Restore Dignity and Decency

Have you no sense of decency?

—Joseph Welch

D o we no longer have a sense of decency as a society? That basic, simple question is central to everything in this book. We are deluged with access to more information than ever, yet millions of people remain woefully misinformed about the vital issues because they believe wrong information. This ignorance has a profound impact on their lives and on all of our lives.

Zealots and demagogues manage to fool some of the people all of the time and trick them into believing they must protect us from "the enemy." Don't these same unimaginative lies get a bit shopworn over time? In reality, they are the treacherous ones from whom the rest of us need refuge. It is not Obama they are smearing; he is just a vessel for their irrational rage. These liars are the verbal equivalent of Holocaust Museum shooter James von Brunn, aiming their wrath at a symbol without regard for who gets hurt. They are smearing you and me; they are smearing our Constitution, our nation, and our traditions. When they wrongly call Obama a fascist or a dictator, they are smearing George Mason, who authored the Bill of Rights, and James Madison, who enshrined them as president. They are tearing down the Founding Fathers who formed our "more perfect" but imperfect union, all with widely differing views but mindful of the big picture and respectful of each other. It is our sacred duty to uphold their legacy and not let demagogues hijack it.

None of Obama's policies come from the far end of a limb. The majority of Americans or significant pluralities are with him on nearly every issue, while the Obama haters and their leaders inhabit Never Never Land, spouting positions held by tiny slivers of the population. It is they who are far outside the mainstream, woefully misinformed, or both, while they try to paint Obama as an extremist.

Republican leaders like John Boehner, Eric Cantor, and Mitch McConnell should be the wise men and disarm the loose cannons. Instead, they fire irresponsible zingers, cheapening the dialogue and muddying the waters when our country needs greater clarity. Instead of making thoughtful, principled critiques of the president's agenda as the loyal opposition, they instead make common cause with the extremists. Have they no sense of decency?

I have cast a light on innumerable lies and liars smearing Obama. They are the latest incarnation of the McCarthy tactics, the "vast right-wing conspiracy," and the Swift Boaters that previously targeted anyone who stood in the way of the right wing's arrogant lust for power. I've tried to find all of the lies that have gotten traction. I'd like to say that my work is done, but I know that once this book has gone to print, the mega-liars will find new ways to attack.

Citizens have a duty to stop the smears when they hear someone repeating a whopper. Pass along this book to friends and family who believe the lies or are perched on the fence. Insist that they do their own research. Nobody should take my word or yours. Complain to news organizations that report the lies unthinkingly, like stenographers, repeating words verbatim without giving it any thought.

Furthermore, next time you hear a smear about anybody in public life, think it through. Does it make sense? What is the motive of the person who made the allegation? Why is it being circulated?

Would you run a business using incorrect information about your market or customers? Certainly not. Then how can we have a strong, vibrant, and truly representative democracy when leaders too often are chosen on the basis of lies and smears rather than the facts and issues?

Before you believe something you read, check it out. Do research. Organizations exist for the sole purpose of sorting information. Appendix C is full of tips about where to determine the veracity of information quickly and accurately. We have access to great search engines like Google and Bing. Use them often.

What will the liars think up next? This book is only a snapshot in time, a look at the smears against Obama during the campaign and his first twenty months in office. The lies use emotional, rather than rational, appeals. Even after being debunked definitively, the smears continue to circulate. The Obama haters are fighting to misinform the uninformed people. As Obama works on his agenda, his opponents remain in the gutter and continue to spew bile, trying to convert more adherents to their vicious cult.

"There was a time when decency, even honor, was an essential part of the American dialogue in its most ideal form, and part of its very identity. There was a time when our culture would have recoiled in horror at the vituperation flowing unchecked from radios, televisions, and the Internet," Michael Rowe wrote at the *Huffington Post.*[1] "There was a time when intellectual honesty was not considered unpatriotic; when compassion for, and understanding of, your fellow man was a sign of strength, not weakness. There was a time when the phrase 'Have you no shame?' meant something."

Rowe appeared to be referring to the classic remark "You have done enough. Have you no sense of decency?" asked of Joseph McCarthy on June 9, 1954, by Joseph Welch, a lawyer for the U.S. Army after the spiteful, reckless Wisconsin senator destroyed the lives of countless people with accusations and innuendo. That simple, honest question was enough to deflate the famous witch hunter's public standing and started his denouement. You want to hear something scary? Some prominent right-wingers today are ready to canonize "Tailgunner Joe."

Ask yourself the difference between McCarthy's shameful tactics and the liars who say Obama is a Muslim or a communist or a fascist or not an American. Why do such filthy misrepresentations continue to have followers more than half a century after McCarthy and his sleazy tactics were shamed and denounced?

Who will be the Joseph Welch of the early twenty-first century and shame the Obama haters into honesty or force them out of the limelight? And when will our society have enough decency to turn off the TVs and radios and stop giving the hatemongers an audience? When will the news channels stop giving known liars a free platform?

Researching this book required that I muck around in the sewer, that I read and listen to and watch loathsome people. I felt as if I were the doctor cataloging all the mental diseases in the asylum, changing David Vitter's diapers, or adjusting Michele Bachmann's straitjacket. I was reminded of the 1964 movie *Black Like Me*, the true story of a white journalist who artificially darkened his skin and traveled through the Deep South posing as a black man in 1959. The film was based on John Howard Griffin's 1961 book, which recounted his experiences of hatred and violence. Years later, I vividly recall a riveting scene in which the protagonist revealed himself to a black man he had befriended during his journey. He confessed that while he tried to truly understand what it felt like to be black, "I can never know any more than you can know what it's like to be inside my skin."

To that, I must say that I will never know what it feels like to be a zealot or racist. As a journalist, I have always worked hard to see both sides of everything.

If the Obama haters obtained information from a wider variety of sources and were willing to consider other views, they would be better informed and not hold such a visceral animosity toward the president. But many, sadly, cling to these beliefs as an essential part of their identity, as outlined in chapter 7, much like a cult.

It's not easy to break the spell. Cult deprogrammers say it is necessary to discredit the cult leader's authority and show contradictions of ideology versus reality, until reality begins to overtake ideology. The subject next recognizes disagreements with the cult and finally declares independence from the cult and opposes it. I accomplish those tasks throughout this book, but will any of the Obama haters realize how they are being duped?

Nonetheless, I remain fundamentally convinced of the unsurpassed genius of our Founding Fathers in designing our precious Constitution and Bill of Rights. I disagree with almost everything I hear spewing from the mouths of Rush Limbaugh, Michael Savage, the trash-talkers on Fox News, and the right-wing bloggers online. Yet I am convinced more than ever that they have the basic right to be heard, right or wrong, until and unless they encourage violence or treason. Some of them come dangerously close and occasionally cross the line.

I experienced the censorship of dictators in Latin America; I clearly see that the hectic democratic free-for-all is preferable to alleged orderliness imposed by military regimes who deny basic liberty. Our republic is fortified by tolerating its fringes and kooks, just like it was at the birth of our nation. It is the duty of the mainstream, however, to push the extremists to the sidelines where they belong and ignore them rather than either mimic or silence them.

"The real challenge is to craft ways to rebuke demagoguery while honoring vigorous political debate and dissent," Political Research Associates published in a 2008 report titled *Rebuking Conspiracism.*

Democratic Congressman Barney Frank did exactly that at an August 2009 town hall meeting in Massachusetts. After a protester called Obama a Nazi, he responded, "It is a tribute to the First Amendment that this kind of vile, contemptible nonsense is so freely propagated."

When I descended into the maelstrom of the Obama haters, I asked myself many questions—why a sliver of the population had such overweening antipathy toward Obama, who was feeding this frenzy, whether it was organized or random, and finally, whether it was an exercise in healthy democracy or rending the fabric of our nation.

I faithfully tried to answer each question as I interviewed knowledgeable people, read books, magazines, newspapers, websites and blogs, watched TV coverage, and listened to opinion makers on the radio. I never stopped believing that vigorous protest is healthy and that it is a fundamental element in democracy. People can and should examine their leaders and their policies, and they should express their disagreement when and where they see fit.

Slander, however, is neither healthy nor democratic. Polls show increasing numbers of people who believe preposterous notions about Obama. Republican leaders know that Obama is a natural-born American citizen, that he is a Christian, that he believes in democracy, that he has not grabbed unprecedented power, and that he vigorously opposes communism, socialism, and fascism. These ridiculous smears have gained far more traction than I ever imagined when I embarked on this project. Clearly, Republican leaders are complicit in stoking the fires of hatred every time an agent provocateur gins people into a frenzy based on pure fabrication, and they weaken democracy by aiding and abetting the herd mentality.

Republican leaders lust for power so blatantly that they have made a pact with the devil under the misguided impression that the Obama haters will pave their return to power. They figure that if they tell a lie often enough, people will believe it. Tragically, the Republicans don't care about the damage they are doing to their nation. Their so-called leadership will live in infamy.

Future generations will judge us harshly for allowing a small minority of fringe elements to block progress for all Americans unless the majority has the courage to rise up and make its voices heard. Americans look back on the stain of slavery and wonder how a free nation ever allowed it. We question why our leaders let robber barons steal the wealth of all Americans for so many years until Teddy Roosevelt broke up the trusts. We are amazed at how McCarthy was allowed to ravage so many lives before he was stopped. We look back at Americans fending off savage dogs and being lynched for seeking equality guaranteed in the Constitution. We can feel pride that we elected someone of African lineage to the highest office in the land, but at the same time, feel shame that a handful of people loudly bleat out one mindless—and harmful—fabrication after another like sheep in need of a good shearing.

Look at the greatest presidents as judged by historians—Washington, John Adams, Jefferson, Jackson, Lincoln, both Roosevelts, Truman, Eisenhower, and Kennedy—and ask yourself how many of them came to power by slandering their opponent. None. How many of them governed through chicanery and demagoguery? None. By trying to topple Obama, the Republican leadership strives to reincarnate Nixon when the nation needs more Lincolns and Washingtons.

Obama has always been more charitable toward his detractors than they are toward him. At an October 16, 2009, town hall meeting in New Orleans, a fourth-grade boy asked the president why so many people hate him. "You've got to take it with a grain of salt. Some of it is just what's called politics, where once one party wins, then the other party feels like it needs to poke you a bit to keep you on your toes, and so you shouldn't take it too seriously," he answered. Obama said the president gets the blame when things go wrong, with people frustrated about losing their jobs, homes, and health care. "So, you've just got to keep on going even when folks are criticizing you, as long as you know that you're doing it for other people."

The sad irony is that if the Obama haters—even those who blindly quote biblical verses calling for his death—met him in person, the overwhelming majority would almost certainly take a liking to their brilliant, charismatic president and realize that they share more in common with him than they originally thought. It's a safe bet that they would see him for the man he is, with both his virtues and faults, rather than the fictional caricature they created.

APPENDIX A

A Plethora of Anti-Obama Blogs and Websites

A liar will not be believed, even when he speaks the truth.

—Aesop

Anti-Obama blogs and websites are so numerous and outlandish that it is impossible to list them all as new ones are born and older ones are euthanized. Reading them sweeps you into the Twilight Zone and traps you there. They range from far-fetched and occasionally amusing to outright nasty, exceedingly mean-spirited, and crude. Some exist solely to promote sheer, unapologetic racism. The one trait they all share is a disdain for the truth and unwillingness to admit when their lies have been exposed.

Reading these sites is like stumbling into a rabbit hole. One link leads to another, which leads to more sites spewing the same, or even more fanciful, inaccuracies. Numerous anti-Obama blogs and websites survived the transition from campaign to his presidency.

Many websites disagree with Obama on single issues, such as abortion rights, religion, foreign policy, and other matters, but they don't demonize him. These websites are part of legitimate political discourse, so they are not included here.

Here is a rogue's gallery of some of the worst blogs and websites that make baseless attacks against Obama:

Accuracy in Media (aim.org): The Orwellian self-proclaimed "Accuracy in Media" website ran headlines such as "Obama's International Socialist Connections," "Washington Post Censors Truth About Bill Ayers," "Pro-Homosexual Media Going Bankrupt," and other tasty morsels. It published one item with the laughable headline "Why is Fox News Protecting Obama?" The so-called grassroots organization gets donations from major corporations and Richard Mellon Scaife, who funded vicious attacks against President Clinton.

Against Barack Obama (againstobama.com): Argued that Barack and Michelle Obama are close friends with Bill Ayers and Bernardine Dohrn and repeated other threadbare arguments without original content. It ran one article that began, "There are 5.3 million votes for Obama out there, the only problem is that they happen to belong to murders, rapists, armed robbers and other convicts and ex-convicts." It features noted liars such as Jerome Corsi, who penned the widely discredited book *Obama Nation.*

America's Independent Party (aipnews.com): Official website for the American Independent Party throws around the word "communist" when referring to Obama's administration.

American Thinker (americanthinker.com): It occasionally pitches sensible notions but gets caught up in too many tenuous connections between Obama and shady characters, such as domestic radicals or Lenin. One headline read "Obama's Court Jews."

Americans Against Obama (americansagainstobama.com): Their mission statement: "Welcome to Americans Against Obama! This site will be a source of news and information about the reality of Barack Obama. The media has shown that they are completely in the tank for Obama, and the only way Americans can see to truth about his policies is through sites such as this. Obama has shown that socialism, appeasement towards terrorism, and bigger government is the solution to our 'problems.' We must get the truth out about Obama and show America what a mistake was made by voting in someone based on a marketing slogan."

Anti-Obamassiah Refuge (antiobamassiah.wordpress.com): Unoriginal attacks against Obama, all of which can be seen elsewhere. Its motto: "Sanctuary for the endangered but growing domestic population of Obama criticism."

AntiObama.net: Its motto is "Barack Obama—A Bad Idea For President." It provides links to the "best" anti-Obama websites. It vilifies Obama and treats Michele Bachmann, the mental pygmy from Minnesota, as if she were a serious person.

AntiObamaBlog.com: After the election, this blog tied Obama and his staff to the crimes of Blagojevich on flimsy hearsay, and it also questioned Obama's birth certificate. The blog reprinted an e-mail from "Operation Screamin' Eagle," which asks "Christian leaders and God-loving patriots" to stand up to Obama and say, "We did not bleed, fight, and die for the freedoms you wish to destroy."

Aprpeh (aprpeh.blogspot.com): Claims Obama is rabidly pro-Palestine and anti-Israel.

Atlas Shrugs (atlasshrugs2000.typepad.com): Pamela Geller is one of the most toxic among Obama haters, full of shrill anti-Muslim rants and smears against Obama that were debunked long ago.

Audacity of Hypocrisy (audacityofhypocrisy.com): Peddles a supposed link between Obama and Donald Young, a gay man who was murdered. Young was a choir director and deacon at Trinity United Church of Christ, which Obama attended until his falling-out with Reverend Jeremiah Wright. It also alleges recent drug use by Obama and claims he was a member of the socialist New Party. It provides no evidence for any such claims or why Obama, one of thousands of people at the megachurch, is linked to the murder victim. It peddles the "Psalm 109:8" shirts calling for Obama's death.

The Betrayal (oilforimmigration.org): Has the motto "Our Heritage Sold Out: Taking America Back – Resist the New World Order." The site says Obama has "a Communist agenda" and America is "being dismantled from the inside out." It hypothesizes that Obama is the son of Malcolm X.

Blogs for Victory (blogsforvictory.com): This blog, tied to the McCain-Palin campaign, stayed alive after the election so it could bash Obama and tie him to Blagojevich. After that, it started running headlines like "Hope for Terrorists" and "Liberal Fascism Strikes Again."

Boortz (boortz.com): The website of conservative radio host Neal Boortz polled its readers, 68 percent of whom said the United States "will fall" with Obama as president. If Boortz offered his listeners accurate information, why would they have this impression? These listeners were woefully uninformed and out of touch with America at a time Obama had the approval of the majority of people in the nation.

Citizen Wells (citizenwells.wordpress.com): Links to a petition to impeach Obama, urged U.S. Attorney Patrick Fitzgerald to indict Obama in the criminal case involving Blagojevich (Fitzgerald found Obama did nothing wrong), and accused Obama of ties to Antoin Rezko's crimes. A poll on this website said 87 percent of its readers believe Obama has knowledge about the Donald Young murder from Obama's former church.

Constitutionally Speaking (constitutionallyspeaking.wordpress.com): A collection of every conspiracy theory, from birthers to Glenn Beck rants.

Debbie Schlussel (debbieschlussel.com): Schlussel's blog claims that Obama's Selective Service registration "raises more questions than it answers. And it shows many signs of fraud." The document on her website shows that Obama registered for the draft on July 30, 1980, less than a week before he turned 19. Schlussel gets bogged down in minutiae using pretzel logic and claims the form was in reality created in 2008. This would require the complicity of Bush administration officials committing a federal crime. Someone not entwined in the universe of conspiracy gibberish would ask why anyone would forge such a routine, inconsequential document at a time when there was no draft.

DiscoverTheNetworks (discoverthenetworks.org): Makes imaginative associations among liberals, leftists, and anyone it brands as leftists. It decries

Obama's "socialist agenda" and claims that a CIA-linked report proves that Obama's birth certificate is fake.

DontVoteObama.net: This website's motto: "Barack Obama: the most popular candidate in the Middle East." The "O" in Obama is shown as a crescent with a star in the middle to look like a Muslim symbol. Headlines: "What do Osama and Obama have in common? They both have a friend that blew up the Pentagon!" "Why the Election of Obama Would Mean the End of America," "Understanding Obama: The Making of a Fuhrer," "Is Obama an Enemy of God?" "Obama Plan to Dismantle U.S. Military" and "Iran Loves Barack Obama."
The website ran this fictive item (that got wide circulation around the Internet):

LETTER FROM THE BOSS . . .
As the CEO of this organization, I have resigned myself to the fact that Barack Obama is our President and that our taxes and government fees will increase in a BIG way. To compensate for these increases, our prices would have to increase by about 10 percent. But since we cannot increase our prices right now due to the dismal state of the economy, we will have to lay off six of our employees instead. This has really been bothering me, since I believe we are family here and I didn't know how to choose who would have to go. So, this is what I did. I walked through our parking lot and found six "Obama" bumper stickers on our employees" cars and have decided these folks will be the ones to let go. I can't think of a more fair way to approach this problem. They voted for change, I gave it to them. I will see the rest of you at the annual company picnic.

This is laughable on many levels, mostly because of the quotation about the "dismal state of the economy," which is the result of eight years of stewardship by the first MBA president. This CEO thinks of employees as a "family" but wants to dismiss those who voted for Obama? How many of us cut loose a "family" member who votes differently from us?

Expose Obama (exposeobama.com): This website is operated by the National Campaign Fund, which is headed by notorious Obama hater Bruce

Hawkins. It pushes for Obama's impeachment. After Blagojevich was arrested for trying to sell Obama's senate seat, this blog headlined "Blagojevich is Just the Tip of the Iceberg," even though the U.S. Attorney in charge of the case said Obama and his team were not involved.

Exposing Liberal Lies (exposingliberallies.blogspot.com): Ran headline "The First Muslim President" with a photo caption of Obama reading "America will bow down to Islam;" considers Sarah Palin to be a deep thinker.

Ezine Blog (ezineblog.org): After listing what it describes as similarities between Hitler and Obama, it showed a poster of Hitler with Obama's "Yes we can" slogan and a poster of Obama bearing the title "Socialism."

Free Republic (freerepublic.com): The patriarch of anti-Obama invective and half-truths allowed people to post the most disgusting racist comments about Obama's eleven-year-old daughter Malia (see chapter 2) and refused to apologize. This is a favorite nesting ground for the nuttiest of nutjobs. Previously, this blog stated, "Obama embodies the fondest dreams of radical socialist organizers over the years—that someday, a candidate with enough broad, personal appeal would rise to lead the United States away from its defense of individual liberty, and into whole-hearted support of World Socialism." It alleges Obama is "literally a plant from within the world of radical Marxism to help achieve their goal of world domination."

Get Out of Our House (topshelf51.wordpress.com): Devoted to the argument that Obama has Muslim ties and is not a natural-born American citizen. Supports the "Where's the Birth Certificate?" billboard campaign by birthers.

Hilary and Me (hillarynme.com): Repeats the birth certificate rumor. Champions a Congressional bill requiring presidential candidates to produce their birth certificates.

Hot Air (hotair.com): Repeats the same old tired guilt-by-association arguments of radical ties. Also accuses Obama of race-baiting and hiding his "hard-left ideology." Founded by Michelle Malkin, who lies about Obama every time she appears on Fox News.

IHateObama.com: This blog operates on the theory that "Barack Obama, his liberal friends and bad liberal ideas caused this economic crisis." This website features amusing graphics, including an organ grinder with a monkey and photo of Einstein scrawling on a blackboard, "Barack Obama+JWright=2 racists." It insults Native Americans by referring to them as "Injuns" and says about blacks, "I wish they'd tell me where in the world they have it better than right here in America." It links to the manifesto by madman Unabomber Theodore Kaczynski as the alleged definition of liberalism.

Infowars (infowars.com): This website, published by Alex Jones, is for people who got lost in psychobabble and never found their way back. "Obama's speeches are a mass of mind-control techniques and neuro-linguistic programming, or NLP, and they are carefully constructed to implant beliefs and perceptions into the mind of the viewers," Jones claims. "All of which brings me to the parallels with Nazi Germany, fascist Italy, and similar regimes throughout history."

Newsmax (newsmax.com): Described by Chris Hayes of *The Nation* as "a clearinghouse for innuendo and rumor." After white supremacist James von Brunn killed a guard at the Holocaust Memorial Museum on June 10, 2009, Rabbi Morton Pomerantz wrote on Newsmax, "Our new president did not tell a virulent anti-Semite to travel to the U.S. Holocaust Memorial Museum in Washington to kill Jews, but he is most certainly creating a climate of hate against us. It is no coincidence that we are witnessing this level of hatred toward Jews as President Obama positions America against the Jewish state and if his views are not vigorously opposed they will help create a danger as great as that posed by the Nazis to the Jewish people."

NewsWithViews.com: Alleged that Obama is planning internment camps in the United States and that Muslims are "turning our country into their country."

No Quarter (noquarterusa.net): Blogger Larry Johnson claimed he had four sources that Michelle Obama had ranted against "whitey" in Trinity United Church of Christ in Chicago. He never produced the promised video.

Nobama Network (nobamanetwork.com): "Nobama Network is a portal site designed to bring together the Grass Roots Movements in America spawned by outrage over this new president and his attempts to destroy the traditional values that makes America great. We work to take back our country from the power drunk Democrats on a spending spree who threaten it!" Linked to the teabagger movement and idolizes Beck.

NobamaZone (nobamazone.com): Repeats the "death panels" canard invented by Sarah Palin that health reforms would lead to government bureaucrats, not doctors and patients, deciding who lives or dies.

Obama Crimes (obamacrimes.com): Devoted to supporting allegations by lawyer Philip J. Berg, who makes a fetish of filing frivolous lawsuits alleging Obama's birth certificate is a fraud.

The Obama File (theobamafile.com): A grab bag of snarky comments with little original content. It "confirmed" that William Ayers wrote Obama's biography *Dreams From My Father*. The most significant thing this website did was to post a picture of Obama made to look like a Vulcan, with the caption: "I Was Spock."

Obambi.com and The Obambi.com Blog (Obambi.wordpress.com): Devised all sorts of fables, including one which purported that Obama and his half-sister Maya Ng faked the death certificate of their grandmother, Madelyn L. Dunham, who died shortly before Obama's election as president. These websites refer to Obama as "the idiot" and use racist terms and imagery.

Power Line (powerlineblog.com): It purported that the left-leaning New Party, identified as being affiliated with Democratic Socialists of America, supported Obama for state senator in Illinois in 1996, and this led the fringe website to declare that Obama "was indeed a certified and acknowledged member of the DSA's New Party."

Prison Planet (prisonplanet.com): Linked to infowars.com, the website of Alex Jones, whose motto is: "There is a war on for your mind!" Jones is a self-described libertarian radio host who rails against the New World Order, alleged moves toward one world government, and the Federal Reserve. Headlines on his website read, "Obama's Dictator Status Expands With Firing of [GM CEO Rick] Wagoner" and "Obama's Elite Agenda: Black Abortion for Profit."

RBO (therealbarackobama.wordpress.com): Itemizes "unanswered questions" about Obama and makes the same shopworn associations between Obama and suspicious characters. Lionizes Beck.

Right Wing News (rightwingnews.com): Their motto: "Kneecapping Barack Obama at every opportunity." Ran these headlines: "Obama Slurs Fellow Americans Yet Again" and "5 Myths the Left Has Created for Itself." Another headline purports that the ABC network is "Propaganda Arm of the Obama White House." An article about women states, "If liberals hated al Qaeda the same way they hate conservative feminist icons, we'd have already won the war on terror by now."

RightPundits.com: Circulated the widely discredited rumor that Michelle Obama had ranted against "whitey" at Trinity United Church of Christ in Chicago.

SlickBarry.com: Says that Obama has flip-flopped on every major issue.

Socialism, Marxism, Communism & Obama (obamaism.blogspot.com): This website shows Obama in front of a colorful hammer and sickle. It goes into a long diatribe listing Obama's purported links to socialism, Marxism, and communism. If viewed as a comic book, this site is more imaginative, amusing, and ridiculous than most anti-Obama sites.

Stormfront (stormfront.org): The white supremacist organization (their motto: "White Pride World Wide") showed a huge spike in readership on its website right after the election. White supremacist James von Brunn, who terrorized the Holocaust Memorial Museum, was a contributor to this site. Its readership spiked around Obama's election and the museum killing. Stormfront said it began in 1990 to back the Senate candidacy of former Ku Klux Klan member David Duke. It claims to be "the first White Nationalist Internet website."

Townhall.com: This website lets just about any nut post just about anything, no matter how far fetched, as long as it pushes the envelope to the far right. This author punked the website with the fictive "Witchcraft in the White House" in August 2009, which was their top blog for five days.

The Traditional Values Coalition (traditionalvalues.org): Although it does not list Joe McCarthy as a contributor, it attacks anyone with whom it disagrees as a "leftist," "far left," "radical leftist," "communist," or "communist sympathizer." This website frequently uses such terms to describe Obama and his supporters. It states, "Bible-based traditional values are what created and what have preserved our nation. We will lose our freedoms if we reject these values."

Vanguard News Network Forum (vnnforum.com): Full of hate speech against blacks and Jews, it prominently featured a swastika at one time.

WorldNetDaily (wnd.com): This right-wing website considers Rush Limbaugh to be thoughtful. It accuses Obama of ties to Chicago political corruption, repeats the often-stated canard that Obama is hiding his birth certificate from public view, and says this could foment a "constitutional crisis." It claims there is a "Muslim Mafia" that must be stopped. This site is a bizarre hodgepodge of mainstream news, crackpot theories, and right-wing conspiracy speculations. Founder Joseph Farah is a godfather of the birther conspiracy.

APPENDIX B

Anti-Obama Books: Dumpsters Full of Rumors,
Lies, Fabrications, and Excrement

False words are not only evil in themselves, but they infect the
soul with evil.

—Plato

If a stenographer went to a beauty parlor or corner bar, dutifully took notes
on every crumb of chatter, wrote it up, and pretended it made sense, the
result would be a book identical to these. The Internet is now the beauty
salon or bar, amplifying every bit of gossip to a worldwide audience without
any care about its reliability or veracity. These books are bizarre hybrids of
fictional accounts about real people.

There are worthwhile books by serious conservative authors, but none
are listed here; earnest conservatives don't accept far-fetched conspiracy theories about Obama and don't make ludicrous accusations. Also note that few
of these have been critiqued by serious reviewers, who ignore such books
because they are not authentic works of journalism or scholarship. This is a
body of work representing the bile of the Obama haters: political screeching
consigned to paper, praised only by the fawning, unthinking right wing.

A Slobbering Love Affair: The True (And Pathetic) Story of the Torrid Romance Be-
tween Barack Obama and the Mainstream Media by Bernard Goldberg:
  Unlike the who's who of disgraceful Obama-hating buffoons who populate this list, Goldberg can be a critical thinker. He's a serious guy with

serious books printed by serious publishers, but this is not one of them. He is sometimes acute and clear with analysis, but this book, published by right-wing Regnery, is an emaciated volume of pure tangent. Goldberg believes that controversial remarks by Reverend Jeremiah Wright and a passing association with 1960s radical Bill Ayers should have demolished Obama, but his campaign was salvaged only by media bias. In reality, these were peripheral characters in Obama's life who were shoved to center stage only by exaggerated media attention. Goldberg relies on stereotypes about media bias with no profound thinking and leaves the intellectual heavy lifting to the twenty-first century's version of Einstein, Rush Limbaugh.

Barack Obama & Larry Sinclair: Cocaine, Sex, Lies & Murder? by Larry Sinclair:
Sinclair is such a liar that the wackjobs who tout the insane theories that Obama was born in Kenya or is a Muslim consider Sinclair a reject. Sinclair self-published this garbage because it was too far-fetched for even the right-wing publishers that routinely pollute the world with books full of absurd notions. Sinclair has been in jail so many times for so many offenses in so many places that readers lose track. He goes into lewd detail about an alleged cocaine-fueled homosexual tryst with Obama, which nobody corroborates. Sinclair also claims that Obama was involved in the death of Donald Young, a gay deacon and choirmaster at Trinity United Church of Christ. Authorities never suspected Obama of any such link.

Bought and Paid For: The Unholy Alliance Between Barack Obama and Wall Street by Charles Gasparino:
Gasparino is a legitimate journalist for a legitimate network, CNBC, who has written legitimate books about high-level financial shenanigans. His tough conclusions in this book counter the frivolous notion that Obama is a communist, but the author takes too much license by extrapolating subservience to Wall Street based on campaign contributions. Obama has gotten a black eye with the financial community after enacting the most serious financial reform legislation since the Great Depression and ensuing comparison to Hitler by Wall Street–insider Steve Schwartzman. The right-wing publisher appears to have tethered this book to the Tea Party Express.

Crimes Against Liberty: An Indictment of President Barack Obama by David Limbaugh:
Levelheaded people would change their name and move to Antarctica if they were related to Rush Limbaugh by a cruel twist of fate, but his brother instead milks the family franchise to peddle farcical theories and indict the truth. His very first breath labels Obama's presidency "the most destructive in America's history," following with the hackneyed smear about Obama's "visceral contempt for America" and a goal "to bring America down to size." The most amusing quote: he calls "Obama's agenda" a "socialist centipede." This repugnant book's false assumptions and tired clichés will crumble as surely as did the Biblical foolish man's house built on sand.

Culture of Corruption: Obama and his Team of Tax Cheats, Crooks, and Cronies by Michelle Malkin:
This book, like Sarah Palin's *Going Rogue*, vaulted to the top of the charts because of heavy preordering by right-wing organizations. *Townhall* magazine offered this book as a freebie for new subscribers. Malkin lays out the premise that Obama's wife, his cabinet, his advisers, allied unions, and organizations such as ACORN are all corrupt, and then relies on innuendo to segue into her predetermined conclusion. This dumpster diving diva refers to the *New York Times* as the "Fishwrap of Record." Is that supposed to be clever? "Evil corporate lobbyists." Is that original? Another doozy: "When it comes to ethical self-policing that puts taxpayer interests above electoral and special interests, Joe Biden doesn't have a serious bone in his body." Correction: When it comes Malkin, she doesn't have a single serious argument.

Fleeced: How Barack Obama, Media Mockery of Terrorist Threats, Liberals Who Want to Kill Talk Radio, the Do-Nothing Congress, Companies That Help Iran, and Washington Lobbyists for Foreign Governments Are Scamming Us...and What to Do About It by Dick Morris and Eileen McGann:
This book by Morris (a former adviser to Bill Clinton, now a Fox News contributor) and his wife is only peripherally about Obama, though his name is plastered on the cover to boost sales to Obama haters. They make sweeping generalizations based on pure conjecture: Obama would "open

the door wide" to illegal immigrants, socialize medicine, weaken the Patriot Act to increase vulnerability to terrorists, "weaken the standards Bush imposed for improved public education," give a "free pass to leave prison" to "our most dangerous drug criminals," and withdraw from Iraq unilaterally. After Obama took office, not one of those things occurred. Morris also peddles the discredited fantasy that Obama will "muzzle" right-wing talk radio through resurrection of the "Fairness Doctrine."

Obama: The Postmodern Coup—Making of a Manchurian Candidate by Webster Griffin Tarpley:

This dense, 120,000-word tome labels Obama a "Manchurian Candidate" and calls him "a deeply troubled personality" and "the megalomaniac front man for a postmodern coup by the intelligence agencies." Tarpley claims that Obama is controlled by that bugaboo of all conspiracy buffs, the Trilateral Commission, and the TLC's co-founder Zbigniew Brzezinski, whose son worked for John McCain's campaign. How can Brzezinski control Obama but not his own son?

Obama Unmasked: Did Slick Hollywood Handlers Create the Perfect Candidate? by Floyd Brown and Lee Troxler:

Brown was the inventor of the most sinister racist ad in the history of presidential politics: the Willie Horton ad against Michael Dukakis in 1988. In a book riddled with grammatical errors, Brown and Troxler trot out the old idea that Obama is a Muslim. One chapter asks whether Obama is the first "affirmative action" president but fails to ask how C-student George W. Bush got into Yale and Harvard through criteria not based on grades. The authors say Obama was "fighting about how best to hate white America" and that Michelle Obama was guilty of "militant racism." This book repeats the oft-stated contention that Obama is a product of "Chicago machine politics" even though authentic news reports revealed Obama to be a skilled opportunist who bucked the machine to his own benefit. Brown and Troxler forecast gasoline will cost $10 per gallon when Obama leaves office. If they want to wager on that prediction, let me be first in line to take their money.

The Audacity of Deceit: Barack Obama's War on American Values by Brad O'Leary:
  Published by WND Books, an arm of Joseph Farah's WorldNetDaily. Farah
  was one of the earliest proponents of the "birther" movement. O'Leary
  repeats all the same old tired arguments ripped from previous reports in
  WorldNetDaily, a clearinghouse for anti-Obama rumor, innuendo, and
  outright lies: Obama is a Muslim, is under the influence of communists, is
  closely associated with Bill Ayers, and had suspicious dealings with Antoin
  Rezko. He bashes Obama's mother as influenced by socialist thinking.
  O'Leary says Obama would declare "war on success." If Obama targets
  successful people, O'Leary has nothing to worry about.

*The Case Against Barack Obama: The Unlikely Rise and Unexamined Agenda of the
Media's Favorite Candidate* by David Freddoso:
  Freddoso, in 234 pages of text, is devoid of a single original thought or
  revelation about Obama. This book has more clichés than a mutt has
  fleas. He describes Obama as a Chicago machine politician who is under
  the influence of Bill Ayers and other radicals, is closely tied to Reverend Jeremiah Wright, committed suspicious acts with Antoin Rezko, and
  would impose radical policies.

Obama Nation: Leftist Politics and the Cult of Personality by Jerome R. Corsi:
  Corsi has no relationship with the truth and a symbiotic relationship with
  right-wing media. He uncritically transcribes every smear from Fox News
  and right-wing radio, websites, and blogs. Then they all quote *Obama Nation* to support their own fabrications. Corsi was a gunner in the right-
  wing conspiracy that torpedoed Senator John Kerry's 2004 run for the
  White House by penning *Unfit for Command: Swift Boat Veterans Speak Out
  Against John Kerry*. That deceitful book quoted ideologues with a political
  grudge against Kerry who never served on the swift boat Kerry command-
  ed. After the Kerry smear succeeded, Corsi belly-flopped when he tried
  the same tactic on Obama. Scores of websites, newspaper and magazine
  articles, and broadcast interviews pointed out hundreds of inaccuracies,
  making it perhaps the most thoroughly debunked book in history. The
  Obama campaign devoted forty pages on its website to meticulously de-
  legitimizing Corsi's misrepresentations and citing sources. FactCheck.org

described this book as a "mishmash of unsupported conjecture, half-truths, logical fallacies and outright falsehoods" and *Time* called it "trash" and "poisonous crap."

Welcome to Obamaland: I Have Seen Your Future and It Doesn't Work by James Delingpole:

Delingpole has an engaging, witty writing style, unlike the turgid prose by imitation authors listed here. This author at least is amusing and original. He paints a wickedly ugly portrait of life in the United Kingdom due to government failures, making it appear to be in worse shape than its third world former colonies. Delingpole, unfortunately, paints himself into a rhetorical corner from which there is no escape by working from the false premise that Obama is determined to turn the United States into another Britain.

APPENDIX C

Where to Go for Help: It's Easy to Think for Yourself

> Believe nothing, no matter where you read it, or who said it, no
> matter if I have said it, unless it agrees with your own reason and
> your own common sense.
>
> —Siddhartha Gautama (Buddha)

Attacks on Obama contributed to a whole new perspective on how the
Internet is a curse as well as a blessing. It can provide instant access to
useful information about prenatal care, recipes, or news from anywhere
in any language; play music; offer ways to buy anything we want; and even
schedule a flight or cruise to anywhere in the world. But the downside is that
it gives equal access to every conceivable kook, liar, and swindler.

It is often difficult to distinguish the veracity of information on the Internet. Some good websites offer help:

ABYZ News Links (abyznewslinks.com): A complete listing of newspapers and
news websites around the world.

American Journalism Review (ajr.org): The online site for the *American Journalism Review* deals with tough issues such as the "Chinese Wall" between
news and advertising at media organizations.

The Campaign Finance Institute (cfinst.org): Analyzes Federal Election Commission and Internal Revenue Service reports to track which organizations fund political campaigns.

Columbia Journalism Review (cjr.org): The *Columbia Journalism Review's* on-line site examines coverage of important news events for bias and accuracy.

FactCheck.org: Investigates claims by politicians and rates their veracity; it points out falsehoods and myths irrespective of political party or ideology.

FAIR (fair.org): The motto for Fairness and Accuracy in Reporting is "chal-lenging media bias and censorship since 1986." It boasts renowned con-tributors such as pollster Peter Hart.

Journalism.org: This site is run by the Pew Research Center's Project for Ex-cellence in Journalism. It examines media bias and issues fascinating data about news content.

Media Matters for America (mediamatters.org): This site archives the worst misstatements made every day by politicians and media organizations, with links to audio and video when available. It was founded by former conservative hatchet man David Brock, who wrote *Blinded by the Right: The Conscience of an Ex-Conservative* and *The Republican Noise Machine: Right-Wing Media and How It Corrupts Democracy*.

Muckety (muckety.com): Shows connections between people and organiza-tions. If you look up the Obama haters, you will see lots of links between them and other shadowy groups.

NewsLink (newslink.org): A handy way to find websites for newspapers and broadcasters anywhere in the world.

NewsTrust (newstrust.net): Critiques the websites that critique the media.

The Nieman Journalism Lab (niemanlab.org): This is a project of the Nie-man Foundation at Harvard University, which describes itself as "a col-laborative attempt to figure out how quality journalism can survive and thrive in the Internet age."

Obama Conspiracy Theories (obamaconspiracy.org): A folksy, independent website is devoted to investigating the many conspiracy theories against Obama.

National Public Radio (npr.org): National Public Radio's Secret Money Project lists roles played by people in numerous organizations.

OpenSecrets.org: The non-partisan Center for Responsive Politics exposes spending by organizations and affiliated groups to influence elections.

PolitiFact.com: Created by the *St. Petersburg Times* in Florida. It has a Truth-O-Meter, "a scorecard separating fact from fiction," and an Obamameter to check the status of the president's campaign promises.

Political Research Associates (publiceye.org): Meticulously documents activities by extremist groups. It said one group pulled "their conspiracy theories into the mainstream media and Congress."

SourceWatch (sourcewatch.org): A project of the Center for Media and Democracy, SourceWatch is a media critic that is also a Wikipedia-type reference about news sources.

Snopes.com: This website is devoted to debunking urban legends. For instance, a search for "Obama birth certificate" links to his Hawaiian certificate of live birth, a copy of his birth announcement from Honolulu newspapers a few days after he was born, and a summary of the smears and frivolous lawsuits. It cites its sources from legitimate news organizations, such as the *Philadelphia Daily News, Honolulu Advertiser, Honolulu Star-Bulletin,* the *New York Times* and *The Economist.*

TruthOrFiction.com: This website looks into rumors that have appeared on the Internet and judges their veracity.

Tyndall Report (tyndallreport.com): Monitors broadcasts of the nightly network news. Andrew Tyndall claims to have not missed a single one since 1987.

About.com: Urban Legends (urbanlegends.about.com): The popular About. com website has numerous interesting links. This one checks rumors to see whether or not they are true.

Wikipedia (wikipedia.org): This volunteer-based website has its share of goofs on occasion but strives for accuracy and is widely regarded for the amount of information it handles in an even-handed way. It tries to weed out incorrect and biased information. Its lengthy entry about Obama's birth certificate states, "these claims are promoted by a number of fringe theorists and political opponents." It scrupulously cites sources. For the birth certificate rumor, it cites 200 sources.

NOTES

Introduction
1. Evan Thomas, *A Long Time Coming* (New York: Public Affairs, 2009), 106.
2. Dan Balz and Haynes Johnson, *Battle For America 2008: The Story of an Extraordinary Election* (New York: Viking Adult, 2009), 361.
3. Balz and Johnson, *Battle for America*, 364.
4. Richard Wolffe, *Renegade: The Making of a President* (New York: Crown, 2009), 230.
5. Michael Oreskes, "Lee Atwater, Master of Tactics for Bush and GOP, Dies at 40," *New York Times*, March 30, 1991.

Chapter 1. How an Unknown Inspired Hope in Millions
1. John Harwood, "But Can Obama Make the Trains Run on Time?" *New York Times*, April 19, 2009.
2. Paul Krugman, "The Politics of Spite," *New York Times*, October 5, 2009.

Chapter 2. Falsehoods About Obama Echo Endlessly
1. Mark McKinnon, "Send Joe Wilson Home," *The Daily Beast*, September 12, 2009, http://www.thedailybeast.com/blogs-and-stories/2009-09-11/send-joe-wilson-home.
2. Erick Erickson, "Barack Obama Wins Nobel Peace Prize: He's Becoming Jimmy Carter Faster Than Jimmy Carter Did," RedState, October 9, 2009, http://www.redstate.com/erick/2009/10/09/barack-obama-wins-nobel-peace-prize.

Chapter 4. Loons and Losers
1. Michael Weigel, "McCain Campaign Investigated, Dismissed Obama Citizenship Rumors," the *Washington Independent*, July 24, 2009, http://washingtonindependent.com/52474/mccain-campaign-investigated-dismissed-obama-citizenship-rumors.
2. Jim Myers, "Inhofe Weighs in on Obama Birth Site," *Tulsa World*, July 28, 2009.

3. "Editorial: Obama birth conspiracy is an embarrassment," *Dallas News*, July 24, 2009.
4. "Editorial: No Doubt About Obama's Birth," *Honolulu Star-Bulletin*, July 29, 2009.
5. "Editorial: The 'Birthers': Don't encourage them, Senator," *Tulsa World*, July 29, 2009.
6. "Born in the U.S.A.," *National Review Online*, July 28, 2009, http://www.nationalreview.com/articles/227954/born-u-s/editors.

Chapter 5. Can You Prove Your Innocence?
1. Bernard McGinn, *Antichrist: Two Thousand Years of the Human Fascination with Evil* (San Francisco: Harper, 1994), 273.

Chapter 6. The Obama Trifecta
1. Hugh Hewitt, "Just Say No to Government Motors and Obamacars," *Washington Examiner*, June 1, 2009.
2. Mark Tapscott, "Furor Grows Over Partisan Car Dealer Closings," *Washington Examiner*, May 27, 2009.
3. Stephen F. Hayes, "Not Right: The Obama Administration Grants Miranda Rights to Detainees in Afghanistan," *The Weekly Standard*, June 10, 2009, http://www.weeklystandard.com/Content/Public/Articles/000/000/016/605iidws.asp.
4. John White, Dan Eggen, and Joby Warrick, "U.S. to Try 6 On Capital Charges Over 9/11 Attacks," *Washington Post*, February 12, 2008.
5. William Ayers, "The Real Bill Ayers," *New York Times*, December 5, 2008.

Chapter 7. Why We Hate
1. Alexander P. Lamis, ed., *Southern Politics in the 1990s* (Baton Rouge: LSU Press, 1999), 7.
2. David Frum, "The reckless Right courts violence," *The Week*, August 12, 2009, http://theweek.com/bullpen/column/99474/The_reckless_Right_courts_violence.
3. Jack Levin and Gordana Rabrenovic, *Why We Hate* (Amherst, NY: Prometheus Books, 2004), 81–82.

Chapter 8. Profiles in Cowardice
1. Bob Herbert, "Impossible, Ridiculous, Repugnant," *New York Times*, October 6, 2005.
2. Lee Atwater and T. Brewster, "Lee Atwater's Last Campaign?" *Life*, February 1991, 67.
3. Joe Conason and Gene Lyons, *The Hunting of the President: The Ten-Year Campaign to Destroy Bill and Hillary Clinton* (New York: Thomas Dunne Books, 2001), 76.
4. Conason and Lyons, *The Hunting of the President*, 72.
5. Michael Rowe, "Death at the Holocaust Museum and the Degradation of the American Dialogue," The *Huffington Post*, June 11, 2009, http://www.huffingtonpost.com/michael-rowe/the-holocaust-museum-shoo_b_214133.html.

6. Ann Coulter, "Obama's Dimestore 'Mein Kampf,'" AnnCoulter.com, April 2, 2008, http://www.anncoulter.com/cgi-local/printer_friendly.cgi?article=243.
7. Frank J. Gaffney Jr., "America's First Muslim President?" *Washington Times*, June 9, 2009.
8. Frank J. Gaffney Jr., "The Jihadist Vote," *Washington Times*, October 14, 2008.
9. Jim Myers, "Inhofe Says Patriotism Question Will Sink Obama," *Tulsa World*, September 6, 2008.
10. Chris Casteel, "U.S. Sen. Inhofe Calls Obama Speech "Un-American," *The Oklahoman*, June 4, 2009.
11. John Chase and Rick Pearson, "Perennial candidate back for another race," *Chicago Tribune*, February 10, 2006.
12. Christopher Hayes, "The New Right-Wing Smear Machine," *The Nation*, October 25, 2007, http://www.thenation.com/article/new-right-wing-smear-machine.
13. Ibid.
14. Ibid.
15. Ezra Klein, "Is the Government Going to Euthanize Your Grandmother? An Interview With Sen. Johnny Isakson," *Washington Post*, August 10, 2009.
16. Kathleen Parker, "A Tip for the GOP: Look Away," *Washington Post*, August 5, 2009.
17. Chris Cillizza, "The Palin Wars: Part LXII," *Washington Post*, October 5, 2009.

Chapter 9. Fox News

1. Jonah Goldberg, "Fox, John Edwards and the Two Americas," Real Clear Politics, March 16, 2007, http://www.realclearpolitics.com/articles/2007/03/fox_john_edwards_and_the_two_a.html.
2. Jeffrey Lord, "Thanks, Uncle Walter," *American Spectator*, July 28, 2006, http://spectator.org/archives/2006/07/28/thanks-uncle-walter.
3. Jason Spencer, "U.S. Rep. Bob Inglis: Glenn Beck, Fear-Mongering Undermines Americans' Faith in Constitutional Republic," *Spartanburg Herald-Journal*, August 7, 2009.
4. David Frum, "What is Going on at Fox News?" *FrumForum*, March 16, 2009, http://www.frumforum.com/what-is-going-on-at-fox-news.
5. Peter Wehner, "Glenn Beck: Harmful to the Conservative Movement," *Commentary Magazine*, September 21, 2009, http://www.commentarymagazine.com/blogs/index.php/wehner/100152.
6. Gabriel Winant and Tim Bella, "Glenn Beck, Republican Strategist," *Salon*, October 12, 2009, http://www.salon.com/news/feature/2009/10/12/glenn_beck/.
7. Jim Rutenberg, "Obama's Personal Ties Are Subject of Program on Fox News Channel," *New York Times*, October 7, 2008.
8. Howard Kurtz, "Worlds Apart: The Great Hannity-Olbermann Divide," *Washington Post*, October 27, 2008.
9. Michael Calderone, "Fox Addresses Baby Mama Drama: Producer Used 'Poor Judgment,'" *Politico*, June 12, 2008, http://www.politico.com/blogs/michaelcalderone/0608/Foxs_addresses_baby_mama_drama_Producer_used_poor_judgment.html.
10. Howard Kurtz, "Out and a Bout," *Washington Post*, August 7, 2009.

Chapter 11. Conservatives with a Conscience

1. David Horowitz, "Get over your Obama Derangement Syndrome," *Salon*, April 2, 2009, http://www.salon.com/news/opinion/feature/2009/04/02/ obama_derangement_syndrome.
2. David Horowitz, "Obama Derangement Syndrome II; A Non-partisan plea for civility and equity," *FrontPage Magazine*, June 2, 2009, http://archive.front-pagemag.com/readBlog.aspx?BLOGID=1026.
3. David Frum, "Why Rush is Wrong," *Newsweek*, March 7, 2009, http://www .newsweek.com/2009/03/06/why-rush-is-wrong.html.
4. Ibid.
5. Ibid.
6. David Frum, "A Kennedy Lesson for Obama Critics," *FrumForum*, August 28, 2009, http://www.frumforum.com/a-kennedy-lesson-for-obama-critics.
7. Molly K. Hooper, "GOP Lawmaker Criticizes Nazi Talk," *The Hill*, August 13, 2009.
8. Meghan McCain, "My Beef With Ann Coulter," *The Daily Beast*, March 9, 2009, http://www.thedailybeast.com/blogs-and-stories/2009-03-09/my-beef-with-ann-coulter.
9. R. Emmett Tyrell Jr., "Fourth Estate Follies," *Washington Times*, July 24, 2009.
10. Michael Medved, "Media Popularity Isn't Political Popularity," Townhall.com, October 5, 2009.
11. Horowitz, "Get over your Obama Derangement Syndrome."

Postscript

1. Rowe, "Death at the Holocaust Museum and the Degradation of the American Dialogue.

SELECTED BIBLIOGRAPHY

Brock, David. *Blinded by the Right: The Conscience of an Ex-Conservative.* New York: Crown Publishers, 2002.

Brock, David. *The Republican Noise Machine: Right-Wing Media and How it Corrupts Democracy.* New York: Crown Publishers, 2004.

Brown, Floyd and Lee Troxler. *Obama Unmasked: Did Slick Hollywood Handlers Create the Perfect Candidate?* Bellevue, WA: Merril Press, 2008.

Conason, Joe. *Big Lies: The Right-Wing Propaganda Machine and How It Distorts the Truth.* New York: Thomas Dunne Books, 2004.

Conason, Joe and Gene Lyons. *The Hunting of the President: The Ten-Year Campaign to Destroy Bill and Hillary Clinton.* New York: Thomas Dunne Books, 2000.

Corsi, Jerome R. *Obama Nation: Leftist Politics and the Cult of Personality.* New York: Threshold Editions, 2008.

Delingpole, James. *Welcome to Obamaland: I Have Seen Your Future and It Doesn't Work.* Washington, DC: Regenery Publishing, 2009.

Freddoso, David. *The Case Against Barack Obama: The Unlikely Rise and Unexamined Agenda of the Media's Favorite Candidate.* Washington, DC: Regenery Publishing, 2008.

Goldberg, Bernard. *A Slobbering Love Affair: The True (And Pathetic) Story of the Torrid Romance Between Barack Obama and the Mainstream Media.* Washington, DC: Regenery Publishing, 2009.

Hoffer, Eric. *The True Believer: Thoughts on the Nature of Mass Movement.* New York: Harper & Row, 1951.

Kessler, Ronald. *In the President's Secret Service: Behind the Scenes with Agents in the Line of Fire and the Presidents They Protect,* New York: Crown, 2009.

Lamis, Alexander, ed. *Southern Politics in the 1990s,* Baton Rouge: LSU Press, 1999.

Latimer, Matt. *Speech-less: Tales of a White House Survivor.* New York: Crown, 2009.

Levin, Jack and Gordana Rabrenovic. *Why We Hate.* Amherst, NY: Prometheus Books, 2004.

Malkin, Michelle. *Culture of Corruption: Obama and his Team of Tax Cheats, Crooks, and Cronies.* Washington, DC: Regenery Publishing, 2009.

McGinn, Bernard. *Anti-Christ: Two Thousand Years of the Human Fascination with Evil.* New York: Harper Collins, 1994.

Morris, Dick and Eileen McGann. *Fleeced: How Barack Obama, Media Mockery of Terrorist Threats, Liberals Who Want to Kill Talk Radio, the Do-Nothing Congress, Companies That Help Iran, and Washington Lobbyists for Foreign Governments Are Scamming Us . . . and What to Do About It.* New York: Harper Collins, 2008.

O'Leary, Brad. *The Audacity of Deceit: Barack Obama's War on American Values.* New York: WND Books, 2008.

Plouffe, David. *The Audacity to Win: The Inside Story and Lessons of Barack Obama's Historic Victory.* New York: Viking Penguin, 2009.

Ridge, Tom and Larry Bloom. *The Test of Our Times: America Under Siege . . . and How We Can Be Safe Again.* New York: Thomas Dunne Books, 2009.

Sinclar, Larry. *Barack Obama & Larry Sinclair: Cocaine, Sex, Lies & Murder?* Fort Walton Beach, FL: Sinclair Publishing, 2009.

Swint, Kerwin. *Mudslingers: The Twenty-Five Dirtiest Political Campaigns of All Time.* New York: Union Square Press, 2008.

Tarpley, Webster Griffin. *Obama: The Postmodern Coup—Making of a Manchurian Candidate.* Joshua Tree, CA: Progressive Press, 2008.

INDEX

ABOUT THE AUTHOR

John Wright was born in 1952 in Flint, Michigan; his family moved to the West Coast when he was eight. He graduated from Humboldt State University in Northern California and later studied at New York University and attended graduate school at the University of Washington.

He wrote for newspapers in the Northwest before moving to Venezuela in 1981 to work as a reporter and editor at the English-language *The Daily Journal.* He traveled throughout Latin America for two years before going to work for the Associated Press as an editor on the international news desk in New York and as a correspondent for Mexico, Central America, and the United Nations. He coordinated a package of stories about Latin American street children that won the prestigious Inter American Press Association's 1989 Tom Wallace Award.

His next overseas assignment was as Brazil bureau chief for Dow Jones Newswires in 1993. He returned to Seattle in 1996 as the Pacific Northwest correspondent for Knight Ridder Financial News, which became Bridge News and closed down in 2001. He joined the start-up Energy News Today, where he works as editor of Latin America news.